Praise for *RETURN TO THE SACRED*

*"**Return to The Sacred** reads like an invitation directly from the spirit to come explore the many expressions of the Divine. Ellerby is a masterful storyteller in addition to being a fine scholar, and the result is a must-read book."*

— **Caroline Myss,** the best-selling author of
Anatomy of the Spirit and *Defy Gravity*

*"Very rarely does a book appear with the power to stir the soul; to remind you of what you know in your bones; to inspire you to connect with Spirit in its many forms. **Return to The Sacred** is such a book. An authentic spiritual adventure, it is lyrically beautiful, stunningly real, and at the same time, resolutely practical. This is a book to read and to cherish. I'm going to buy a carton for my family and friends."*

— **Joan Borysenko, Ph.D.,** the best-selling author of
Your Soul's Compass and *It's Not the End of the World*

*"People everywhere are experiencing a spiritual hunger as never before. **Return to The Sacred** is a magnificent way of answering this need. This is an elegant, enchanting book. Jonathan Ellerby's spiritual path has taken him inside many of the world's great spiritual traditions, which he now shares. If you are ready for growth and trans-formation in your spiritual life, this book is for you."*

— **Larry Dossey, M.D.,** the best-selling author of
Healing Words and *The Power of Premonitions*

"Jonathan is one of those extraordinary people who makes an impact everywhere he goes. Not only is he an accomplished, well-credentialed, and knowledgeable expert on seemingly all things spiritual, but he has proven himself to be a master healer and someone who lives what he teaches. We at Canyon Ranch have been blessed to have chosen Jonathan Ellerby as our Spiritual Program Director.

*"**Return to The Sacred** is a reflection of Jonathan's rare gifts: it is warm-hearted, engaging, and sure to challenge and enhance the way you see yourself and the world. If you are seeking wellness and peace, it's got what you are look-ing for. This book offers an invaluable perspective that will enrich your life."*

— **Mel Zuckerman,** founder of Canyon Ranch Health Resorts

blessed journey! Dr. Ellerby demystifies ancient cultural systems and inspires us to journey down the path that is calling to us. We give thanks for the fact that Dr. Ellerby has been true to his own internal muse and, in so doing, has delivered to us a gift that will nourish generations to come."

— **Kamau Kokayi, M.D.**, integrative physician and the host of Pacifica Radio's *Global Medicine Review*

"Jonathan Ellerby has written an insightful, compassionate guide for all spiritual seekers. A must-read for those seeking to remember that all paths lead to God."

— **Colette Baron-Reid**, the best-selling author of *Messages from Spirit* and *Remembering the Future*

"If you want to understand what the spiritual journey is really like, this is the book for you. Dr. Ellerby has given us an intimate, exciting view of walking with Spirit. It is a true inner look at the spiritual world along with 12 powerful spiritual practices that will greatly assist your own passage. This is a great introduction to what spirituality is all about. If you are ready to graduate from traditional religion to spirituality—this is your road map. What a delightful book Jonathan has given us!"

— **Leland R. Kaiser, Ph.D.**, spiritual coach and the co-founder of Two Worlds Wisdom School

"Jonathan Ellerby is to spirituality what I am to comedy—the best! He not only cleaned my spiritual clock time and again, he shook it up and wound it, too. If it weren't for Jonathan, I might still be a soulless, cruel insult comic with no regard for what is right and what is wrong. Thanks to Jonathan, I've ditched the 'soulless' part."

— **Lisa Lampanelli**, Grammy-nominated comedian

*"In this gracefully written and inspiring book, Dr. Jonathan Ellerby teaches us how to discover a deeper dimension of the sacred in ourselves and in the world around us. His unifying vision of spirituality awakening heals our hearts as it enlightens our souls. At whatever your stage of spiritual journey, your path will be enriched as you explore—and experience—the **Return to The Sacred**."*

— **Gary E. Schwartz, Ph.D.**, professor at the University of Arizona and the author of *The Energy Healing Experiments* and *The G.O.D. Experiments*

*"Jonathan Ellerby guides our hearts and minds into the venues and visions of the sense of the sacred. He reminds us of the many signposts that lead us to the heart of being with clearly inspired stories. **Return to The Sacred** helps us all remember the importance of orchestrating the Great Source of life into our daily routines and rituals."*

— **Don Campbell,** the best-selling author of
Sound Spirit and *Creating Inner Harmony*

*"As Joseph Campbell inspired us with the unity of the great myths, Jonathan Ellerby guides us on a remarkable journey of our shared spiritual heritage and the many paths open to us to experience The Sacred. No matter what your heritage, this book illuminates the many paths you can follow to search for the Divine and reach spiritual enlightenment. **Return to The Sacred** is the journey of a lifetime and Jonathan Ellerby has the understanding, experience, and education to guide us along the ancient routes to personal enlightenment in the here-and-now."*

— **Consuelo Mack,** the anchor and managing editor for public
television's *Consuelo Mack WealthTrack*

*"If you are seeking to change your life, the wisdom of the ages can guide you and rebirth you. Reading **Return To The Sacred** will introduce you to the ancient pathways to awakening that lead us to transformative experiences so that painful personal times do not have to be your teacher. It makes ancient wisdom practical, personal, and easily accessible in modern language and stories that teach and inspire."*

— **Bernie S. Siegel, M.D.,** the best-selling author of *Prescriptions for Living* and *365 Prescriptions for the Soul*

*"**Return to The Sacred** reminds us that in our busy modern lives, nourishing our soul is central. Ellerby's exploration of ancient and contemporary spiritual practices reflect his vast knowledge and profound experiences that enable him to be a wonderful teacher, healer, and guide for anyone seeking a deeper connection with the world."*

— **Rabbi Sherre Hirsch,** the author of *We Plan, God Laughs*

RETURN TO
THE
SACRED

HAY HOUSE TITLES OF RELATED INTEREST

RETURN TO
THE
SACRED

ANCIENT PATHWAYS TO
SPIRITUAL AWAKENING

Jonathan H. Ellerby, Ph.D.

HAY HOUSE, INC.
Carlsbad, California • New York City
London • Sydney • Johannesburg
Vancouver • Hong Kong • New Delhi

Published and distributed in the United States by: Hay House, Inc.: www.hayhouse.com • *Published and distributed in Australia by:* Hay House Australia Pty. Ltd.: www.hayhouse.com.au • *Published and distributed in the United Kingdom by:* Hay House UK, Ltd.: www.hayhouse.co.uk • *Published and distributed in the Republic of South Africa by:* Hay House SA (Pty), Ltd.: www.hayhouse.co.za • *Distributed in Canada by:* Raincoast: www.raincoast.com • *Published in India by:* Hay House Publishers India: www.hayhouse.co.in

Editorial supervision: Jill Kramer • *Design:* Riann Bender

Poem on page 229: From *Yoga Beyond Belief: Insights to Awaken and Deepen Your Practice,* by Ganga White, published by North Atlantic Books. Copyright © 2007 by Ganga White. Reprinted by permission of publisher.

Library of Congress Cataloging-in-Publication Data

Ellerby, Jonathan H.
    Return to the sacred : ancient pathways to spiritual awakening / Jonathan H. Ellerby. -- 1st ed.
        p. cm.
    ISBN 978-1-4019-2155-2 (hardcover : alk. paper) 1. Spiritual life. 2. Spirituality. I. Title.
    BL624.E455 2008
    204'.4--dc22
                                    2008027514

Tradepaper ISBN: 978-1-4019-2156-9
Hardcover ISBN: 978-1-4019-2155-2

13 12 11 10   5 4 3 2
1st edition, January 2009
2nd edition, January 2010

Printed in the United States of America

For my Mom,
and all the
Divine Beings
who have
guided me along
The Way.

CONTENTS

Of all that God has
shown me
I can speak
just the smallest word,
Not more than
a honey bee
Takes on her foot
From an overspilling jar.

— Mechthild
of Magdeburg

INTRODUCTION

"To find God, you must welcome everything."
— Rabindranath Tagore

See for Yourself

If you want to understand the stars, you will need to use a telescope. If you want to understand a molecule, you will need to use a microscope. If you want to understand the ocean, eventually, you will need to get wet. If you want to understand the spiritual nature of the world, you will need a spiritual practice. In the center of all of the philosophy and science that explains and debates the existence of the soul and God lies one simple truth: spirituality is an experience. It's a journey that no one can take for you, an understanding that no one can give you.

The greatest challenge Galileo faced when he discovered the truth about the organization of our solar system was that the "experts" and "officials" of his day refused to look through his telescope to see what he could see. Many of us reject the Galileos of our time; we avoid spiritual ideas that challenge the way we see the world, or we swing to the opposite extreme and believe them without a second thought. We look to the experiences and ideas of others to tell us what to think and feel. We make decisions about what we believe without investing ourselves fully in the questions.

We've forgotten that the mind is only a small aperture through which we acquire limited kinds of knowledge; and that the body, the heart, and even the soul itself, have ways of perceiving what is true and healing. Wisdom is much more than an idea. Spiritual enlightenment asks that we awaken our spiritual senses so that we might personally discover and remember what is sacred in ourselves and the world.

This book is about the ancient pathways that have led history's great saints, sages, shamans, and mystics to spiritual awakening. It is about the way we directly experience The Sacred, and always have. It is about how we develop and refine our consciousness. There are time-tested practices that will help us along the myriad roads to the One Spirit we call by many names. These are the paths that reveal our truest selves and deepest knowledge of a Higher Power; furthermore, these are the ancient pathways of peace.

There are millions of ways of explaining consciousness, God, and The Sacred. There are countless ways of seeking an understanding of these profound mysteries; however, the core spiritual practices have remained the same throughout time. In this book, you'll encounter the 12 Master Paths that will cultivate your soul and guide your way. Once you understand the essence of the many pathways of the Spirit, all that remains is your willingness and choice.

This book is not about telling you what to believe; rather, it shows you the ways that you can learn for yourself. Its purpose is to help you find or affirm the path that's right for you—right now. This is about experiencing the infinite nature of being—in yourself and in the world. It's about your most profound potential to embrace your True Self, God, and the Spiritual World. You'll see how spiritual maturity is not only good for yourself, but also for your relationships, society, and the restoration of the natural world.

Prepare for a Journey

When I reflect on spiritual practices that I've experienced, my mind doesn't turn to textbooks and complicated instructions. Rather, my attention shifts inward and my heart opens. There's a light that burns brightly within, and the mere thought of it causes it to grow. I can feel it now. The memory of the sensation transports me through time to a simple practice, a profound moment.

🐞 🐞 🐞

It is an early summer morning. I'm 14 years old, and I'm standing at the edge of a wooden dock, overlooking a beautiful lake in Ontario, Canada. Slowly shifting shades of greens and blues surround me. This is the dock that I played on, slept on, and swam from ever since I was a baby. The sun is still low and rising in the east; the sky is pale around the brilliant solar light and fades into the deep waters around me. A few wisps of clouds wander off in the distant south.

I close my eyes and focus on my breath. Only my breath. Deeply, I breathe in the light of day. I imagine it rushing through my body, through veins, muscles, bones. The light touches every cell within me. I breathe out, long and slow.

I imagine that I'm releasing anything that stands between me and my full awareness of The Sacred. I release anything that doesn't help or heal, or that's not for my highest good. I visualize the energy of those things departing with my exhalation. The early sun is causing them to evaporate from every pore in my skin. I breathe in the light again. The cycle continues. After a short period, I open my eyes.

Below me is a reflection of myself, peering over the edge into the gently moving mirror of the lake. The water moves, and I see myself as if I'm dancing, swinging from the infinite space above me. Then a flash of life below me: a small family of fish, green and black striped perch, dart past. My awareness shifts beneath the surface into the cool world of seaweed, algae, and the smooth stone bottom covered by slippery soil and sand. For a moment, I'm one of those fish; I see the tiny particles of green floating past, feel the cool water against my scales, and move effortlessly into a shadow.

I hear a splash in the distance and look up. Rings of ripples slide over the surface of the lake about a hundred feet away. My awareness is pulled up and out toward the ripples and then to the beautiful green islands beyond. I see the silhouette of pine trees and the familiar shapes of fallen trees and rocky hills. I see the grassy shoreline and the little sandy beaches. Again my awareness travels beyond my body. I see a small shorebird looking for breakfast, and I become the dragonfly humming nearby watching to see if she's successful. I fly among the reeds, touching the water's surface momentarily. Compared to my light body, the water is a dense, almost solid world that I play upon. Diving low, I search the shore, watching patterns among the stones, sand, and driftwood; the flowers of summer; and the footprints of deer and large birds.

I hear the sound of another splash, and I'm back in my body, looking out over this breathtaking scene; feeling every detail; and experiencing the magnificent orchestra of sound, light, color, and form. I'm drinking in a moment of bliss: a true ecstasy that I feel in my bones and muscles, as if I were sunshine myself. I become a warm, life-giving ray of light.

I breathe deeply, returning to my senses, and say a prayer in my heart: *I imagine this water is the Sacred World, the One Original Source. Let this water be the light of God; let us be one.* I dive in.

The water is just cool enough to wash the warmth from my skin, revealing a new sensation. I'm swimming, staying long below the surface. Eyes wide open as I pull myself, stroke after stroke, into deeper water, farther from shore, out into the very depths of Spirit. I look to the light as I rise toward the surface and know, as sure as I know that I'm alive, that there's a Divine and Sacred Presence always just beyond the surface of things. I pray to receive it when I break through. Coming into the light again, I gasp and feel the vitality of the air. I breathe as if for the first time ever, and my spirit is new, again.

Return to The Sacred

There are no words to properly describe experiences like this one. It is more than visual, more than imagination. These moments are full of feeling, emotion, sensation, and a quiet sense of knowing that carries a timeless wisdom. It surpasses appreciation or pleasure: it's insight, peace, and a sense of connection. In such a moment, the oneness of life and the divine rhythms of nature aren't ideas, but realities as evident as our own bodies and breath. The presence of a greater force in the world is no longer an abstract concept; it becomes a clear and undeniable quality that we can experience directly. A simple practice regularly done clears the mind and opens the heart to such moments.

At times, the shift in perception may be subtle. It may be just a flash when we look at things differently—that is, when we change our perspective. It may come by surprise in an unexpected moment of beauty or inner silence. Suddenly a veil is lifted, and something sacred is revealed. We know that there's more to us than what we show our friends and family; and we know there's more to the world than what we can see, hold, and measure. Experiences like this taught me from very early on that spirituality isn't about a belief system. Spirituality is deeply personal, intimate, and beyond religion and dogma. It's an experience that awakens us to a way of being.

The spiritual path is one in which we explore questions of ultimate meaning and our relationship to the most amazing mysteries of life. Through spiritual practices, we engage and expose the deepest dimensions of our identity and directly encounter a force within ourselves and this world that we can only call "Sacred." It holds a quality that's purely transcendent; it *feels* divine—expressing qualities not of this world. It's real and life changing to encounter The Sacred, yet it's impossible to completely explain.

The spiritual journey may sound abstract or even strange at first, but its power is as real and practical as anything else we know. Without a sense of The Sacred, life becomes small and disconnected, and our vitality diminishes. In the absence of The Sacred, fear and worry have fertile ground to take root, and we feel like something is missing. Until we return to The Sacred, we live with a longing for something more.

This book will help you recognize and embrace the spiritual dimension of your life.

Consider the Source

My spiritual journey began when I was about ten years old. For some, spirituality begins with curiosity and study, and for others, it starts with a teacher or someone else who inspires the desire to learn more. However, my spiritual life began with experience. Many were like the one I just described. They were vibrant, unexpected, and as real as anything else I knew. Through such experiences, I gradually became aware of an extraordinary presence in my life and the world around me. Frequently, I'd encounter a way of seeing the world that felt magical and transforming—it was a way of listening to the spirit of things, of feeling the connection of all things. It felt like the direct perception of a divine force uniting it all, something that many people call "God." When I was young, I simply knew it as the One Spirit that was within and beyond all things.

Such moments are amazingly common for children since their spiritual senses such as intuition, vision, and symbolic thinking remain intact. Most will have frequent spiritual experiences until these senses are taught and sometimes ridiculed away by misunderstanding parents and teachers. When children talk of seeing ghosts or speaking to spirits or fairies, they're often told that they're being foolish or imaginative. Sometimes when children react to the energy of a person or a place, they're reprimanded for acting fussy or silly. Rather than engaging the intuition and spiritual senses of children, most adults become uncomfortable and try to train them to think and act in more socially acceptable ways. Eventually, like any sense or skill unused, a child can be taught to disconnect from The Sacred.

In ancient cultures where the Spiritual World is assumed or taken for granted, these senses are often celebrated or encouraged. Yet, for me, I kept most of these young visions to myself, and they didn't end with my childhood. The experiences of shifting consciousness, spiritual sight, and intuition continued throughout my life. These radical shifts in awareness have changed in form and frequency over the years, but have never left me to this day.

By the age of 13, I became more self-aware of the incredible experiences I was having and curious about whether other people saw or felt the same things. It finally occurred to me that I was aware of something that no one seemed to be talking about. Today, I can't say who actually knew of the mystical world or who did not, only that it was never spoken of.

Even when I went to synagogue with my family (or church with my friends), I never heard anyone talk about how we can not only talk to God, but also receive direct answers and intimate experiences that empower us no matter what religion or culture we identify with. In those early religious encounters, the only visions or mystic feelings I heard about were those of prophets, saints, rabbis, and priests long dead. It seemed that the living experience of Spirit was a secret reserved for a precious few. Modern religious spiritual practices seemed more about fitting in than transcendence.

My self-awareness of my spiritual experiences grew along with a sense of isolation and sadness. There came a time in my adolescence when I felt estranged from my classmates, friends, and the world I saw on television. I felt as if I were living on a different planet than they were. I began to wonder why they didn't see what I saw or feel what I felt. I felt heartbroken by the fact that the greatest source of joy in my life appeared to be of no interest or value to those around me. I had no context, no explanation or guidance. I only had the experiences: enchanting, blissful, and impossible to explain.

In retrospect, my first spiritual practice involved meditating in the wilderness. This came to me spontaneously without direction or instruction. In time, however, it didn't seem enough. The next practice I engaged in was what I call "sacred study." I dove into the world of spiritual literature with all of my attention and focus. I looked for books that might help, but the scriptures that I knew of in my Jewish heritage were difficult to read and more difficult to understand. Today, I'm aware of other options that would have spoken to me, but I didn't know of them at the time.

I don't recall how, but one day when I was about 13 or 14, I encountered three texts that changed my life: an ancient Indian Vedic text called the Upanishads, an old Buddhist scripture called the Dhammapada, and a Taoist book called the Tao Te Ching. Reading the texts was like finding my own soul uncovered. There was a simple poetry in these profound works that felt familiar despite my lack of previous study. It was astonishing, like seeing my own face in the mirror for the first time. How could these texts, thousands of years old, be describing my innermost feelings? I felt that I'd seen what they wrote about and that they wrote what I had come to understand.

Every word felt clear and true—a perfect articulation of everything I was experiencing and all that I felt I knew. These books gave me language and concepts I'd never known. For the first time, I was introduced to the notions of *nirvana, moksha, satori,* and *God-realization.* These are all words for "enlightenment": the idea that the deepest encounter of God is actually a state of mind and perception.

Suddenly it was clear that "God" is as much an inner awareness as an outside force. I saw that enlightenment is about discovering the true nature of reality, a purity of awareness that reveals the roots of suffering and a mysterious essence that is the source and substance of all things.

Through those readings, my world had been changed forever. I realized that there are hundreds of thousands of teachers, cultures, and traditions that have long been dedicated to the knowledge and experience of the Spiritual World. They all spoke of practices that could maintain and deepen the feelings of the sacred connection I had. I needed nothing more to spark an endless passion to explore the ultimate nature of reality and the many ways people seek to encounter and explain the magnificent Sacred Mystery that is called by so many names around the world.

Some call it the journey of awakening, some call it the exploration of consciousness, and others see it as the religious quest for communion and union. It seemed evident to me that the differences between the great mystical teachers and teachings were mostly linguistic, yet each variation also indicated something of importance. Each tradition and philosophy was like a facet of the same astounding gem. The world's mystics and modern philosophers such as Joseph Campbell, Huston Smith, and Aldous Huxley held firm to the affirmation: *many paths, one source.*

Those young and naïve beginnings were the roots of my lifelong search and still hold great power and meaning for me. I've explored the topics of "enlightenment," "healing states of consciousness," mysticism, psychology, and comparative religion through as many avenues as I could. The passion to comprehend the ways people understand and encounter The Sacred became an adventure that has taken me around the world and deeply into myself. It has taken me to the feet of many incredible teachers and healers, and still continues to this day.

Cross-cultural studies of spiritual beliefs and healing practices were the focus of my bachelor of arts, master of arts, and doctorate degrees. I completed a two-year interfaith ministry program with a focus on cross-cultural healing and counseling, and studied to work as a chaplain. I even explored spirituality and consciousness in the world of business development, and trained and worked for several years as a management consultant. Of course, I'm still learning and remain open to change and growth.

In time, I've come to understand that The Sacred is everywhere: within you; within me; within all things; and far, far beyond. Although I'd always struggled with doubt, skepticism, and disbelief, my commitment to spiritual practice has led me deep into a world of sacred experience. And experience is the evidence of a world that can only be measured by the heart. The volume and force of these experiences have carried me to a place where I live my life with certainty that the invisible world of Spirit is every bit as real and necessary to health, peace, and meaning as anything tangible or subject to the lens of science or physical proof.

My connection to The Sacred has always guided and helped me find hope and empowerment, guidance, and healing. When I've faced setbacks, suffering, and loss in my life, I've found that the lessons of Spirit were a constant source of love and discernment that I could always rely on. I can only hope that others will find their own experience of The Sacred and the healing wisdom that lives within.

No One Does It Alone: Teachers, Family, and Friends

The stories of wonderful experiences and enchanted moments, such as the ones featured throughout this book, are only the glimmering edge of the Spiritual World. At times, the spiritual path can be as scary as it is joyful, or as hard as it is rewarding. If it weren't for gracious guides and supportive family members, the practices would have been much more challenging.

Don't underestimate the importance of mentors, friends, and community along the way. You may have to seek out guidance, but that, too, is part of the process.

> "If on the great journey of life a [person] cannot find one
> who is better or at least as good as himself, let him
> joyfully travel alone. . . . Have for friends those whose
> soul is beautiful; go with [people] whose soul is good."
> — from the Dhammapada

I've been blessed to have met a great number of powerful and gifted spiritual teachers who have guided me in the world of spiritual practice. The guidance of wisdom keepers and spiritual teachers—people who'd journeyed through the realms of Spirit— was more precious than I can express.

I look back with a deep sense of gratitude for the teachers and spiritual leaders I've encountered in Hawaii and other parts of the U.S., New Zealand, Australia, Peru, Mexico, China, India, Canada, Israel, Swaziland, Botswana, South Africa, and Zimbabwe. I was also fortunate to meet and learn from spiritual teachers and healers from diverse cultures in the many workshops and conferences I've attended through my involvement with integrative medicine and Indigenous healing projects.

Some of my relationships with the spiritual teachers I met were brief and others have been prolonged, but none are forgotten. In all of these encounters, I've been fortunate to have experienced sacred places and teachings that have shaped my life. Among these incredible people and cultures, I've been especially blessed by the intensive practices and enduring relationships that have taken me deeply into myself and the Spiritual World. More often than not, the longer and more committed I've been to a practice, the more I've matured from it. At the same time, exploration, experimentation, and endurance are all a part of learning from spiritual practices.

Some of the shorter periods of training and practice have been life changing, such as my first trip to India during a transformative six-week period practicing Shivananda yoga and meditating with Tibetan Buddhist monks. Similarly, my weeks being introduced to traditional Spirit Medicine in Kauai, Shamanism on the upper headwaters of the Amazon, and Jewish Kabbalistic wilderness teachings in New Mexico were all unforgettable.

It's important to recognize that the longer mentored relationships and practices that I've followed for years have taken me deepest into myself and my understanding of The Sacred. These incredible and still ongoing relationships include more than 15 years of participation in the amazing ceremonial ways of the Lakota Sioux; more than seven years of apprenticing to a Venda African traditional healer; an intense three-year training with an international business consultant and executive coach who was also a master of energy and awareness; and my two-year training and internship as an interfaith minister.

A Spiritual Practice Will Take You There

If spirituality is about understanding the limits and extent of our identity while awakening to the mysterious power of the universe and the Spiritual World, how then do we explore it? Many modern paths of healing will take us beyond the limits of our beliefs and self-concepts, but eventually the water deepens, and we can no longer touch the bottom with our feet. The conventional worlds of psychology and science cease to explain all that we encounter, but spiritual practice allows us to safely explore the deeper waters and can provide a lifeboat when we're overcome by the force of the great ocean of Spirit.

When you examine the lives of the world's greatest spiritual teachers, you'll find that next to grace—the unexpected and spontaneous experience of the Divine—the most common factor in what created and sustained their awakened consciousness was having a spiritual practice. Each fostered and maintained their sense of connection and grace through a conscious and intentional spiritual life, built on intentional spiritual activities.

Jesus practiced the paths of service, prayer, meditation, and wilderness asceticism. The Buddha tried numerous practices before his awakening; and even after his great enlightenment, he still practiced various forms of meditation. Mohammed practiced prayer, meditation, pilgrimage, ritual, and fasting. We can go through the lists from around the world and still find that all great beings were committed to one practice or another. Martin Luther King, Jr., the Dalai Lama, Gandhi, Ba'al Shem Tov, Confucius, Rumi, Guru Nānak, Black Elk, Paramahansa Yogananda, Lao-tzu, Krishnamurti, and each and every Pope all used spiritual practices. In the lives of these and similar masters, we find prayer, meditation, sacred study, wilderness contemplation, and the 12 Master Paths playing a critical and formative role.

The missing link for many spiritual seekers today is recognizing that the mind can only take us so far into the world of Spirit. Books, CDs, and conferences are important, but regular and daily practices will create the lasting change that most are hungry for. When we look to the inspiring saints and sages throughout time, we love to focus on their brilliant words, deep wisdom, and comforting philosophy.

Often we forget to ask ourselves, *How did they get there?* For some, it's enough to allow others to be the masters and mystics. They're content to read and observe from a distance; and rather than truly challenging their understanding of reality, they deny their personal capacity to be their own source of wisdom and awakening.

It's easy to glorify spiritual teachers and claim that they're "special." Such an attitude absolves us from the commitment and work necessary to mature to their level of insight and integration. That's a dangerous attitude, however, because it places the source of spiritual authority in someone else and robs us of the transforming power of a personal journey. It's true that some people have special aptitudes and talents that make them excellent teachers or allow them to awaken more readily, but virtually all of the great masters shared the conviction that every person has the potential to become enlightened: fully awakened to the love and wisdom of our Sacred Source and Universal Life Force.

True spiritual maturity isn't regulated by status, wealth, nationality, intelligence, or vocation. It emerges through a mysterious process of grace, practice, and direct experience. You'll never understand the world next door if you never leave your home. We all need vehicles to travel, especially in the spiritual landscape of the world.

Just Words: The Limits of Language

When describing their spiritual experiences and beliefs, people use words and phrases such as *consciousness, Spirit, God, the ultimate nature of reality,* and *the spirit world* to explain what they're encountering. They use descriptions such as "a Higher Power," "a Sacred Force," "Great Mystery," or "Divine Energy." A person's history of experience is the key factor in shaping the words that feel appropriate. Culture and experience don't dictate what's right—just what's right for you.

Throughout this book, I'll be using terms such as *The Sacred, The Divine Mystery, God, Soul,* and *Sacred Source* interchangeably to refer to the astounding and complex dimensions of the Spiritual World and the Ultimate Source Energy/Force/Being. My preference is simply to use the term *The Sacred,* which may be interpreted as

"God," "The Divine Energy of All," or "Consciousness." I do *not* refer to God according to any one religious tradition or as a being with humanlike qualities.

Please don't be distracted by words. Every culture in the world has names for The Sacred and its many aspects. Some cultures have only a few names for God; and others have hundreds, each offering insight into a different aspect of consciousness. If one term for The Sacred works for you, use it. If another term I use doesn't work for you, let it go and replace it in your mind with one that feels right. Ultimately, words are only symbols.

As you explore the stories and practices within these pages, find the balance between using the words that are comfortable for you and being willing to consider new terms and the realities behind them. Remember the wise admonition of Joseph Campbell, who wrote: "God is a metaphor for that which transcends all levels of intellectual thought. It's as simple as that."

A Million Stories: Speaking for Myself

Being a spiritual teacher has always been an interesting tight-rope to walk. It's important to share conviction, personal truth, and information about the world and its many paths, philosophies, and perspectives. Facts and theories can only take you so far, and then you must take it the rest of the way. In this book, much of what I share about spiritual practice is presented in stories. The personal accounts I share are all essentially true: based on true events, people, and places. In most cases, however, I've changed names and distorted or edited some facts to ensure the privacy and anonymity of the people I write about. In a few cases, I've condensed the timelines of true events for ease of reading or to protect the privacy of the individuals involved.

I've chosen stories over facts and analysis, for in stories we find the heart and color of life. I hope that reading descriptions from my own spiritual adventures will awaken in you a clarity and longing to explore the equally amazing and significant stories yet to be found in your own life.

As you explore the world of spiritual practice, remember that it's not only great masters who teach and heal. The friends and family around you are also great spiritual teachers, each expressing their truths about the world as they understand it. If you truly seek growth and healing, then respect each voice you encounter in life: neighbors, co-workers, friends, family, trees, rivers, fire, wind, and our animal relatives. Everything teaches if we're prepared to listen with the heart. Everything sings its own song, completing the fullness of life.

If you are to find your own song and harmony with The Sacred, you'll only come to know it through the lessons and lenses of your own life. It doesn't matter if you're atheist or agnostic, psychic or pious, or religious or spiritual; the experience of the ultimate nature of our mysterious world is life changing and available to all.

How This Book Is Organized

This book is divided into six sections. In Part I, you'll explore the nature of spirituality and spiritual growth, including an explanation of what spirituality is and why it's important. As you move through its definitions and connections to health, healing, and enlightenment, you'll finish with an understanding of why spiritual practice is valuable to all people, and critical to those who seek spiritual and personal growth. In this first section, you'll also be introduced to the timeless 12 Master Paths that form the core of this book. The Master Paths are universal practices that I've encountered again and again around the world. They recur in sacred texts and accounts throughout time, and resurface in communities whenever they've been pushed aside long enough. Although there are thousands of spiritual practices, these are the 12 essential forms that have shaped and fed the human spiritual journey.

Then, in Parts II though V, you'll journey into the nature and experience of the 12 Master Paths. These sections are arranged according to the four essential dimensions of spiritual personality that they focus and draw upon: body-centered practices, mind-centered practices, heart-centered practices, and soul-centered practices, respectively. Each of these Parts comprises three chapters; each chapter discusses a Master Pathway through stories and teachings that reveal the lived experiences and common lessons that emerge from them.

Part VI, the final section of this book, concludes with a chapter that summarizes the benefits of a spiritual practice and its application in daily life. I also address the relevance of spiritual practice in the grand scheme of global challenge and change. You'll find the invitation and inspiration to awaken to a deeper experience of life and love for the transformation of yourself and the healing of the world.

You'll see that no matter where you're at in your personal life—high or low, rich or poor, sick or well—this is the perfect time for you to embrace a spiritual practice and discover the ever-present power of The Sacred. Everything you've gone through up to this very moment has been exactly what was necessary to prepare you for what comes next. You need nothing more than what you have with you right now to experience the most profound peace and wisdom of your life.

I see through the ancient archways
the sacred door is open
in the distance a traveler comes
through time
and from the heart of spirit
I know the journey well,
I watch the moving form, though
I cannot tell if they are coming or going
is the sun rising or setting
is it man or woman
the path shines like a thin deep river
shadows and light play tricks on the mind
but none of this matters
this is the arrival and the departure
there is only one direction:
inward
the road is littered with scrolls and beads
talismans, scriptures, rattles, and robes
every step is sacred
and none of it matters
for the road only leads one place:
home.
— J. H. Ellerby

PART I

Understanding Spirituality

God approaches
Like sunrise.
As the light draws near
Life awakens
in the pale and flowing
Blue light of dawn
Birds prepare the day
It is impossible to sleep now
With the promise of light so near

I stay awake, waiting for the arrival
I'd give my life just to wait for you
Every step a prayer for you
Every step a moment closer to you

I am so lost now,
I cannot distinguish my love for you
From my love for the path toward you
In through the beauty
of nature's color and dancing energy

Into a force and presence within all.
Each is illuminated in The One,
And we merge
I, too, become the love and clear light that you are
I seek you until
Nothing is left
but you, and then
Only Love and Light remain.

— J. H. Ellerby

Chapter One

SPIRITUALITY IS
NOT RELIGION

Absolutely Nothing Happened: The Quest

The summer after I graduated from high school, I set out on a road trip on August 5, my 18th birthday. This was the first chance I had to make my own truly independent and epic quest. I'd go alone, with no plan and no hindrance. I was determined to make a direct and deeper connection with The Sacred than ever before.

Filled with years of spiritual experiences, mystical longing, and the insights of a range of sacred texts and modern thinkers, I set out to find nirvana within. Looking back, it seems absurd and perhaps naïve, but at the time there was no doubt in my mind that a deeper awareness was possible and waiting for me. Nature had always been my greatest source of spiritual inspiration and connection, and I was committed to immersing myself in months of spiritual practice in the beauty and grace of the wilderness.

In preparation, I'd spent a great deal of time reading about Indigenous traditions to understand how I could incorporate ceremony in my time away. I read about Zen Buddhism to learn how I could involve meditation in my journey. Vedic texts and the work of Joseph Campbell helped me understand the language of prayer and the power of intention. I also began to explore ascetic practices and read a fantastic book called *The Roaring of the Sacred River* by Meredith Little and Steven Foster about the process of seeking spiritual wisdom through solitude in nature.

I tried to complement all of this study by meeting with people who had experience in each of these areas. In some cases I was successful; in others, I wasn't. One thing was clear: all of these writings talked about the importance of separating from the familiar and immersing oneself in a spiritual practice. Isolation, contemplation, and strong intent were essential.

At the heart of these ancient pathways is the call to surrender everything to the process of transformation. It asks nothing less than a "letting go" that is so profound that it's like death itself. I was willing and determined to do all I could to break the illusions of my own mind and ego. Even though I didn't fully understand what I'd encounter or how it would change me, only one thing mattered: awakening to the Spirit of The Sacred. If it was possible for thousands of other people over the centuries, I was sure it could happen for me, too.

The journey was fun and full of surprises. I was fortunate to be at a time in my life when I didn't mind sleeping in my car, driving long hours to lost campgrounds, or eating sparsely from time to time. I met many characters and followed signs and synchronicities. I camped alone in the western national parks of the United States. I wandered riversides and mountain trails. I searched out the places that caught my attention and invigorated my spirit. I attended gatherings, workshops, and ceremonies that I found along the way. It was a compelling and liberating time.

Unlikely Guidance

While camping on a beach in California, I was befriended by two drunk prospectors. They recounted the most outrageous tales of their misadventures in the High Sierra. Their laughter and storytelling flowed like the cases of beer they were draining at an alarming rate. Late in the evening, they poured out a story of a place accessible only by off-road vehicles that was so remote and wild, they'd never seen a trace of another human being there. Their demeanor changed and they sobered up as they talked about the tranquility, the rugged beauty, and the silence that was deafening: "It gets so quiet up there, you'd think the sound of your beating heart could scare off the birds."

Against all the better judgment that my parents had tried to impart about taking risks and talking to strangers, I was sure these were my mythical guides, and I decided to set out in search of this American Shangri-la. A feeling within told me that there on that mountain I'd find what I was looking for. There I'd create my ceremony, my sacred rite. In that place, I'd meditate and pray until I saw the naked face of God—if only I didn't get lost following the directions of two intoxicated strangers!

Remarkably, the drunken directions were both clear and easy to follow. Within a few days and after traversing some hair-raising back roads that were more like hiking trails, I arrived. The place was truly extraordinary. It was extremely high in the Sierras and from the ridges of stone and pine, I could see far and wide into a vast range of mountains and valleys to the east. The air was notably different as well; it felt cleaner, thinner, crisper. There was a sense of isolation that was inescapable and a secret thrill in the danger of a location beyond easy rescue. I set up my camp and began to plan my "great spiritual quest."

Expect the Unexpected

That first night after dinner, I decided to go for a walk in the moonlight. Nearby was a large area of exposed rock. It was a wonderfully smooth hilly outcrop that shone in the pale blue light of evening. I decided to take an old blanket with me so I could sit for a while. I felt that I needed to go and pray for guidance and help in the days to come—to take a last look at the world as I knew it.

I wanted to pray for the insight I'd traveled so far to experience. I was growing nervous about what I was committing myself to, and so it seemed wise to take some time to be still and receive guidance. I wanted to be sure that my intention came from my heart and not my ego. I wanted to approach this next journey with reverence.

After a short walk, I found myself at the foot of the bald rock outcropping I'd seen from my camp and walked up and over the smooth granite surface to the highest point. The stone face was glowing beneath the moonlight. I noticed that the moon was almost full and thought, *Tomorrow would be a perfect night for my passage into spirit.* I felt the rising force of fear as I wondered how many days I might have to spend in isolation: waiting, fasting, and praying. I chased the thoughts from my head as I placed my folded blanket, like a pillow, on the ground.

I knelt down facing the moon and took a moment to relax. I knew that the passion I felt for my spiritual path was essential to cultivate the energy and focus that would be the gate to deeper awareness. I also knew that the desire to control the experience, or any emotion of anxiety or impatience, could douse the very fire I was building. I took a deep breath. Every day of my trip I sat in meditation at least twice and kept a daily ceremony of gratitude and intention. I sang, read, danced—whatever seemed right. That night, I resumed my evening ritual of prayer and meditation.

Looking around, I could see the way the sky became darker and the stars appeared brighter the farther they were from the moon. The whole world around me was like a dark lake of deep shadows. Silhouettes of tall pines and patches of moonlight were scattered on stones and open spaces. I surrendered my senses to the beauty that flooded my vision. This wasn't a time for thoughts or analysis, nor was it a time for poetry or metaphor. I sat for a while and allowed myself to become still.

With each moment of silence, the energy of the world grew stronger. I could hear distant frogs by a pond, crickets, and the occasional night bird. I heard the twitch and rustle of the smallest animals searching for food among the pine needles and grasses. The sound of my breath was overwhelming . . . my heartbeat was like thunder. I wondered if the creatures would be scared off by the noise of my simple existence. I tried to soften my breath and was floating on the slow depth of the night. The stillness was intense.

A surge of profound gratitude filled my body. How could I be so blessed to have this perfect moment on Earth? Just to have the opportunity, the luxury to make such a quest, was a gift beyond measure. I remembered abruptly that I'd come to pray and took the time to bring my attention back to words, thoughts, and feelings.

I stared up at the moon as if she could hear my soul, as if she were the face of The Sacred in this moment. The giant, white silver disk was more than a distant celestial body, but the very light and presence of God made manifest. I spoke my prayers of gratitude to her. I felt her loving attention, like a grandmother listening to her dear grandchild.

I gave thanks for the vastness of this world, honoring the four directions of the universe. I gave thanks for my family, for my life, and for the one fragile moment I sat within. I became absorbed in the moment. I forgot about the quest I'd planned for the next day; in fact, I'd forgotten about everything except the pure beauty of the moment and the infinite gratitude that I was overflowing with. And then, something happened.

As I stared at the moon, the world in my peripheral vision began to dissolve. I became aware of it for a moment, blinked, and it all returned. I hadn't consumed any alcohol or unusual foods. And I hadn't taken drugs of any kind, nor had I anytime prior. I was a bit confused by this experience. I felt so alert that it seemed my eyes were playing tricks on me. It was an odd sensation and made me a bit nervous.

I tried to relax and took a deep breath in and out. I returned my gaze to the moon, and the earth around me disappeared once again. My eyes were open, and I watched as slowly the sky, too, began to dissolve. I started to lose awareness of my body. Stars faded into the night sky; eventually, there was only an infinite field of dark and the sacred white light of God shining through the moon. My attention was transfixed: there was nothing in existence but that brilliant light in infinite space.

I became the light for a moment, a taste of Formless Spirit. It was vibration, life force, and joy—only for a moment. Then unexpectedly, the moon also vanished. The sense of Divine Energy dissipated along with it. Wide awake, my eyes still wide open, there was absolutely nothing in the world to see. Everything had become one dark blue awareness. Then my awareness of Nothing itself collapsed into an experience beyond experience. It was as if *everything* dissolved . . . absolutely everything.

What happened next, I can only describe in retrospect. I experienced a moment without time or space or content of any kind. There was no awe, no love, no unity, and no presence. There was no God, no Web of Life, or Sacred Voice . . . nothing. There was no Spirit World or Divine Energy. There wasn't even the experience of Love or Joy such as people encounter in the mystical awareness of pure Spirit. It was the experience of the cessation of all perception while fully awake. It was the vastness that embraces all that is and all that is waiting to be. Even the words *eternity* and *infinity* seem too small for time and space, for these are concepts that can't be held up to such a moment of Sacred Awareness.

There was only an awareness so clear that there was no awareness at all. It was void, it was emptiness, it was more than infinite, and it was eternal and beyond any dimensional quality. There was no self, no subject, no ideas, and no feelings. What existed was nothing more than awareness reflecting awareness: the absolute insubstantial substance of all being. It's pure silence, pure stillness. It is a radical emptiness that obliterated all self-awareness and consumed all reality. What it really is, is impossible to describe.

When Nothing Can Be the Same Again

After what could have been moments (or hours), I suddenly became aware of the emerging presence of the sky. It was surfacing in my field of vision, as if rising out of a dark sea. First I noticed a few stars, then the moon. There wasn't a cloud in the sky, nor had there ever been that night, but it was as if the moon and stars were materializing from thin air or from behind a cloud. From Pure Consciousness to the resonant Love of a Formless Spirit, to the subtle vibrations and flow of Divine Energy.

Eventually, I became aware of the dark earth: soaring ponderosa pines, spruce, and the rocky hills atop the mountain. Finally, I gasped. I'd completely forgotten my body or that I had one. I don't even know if I'd been breathing. It was only very slowly that I realized there was an "I" sitting on a rock, praying in the night. It came as a surprise to recognize my body again, as if the great void was more familiar than my own skin. It felt as if The Sacred Void was the true reality and that all of the emerging world were but a dream.

I began to move my tongue over my teeth as if for the first time. Each surface felt so foreign and unusual. I slowly flexed a finger with amazement. I felt alien to my own body; it was like a heavy robe, and I—my awareness, my spirit—was naked inside. I watched my thoughts form like clouds, brief rains of impulse and intention, and then the body followed as willed. Slowly, as if recovering from amnesia, I recalled my name; and then the awareness of my life and history gradually returned.

Every aspect of "who" I'd been prior to that moment was clearly absurd. I'd confused my "self" for my body, my family, my name, my journey, my emotions, and my thoughts. I thought all of those things were me. I called them "mine" as if I was inseparable from them, but now I knew that, in the one true reality, *nothing is mine and nothing is me!* The shocking frailty and limits of my ego were radically exposed and exploded in a way I would never forget. Every mystic riddle I'd ever encountered suddenly became clear to me. Everything made sense, now that nothing did. It was the most natural moment of total paradox.

I sat in sober shock, as ideas and feelings filled my being. In that most transparent, translucent moment, I experienced myself as *one* with the true nature of being—the essence of God beyond form, thought, *or* feeling. The world had become meaningless and profound. Everything seemed broken and out of balance, yet everything felt perfect and peaceful. Every question in my life was answered. Every spiritual passage, scripture, and poem that I'd encountered had fallen into place, like a jigsaw revealed before my inner vision. Yet *in* the moment of Clear Awareness, there were no words, no ideas, no thoughts, and no feelings.

The melting of the world around me into the nothingness wasn't an optical illusion, but a revelation of the true essence of all things as expressions of One Spirit beyond concept. It was clear that this was showing something other than one system of things, but literally an essence and substance within and beyond everything and nothing. Rather than an immediate feeling of "emptiness" afterward, what I felt instead was a profound fullness and exquisite sense of union and communion with the "Sacredness" that is absolutely all and everything.

This was a moment more incredible than Divine love and connection; it was true dissolution and identification at once. It has shaped and touched all other moments of my life and has become the foundation of my understanding of self and meaning, for within it, there was no discovery, only a deep sense of knowing. It was an awakening to the field of Living Energy that is the world, the watcher, the wisdom, the source, and something yet beyond all that. In the experience of Nothing, I felt as if I'd realized everything.

This encounter wasn't only of the life behind life and the energy within energy, it was the permeating Awareness that is everything, nothingness, and more. As I looked around, not only did I see and feel that all things were from the Divine Source, but I saw and felt that all things *are* Divine. Every stone, every breath of wind, every thought, and every moment—everything is sacred.

When it was all over and I was present enough to move, I experienced a state of complete calm and peace. My body felt like it was gently vibrating to an imperceptible hum, and I began to make my way back to my tent. Still overwhelmed, I lay down and again an immense sense of gratitude emerged in me—a joy and thankfulness for this experience, this revelation.

It felt like everything in my heart and mind had been cleared and washed clean. The feelings came so strongly, I burst into tears. I wept for a long time, as my body shook with deep sobs of love and thankfulness. There were no thoughts to contain my joy, only feelings that exploded within me. That night the entire universe felt perfect, calm, and serene. It changed my life forever.

Self or Spirit: Which Way Are We Headed?

*"When you look at the unchanging Existence from the outside,
you call it God; and when you look at it from the inside,
you call it yourself. It is but one."*
— Swami Vivekananda

This profound experience came unexpectedly and as a result of a deep commitment to the practices that lead to a greater experience of Spirit and the self. We can't always count on such moments in our spiritual practice, yet when we understand the potential that lies ahead, all we can do is make the commitment and take a step.

This personal account reminds me of a well-known Hasidic Jewish story of a wise king who was wealthy and powerful beyond imagination. He had a very young son who, growing up in the royal palace, began to become spoiled, poor tempered, and ungrateful for the abundance and opulence he lived in. Fearing that his child would grow to be a terrible and heartless man, the king decided to send him away from the castle. Although the child was only five or six years of age, he was sent to the farthest reaches of the kingdom to live with a good-hearted and humble family of peasants. The decision was painful for the king, but it was the most loving thing he could think to do.

The boy soon changed dramatically. Forgetting the palace's comforts, he learned to love to work the land, care for his new brothers and sisters, and help out in the local village. He was a fine young man. As he passed through adolescence, however, he began to have dreams that haunted him. In his dreams, he was a prince in a regal palace, and his father was a great and wise king. Soon the dreams tormented him so much that he came to believe that it was in fact a memory of the past or a vision of the future. He was of royal blood, and he knew it.

Although his kind guardians tried to evade his questions about the past, he knew in his heart that his true parents and home were somewhere far from where he lived. One day he confronted his family and said, "You have been nothing but generous and loving parents to me. I will always love and be grateful to you, but there's a part of me that I have forgotten. A part that I must find, no matter what it takes. Nothing you say can stop me, for I'm certain that these dreams are true. I must reclaim my birthright. This is not for power or wealth, but because it's my truth, and without living that truth I will die."

The young man set off. His guardians immediately ran to the village representative for the king and sent urgent word that the son was seeking his way home. The king's messenger raced across the countryside on horseback, and the king soon received the news. The court advisers panicked and exclaimed, "What should we do, dear king? Shall we have him diverted, distracted, or misled? Maybe we could send forces to restrain him or to convince him he is mad?"

With tears in his eyes, the wise king rose to his feet. "No, my son has been away from home long enough, and he has learned well. Prepare my carriage for travel, for we'll leave immediately and meet him halfway. I long to have him home again, by my side."

☆ ☆ ☆

In many ways, each one of us is like that young boy. We've been caught up in lives that have taught and challenged us, but something deeper calls to us, asking us to remember who we really are. Many of us come to believe that we are defined by our situation. However, something within us longs to return to our sacred birthright—to feel at home in ourselves, at home in this world.

We are tested and challenged. When will we begin the quest? When will we admit the longing, the dream that lives within us? Our spiritual paths are like the journey of that young man. No sooner do we make the effort and feel the certainty of our direction and life begins to respond. Our Sacred Origin works with us to bring us home.

The Sacred Power in this world is much like the king in this story: wanting what is best for us, willing to allow us to endure all the lessons that life will send. Yet it remains ever ready to reach out, whenever we're ready to return. It begins with a feeling and then a step in any direction. We were gifted the royal blood, a spark of the Divine. Each of us carries the memory of our sacred origin. We've all been given enough of a vision to find our way back. When the student is ready, the lessons appear.

From this story, we see that spirituality is about both the recognition of the "true self" and the memory of our sacred origin—a higher power. Amazingly, on the spiritual path we find that the journey to know the self and the journey to know God are really one and the same.

On that incredible night high in the Sierra Nevada mountain range, what I experienced was the unity of the self and the Spirit. There was no way to discern God from self or self from God, or Spirit from energy or energy from Spirit. It was an instant of pure awareness. In a moment more radically empty of thought, feeling, or form than I can express was the simple realization that our day-to-day senses perceive a very important but limited dimension of what is "real."

In the most profound moments of spiritual practice, regardless of the practice, we awaken to a reality that feels more true, more permanent, and more substantial than anything else we've ever experienced. What burns away in such flashes of brilliant Light are all the falsehoods that limit health, self, and society. For a moment, we touch the eternal. The more we expose the limits and false elements of our identity, the closer we come to understanding ourselves as an expression of a Great Miracle and Divine Spirit. The further into the nature of The Sacred we go, the more it teaches us about ourselves.

Many of us have had moments, glimpses, or immersions— like that magical moonlit night—when we *know* that the division between the self and The Sacred is simply a matter of perception. As I experience new dimensions of my own identity, I'm able to release old expectations and gain new awareness of my limiting beliefs.

The intent of our spiritual practice isn't to escape life but to embrace it. The content of our spiritual experiences isn't disconnected from our everyday life; rather, it's vitally important to it.

When we choose to integrate the wisdom we encounter through our spiritual practices, our lives are healed in a radical way. When individuals and communities of people deepen their direct experience of the spiritual nature of this universe, the world is transformed to reflect the qualities of those experiences: peace, connection, love, and cooperation. We begin to see that The Sacred is *not* a separate being; it is our own nature. We experience the "oneness" of all things.

What Is Spirituality?

Years ago I spoke at a women's health gathering in a small town in Ontario, Canada. On that cold winter's night, the small lecture hall was full. It was clear to me that not all the people attending were passionate about my topic or even interested in me. The town was small enough that I expect many came simply for something to do. For some, it was a warm place to see friends and pass the evening.

I spoke about the importance of spirituality as a foundation of health and well-being. Seeing many elderly faces, I tried to emphasize the message of connection and compassion because for many single elderly people, loneliness and a sense of spiritual emptiness can be crippling. I've also experienced that some elderly people become trapped in stagnant ideas of religion that foster a sense of fear and keep them from trying new things and meeting interesting people.

One woman in the audience seemed to be a perfect example. She looked concerned by my comments and sat with a grumpy expression on her face until I finished. She was hard to ignore, as she was dressed in an odd outfit of mismatched colors and exuded something I couldn't make sense of.

Afterward a small group of interested people gathered around to speak with me and each other. The older woman I had my eye on was one of them. I was surprised, and immediately went to greet her.

"Thank you for coming," I said. "Do you have any questions?"

"Yes," she said sternly. "I spent my whole life getting in trouble with my family and friends for not going to church with them, but I was never into religion. Where I grew up, there was too much hypocrisy and judgment. I found that all the interesting people were from somewhere else. You know, I befriended all the immigrants in our little town. That was back in the days when there weren't too many of them in these parts."

She went on, "I recall there was the Chinese couple who moved in for a time and the big East Indian family, too. My goodness, could they cook up a storm! My best friend was a Native American lady. We used to sew together, and sometimes I'd go to her community for those gatherings they have. What a pleasure! You know you don't need to travel far if you just open your mind to the people around you.

"But I became the black sheep in my family, and I still am. My family didn't trust those people and just wanted to stick together. To me, life isn't about making your world smaller and smaller. It's about making friends, you know? Being kind, helping out, and having fun while you do it. If you can't enjoy the little things like the crisp winter snow and the smell of the summer breeze, then you may as well be dead.

"I just don't have patience for people who are busy telling others how to be. They should just love and let live. If the world gives you lemons, you make some lemonade and take it next door. Do you understand what I'm saying?"

She seemed lost in her thoughts, but I was very attentive. "Of course I know exactly what you're saying."

"So then you come here talking about this 'spirituality'—now, what am I supposed to do with that? Is it a religion of some kind? It sounds all right, but I can't figure how to make it work for me. I'm sure that I'm too old to start something new."

"Well," I responded carefully, "if you don't mind me saying so, I don't think you need to change a thing. You know the 'way of living' that you're talking about: kindness, curiosity, an appreciation of the little things, and making the most of each day. *That* is spirituality, and it's a natural part of being human if you can let go of all the junk that life piles on you. I mean things like roles, expectations, assumptions, and fears. It sounds to me like you don't need anyone to teach you anything. I'd say we could all learn a lot from you. *Spirituality* is just a word. It's about how you make your way in the world. The idea isn't important; it's the living expression that matters most."

She smiled and looked me in the eyes. "It's like once you've bought your groceries, there's no need to keep the list, eh? That word *spirituality* just helps you get somewhere. Right? You educated kids, you've got a word for everything. I just hope you do more than talk about it."

This woman reminds us that spirituality and spiritual growth is so natural to being human that we don't need all the words and concepts to take the journey. Spiritual growth is about the movement toward the realization of our truest identity and most integrated awareness of The Sacred in the world around us: self-knowledge and Divine Connection.

These are qualities that some people naturally move toward—without special languages or instruction. Many are already living a deeply spiritual life but doubt themselves because their actions and beliefs don't fit a familiar "box" like religion or some established philosophy. Defining spirituality is a task of the mind and can become a distraction. The concept can be more confusing the more we try to define it. Communication, however, is also important, so it's worth defining our terms.

Defining Spirituality

The very definition of spirituality is a personal process. The definition that's comfortable for you today will evolve over time if you're growing and maturing. Nevertheless, to help in the process of discussing spiritual matters, you can think of spirituality as: *your relationship to whatever you consider to be most sacred*. In this case, the term *sacred* refers to things of ultimate meaning, power, and value: worthy of deepest reverence. It's impossible to examine your relationship to The Sacred without being led to the challenging questions of identity and higher power. You may consider these the central elements of "spirituality."

If spirituality is new to you, you can simplify your understanding by thinking of spirituality as: *your deepest personal sense of meaning, identity, and connection.* This definition will take you down the same path as the one previously described. Everyone lives from a personal sense of meaning, identity, and connection. These core elements are what guide each of us, whether we manage them wisely or not. Meaning and identity are as necessary as blood and breath. They're essential to who you are; they shape your choices and attitudes. Your spirituality is the foundation of your well-being and health. You might call your spirituality your worldview or consciousness—it's how you understand the ultimate nature of being. A healthy spiritual practice will help you deepen these things.

Spirituality Is Not Religion

If we think of spirituality as our deepest experience of The Sacred, in the world and within us, then we see that religion may be a support to exploring and experiencing these elements. The religions of the world are vast repositories of practices and philosophies that point us toward The Sacred. They offer timeless wisdom and sophisticated systems that can advance the soul. Yet if we understand that spirituality is ultimately about a person's sense of identity, connection, and meaning, then it's equally true that religion is *not* necessary and may sometimes even be an obstacle to spirituality.

A religion is typically a social organization built around common beliefs and practices that reflect a shared assumption about the nature of The Sacred and the self. There are many people who find their spirituality ignited and fed by their religion. Spirituality and religion may function in harmony; and we must not forget all the good work, charity, and service that's done in the name of religion. There's also great value in understanding and honoring your heritage: your language, ancestors, and traditions. These strong foundations can bring great meaning and stability to a spiritual path.

In contrast, spirituality, for some, will never closely follow a religious community or prescription. For many, religion becomes a barrier to spirituality and feeds off fear; a desire to belong; and a lack of willingness to truly question and explore the nature of life, the self, and The Sacred. The gift of religion is its capacity to preserve and transmit teachings of philosophies and practices that, if engaged with a spiritual focus, can serve as powerful vehicles of connection and awareness of The Sacred. When politics and ego get involved, religion can be dangerous. While I believe that a conscious spiritual practice supported by guides and community is essential to a life of peace and balance, I haven't found religion to be necessary. There are many ways to find these elements.

This is difficult for some people to accept. Whether out of true belief or fear, many religious leaders claim that "their way" is the only one. Old mind-sets such as this only impair the spiritual path and stunt personal maturity. Individuals can only know the "right path" for themselves. Spirituality is so personal, so intimate; it isn't for one person to tell another what his or her spirituality should be.

There can be no one "right religion" for all, just as there's no "perfect" path or practice. In fact, such ideas defy all logic when we see how profoundly personal spirituality is. Because judgment and fear are so contrary to maturity, healing, and growth, the merits of spiritual elitism, fundamentalism, and extremism should always be questioned. It's possible, however, to present a religion, philosophy, or idea of The Sacred to others. After that, we must leave them to their personal choice. Throughout history, spirituality has never been successfully forced on individuals or groups without great pain and loss. Religious practices and statements of faith are extremely external, and certainly can be imposed on people—behaviors can be demanded but genuine feeling cannot.

The actual lasting and meaningful changing of a person's heart and mind is something that only an *experience* of The Sacred can do. Looking around the world, we find endless examples of traditions of all kinds being forced upon others. Anywhere we find spirituality imposed or prohibited, we find a decay of the spirit. Life loses its vitality and meaning when spirituality is controlled or contrived.

Human history and human nature have demonstrated the absurdity of seeking one true religion. Change is inevitable, diversity is natural, and so is the integration and evolution of tradition. In both Judaism and Islam, each contain nearly 200 movements and branches. In Hinduism and Buddhism, there are only a handful of major "schools" or "sects," but when we look further, we find thousands of Buddhist variations, schools, and branches. There are perhaps millions of subcultures of Hinduism. In the Christian world, more than 2,000 sects have developed in less than 2,000 years. Diversity is the essence and nature of life on Earth. Spiritual expression is no exception.

The End of Religion?

As you learn that spirituality is cultivated by personal practice and defined by direct experience, you begin to realize that religion isn't necessary in order to be spiritual. Spirituality can be cultivated in groups, traditions, communities, and religions; or it can exist spontaneously, finding form as needed to grow. It will need certain basic elements to grow; and spiritual practice is like the soil that grounds, feeds, and creates a foundation for the plants that reach for the light. The key is practice and the evolution of consciousness—not religion. Regardless of whether you have spirituality with or without religion, what's important is to immerse yourself in the experience of the path that's right for you. Experience your lines of connection and intimacy with the Divine with depth, honesty, and complete vulnerability.

In the terrible wake of destruction that religiously motivated wars, persecution, and politics have left behind, many people struggle to find meaning or the depth of spirituality that they crave within their religious traditions. At one extreme, we find people clinging more fervently to religion as a means to weather the storm. However, many people are turning away from religion or are at least questioning its true purpose. The problem isn't religion, but how it's used.

This book is neither an endorsement for nor against religion—that is your personal choice. As people understand the power of spiritual practice, then community, guidance, and history can be a great help. The healthy role of religion is to serve as a source of guidance: well-maintained vehicles of awakening and a community of support, love, and accountability. It's important to note that this powerful role is still possible and fulfilled by religious communities everywhere. Sadly, religion has also become a breeding ground of fear, control, judgment, intolerance, and the many ills of a persona-driven life.

Debating the success or failure of religion is to be caught up in a mind game of judgment. Your energy is best spent on becoming the qualities you wish to see in the world. If you work toward being free, peaceful, and fulfilled, the world will change around you. If religion helps you, honor that and follow with integrity and deepest intent. Arguments about faith and religion don't help to heal or awaken. It's time to turn your attention to your experience of The Sacred and to listen to what those moments are whispering to your heart. What calls you? Where do you feel connected?

More Than Feeling Good: The Supernatural Is Natural

For many people who do embrace spirituality today, their focus is only about self-knowledge and self-awareness. It is about the betterment of one's personal life. This is one of the natural healing directions of the spiritual journey: the realization of our deepest sense of self. The idea of acquiring new freedom, peace, and power is tempting and exciting. Spirituality can help us break the boundaries of our false limits and find a sacred center from which to live with inspiration and intention. All these promises are true, but they come with their own challenges and new problems. The journey never ends.

Spiritual awakening doesn't mean that we'll cease to experience loss, pain, or life's problems; and it isn't about getting everything that we desire. Spiritual awakening is about learning to love what already is and finding the clarity and power to make intentional choices when we need to. It's the daily balance between being masters of change and masters of acceptance.

Through years of friendships, teachers, and working with thousands of people on their healing journeys, I've heard the stories of many who've risen above oppression, trauma, illness, and poverty because of their spirituality. I've seen how their spiritual practices have helped them better understand themselves and their place in the world. Moreover, it's developed critical qualities in them, such as patience, endurance, and self-awareness.

Spirituality is also about the experience and understanding of the astonishing dimensions of Spirit that defy the mundane and material world. Altered states, spiritual beings, miracles, and mysterious energy fields are all a part of the vast world of The Sacred. Some choose to turn their attention away from these aspects of life because their mind can't or won't fully grasp its nature. The fact that the Spiritual World confounds science and defies thought doesn't excuse us from its exploration.

There are many dimensions and layers to The Sacred. The spiritual journey may take us into the depth of who we are as individuals, revealing limiting and false beliefs. It may take us into the complexities of the metaphysical world where we encounter angels and Divine Energy. Or it may take us into the Sacred Life Force and Source that transcends all things, even all thought. These are all aspects of the same Sacred Power, expressed in different ways.

Regardless of how you name it, The Sacred is something we most fully perceive with the heart and with senses long neglected in the Western world. Dreams, intuitions, gut feelings, visions, and subtle sensations are the eyes and ears of the soul. These felt-senses and similar spiritual senses aren't measurable, but they're clearly felt in the body and in subtle ways that can only be described as inner feelings. Although many of us have been trained to overlook these senses, to deny them is to deny the fullness of our humanity. To shun these senses and the world they point us toward comes at our own cost. We need the supernatural world as much as we need the natural world.

I'm reminded of the clients I've met over the years who've placed all their attention and energy on their work, neglecting the needs of their body. Diet and exercise are forgotten in favor of career. Years later they pay the price of their neglect and struggle to manage chronic health conditions, illness, and vitality. Similarly, I've met many people who've ignored their emotional needs in service of vocation, children, and family; and after decades of overlooking those inner needs, their work life changes, their kids move away, and their own aging parents pass on. These people are left with a profound sense of emptiness, grief, and confusion. They wonder, *Who have I become?* The heart longs for its renewal and restoration. The mind is unsure of what's next and begins to turn toward fear.

In much the same way, a life without the expression and experience of the soul grows numb beneath layers of stress, fear, and disconnection. Having forgotten our birthright, we're puzzled by the subtle, nagging sense that there must be something "more" to life. We long for experiences of the things we call "Spirit," "God," and the "Spiritual World," yet we're caught in a self-perpetuated trap of materialism and unconscious patterns. Our tribal taboo keeps us from wandering beyond the village of the mind into the wilderness of the heart and soul. The communal warning haunts us: "If you can't prove it, it's probably not really there." But mystery is no reason to fear the journey.

Every day, every one of us experiences things that we don't understand but, nevertheless, rely on for our existence. Gravity, electricity, global politics, economics, light, heat, radio waves, and even the mechanics of our own breath and blood are all examples of what few of us fully comprehend yet are necessary to the foundation of our lives.

We use cell phones and can't touch or see the signals; we eat foods that we've never seen growing in the earth; and millions of people participate in commerce through computers and the Internet every day with people and places they'll never know, using technology they can't begin to comprehend. It's common for us to be unaware of the nature and origin of the things we're experiencing, and it doesn't prevent us from having useful and meaningful experiences. The great Hindu saint Ramakrishna reminds us: "You see many stars at night in the sky, but find them not when the sun rises. Can you say there are no stars in the heaven of day? So, . . . because you behold not God in the days of your ignorance say not that there is no God."

Understanding the metaphysical world is necessary to fully understanding the physical reality we live in. Ironically, in facing the profound depths of Spirit, we find the secrets of everyday life. From the supernatural and the extraordinary, we receive the keys to transform our lives. This is a part of the mysterious nature of The Sacred. In going inward, we understand the world around us; in going beyond material things, we understand our most intimate self.

A full spiritual life seeks to understand the sacred self within an eternally complex Spiritual World around us. A balance of the two is necessary to prevent us from misusing our understanding of either. A deep relationship to a Higher Power combined with egotism and judgment can become cruel and dangerous to others. A deep relationship to our "self" without awareness of our connection to a Higher Power can turn us toward selfish and self-serving tendencies that can disconnect us from our relationship to the world and a sustainable way of life.

What Does It Take?

If a spiritual practice is so essential to spiritual growth, how do we know if we're equipped for the journey? How do we know that a spiritual practice will work for us? There's a wonderful old Buddhist story of a man who struggles to find spiritual peace and awakening. He's sought out many teachers, and finally, in frustration and desperation, he visits a monastery. Pounding on the temple door, he attracts attention and is taken to see the head monk, the abbot of the monastery.

The man explains that he's sure he'll never find spiritual peace and will never truly awaken, even though it's his greatest desire. He feels worthless. The kind old abbot asks, "Isn't there anything you feel proud of? Anything you've done well?"

"No," replied the man, "not unless you consider playing chess a gift? I'm the greatest chess player in my entire region, but what good is that?"

With that, the abbot ordered a nearby monk to bring a table, two chairs, and a chessboard. In one chair, he sat a gentle-looking senior monk, and in the other, he instructed the man to sit. Then he ordered his monks to bring him the sharpest sword in the monastery. A menacing, razor sharp sword was quickly brought to the abbot.

"Now," he said to the man and monk across from him, "you'll play this game of chess and whoever loses, I'll cut his head off!"

The man protested, "But this monk has done nothing wrong and is valuable to your people. He's a teacher!"

"Don't worry about him," the abbot replied. "He's been a devoted servant of the community and a dear student of mine. He trusts me and knows that he'll receive safe passage and blessings into the afterworld for all of his good work."

The abbot grew stern, and the game began. The man from the countryside quickly established a lead. After all, he was playing for his life: his mind was intent, his focus extreme, and every move was made with perfect determination. The senior monk played his best, too, but soon was at a major disadvantage, and his loss was becoming apparent. The man was now sure to win the game.

But the man couldn't help but notice the situation and looked up to see the kind, intent face of his opponent. He began to think, *What has this man done to deserve to die before his time? He is clearly respected and helps so many. I do so little—why should I live and not him? Why is my life worth more than his?*

The man continued to observe the monk seated across from him and felt a deep and growing affection for this person who'd give his life so willingly. His heart ached for the monk, and soon he made the decision to intentionally lose the game. One move at a time the man disarmed himself, and one move at a time the monk took the lead until *he* was now sure to win.

In that moment, the abbot approached the table and grabbed the chessboard, casting all the pieces to the ground. The man sat astounded.

"You've shown the two most essential qualities necessary to the path to awakening," the abbot said. "They are absolute determination and absolute compassion. Use these and you'll soon be enlightened." The man remained at the monastery, and following the abbot's instruction, soon attained an enlightened state.

It's impressive that the centerpiece of this story isn't an ancient spiritual practice but a game of chess. We're shown that the power of our practice lies not in which one we choose but how we apply ourselves to it. Willingness, sincerity, and discipline are all essential to the path of awakening. The extreme concentration shown in this story is necessary, and frequently, it's a missing element for modern seekers.

In today's world, many place wealth, health, and control as priorities above their spirituality. The Sacred takes a backseat to the business of life. However, if you truly understand the spiritual self and the Spiritual World, you'd realize that The Sacred is the foundation for all we seek.

Before diving into the 12 Master Paths, let's take one more step toward understanding the importance of your spiritual life. The next chapter will help you find your motivation and willingness to make a lasting commitment to the wild and wonderful terrain ahead.

Chapter Two

THE HEALING POWER OF SPIRITUALITY

Why a Spiritual Practice Matters

Entering the Magic

It was late evening, and I was sitting in the basement of a small home on a Native American reservation in Pine Ridge, South Dakota, the land of the Lakota Sioux. It was a fairly large rectangular room, windowless, and without furniture. Around the perimeter, community members sat against the wall on pillows and blankets. I was the only nonlocal I could detect.

The room was dimly lit, and people were talking and joking quietly while waiting for the ceremony to begin. They came seeking healing, connection, and blessing, as well as having a desire to support those who were there for help with their own prayers. In the middle of the room, a blanket was laid out, and on it was an elaborate and intricate arrangement of ceremonial objects.

The *Wapiye*, the healer, was busy preparing himself and the ritual items. He seemed to be slowing down his movements with each moment; in fact, it seemed as if his actions were becoming more precise, more contemplative with each passing second. This man, whom anthropologists would call a "shaman," was well recognized throughout the surrounding areas for his amazing abilities to heal through a special ceremony known as the *Yuwipi*. The Yuwipi is a ceremony in which the healer communicates with the Spiritual World—sacred forces and spiritual beings—to assist in the help and healing of individuals and the community.

At one side of the room, his assistants and the ceremonial drummers prepared themselves, as the lead assistant moved around organizing people and protocol. I was sitting in a sort of "honor seat," which was located at the head of the room. This was the position for the person who called for the ceremony, the main sponsor who requested the healing—that was me. I'd never experienced anything like this before; I was filled with a mixture of excitement, anxiety, fear, uncertainty, and a strange undercurrent of peace. Years ago when my problem first began, I'd have never expected that this is where it would have led me.

When I was an infant, the doctors noticed that I was pigeon-toed and wanted to "correct" the "problem" with leg braces. They were sure this course of action would prevent me from future difficulties. Until I reached adolescence, I had no obvious problems or pains in my lower extremities, and I enjoyed an active childhood. At the age of 13, however, I developed problems in my feet and legs.

I experienced sharp pain in my knees and hips when running or walking long distances. I continued to play sports but began to sprain my ankles repeatedly. Soon I was forced to withdraw from many of the high-intensity physical-activity programs in my high school. That's when my parents and I sought medical help. It was quickly revealed that when I was a child, the problem in my feet was "overcorrected"; as a result, my legs were turned outward, which caused misalignment of my ankles, knees, and hips.

During high school, my parents pursued many options and all the specialists we could track down. The choices were always few: prosthetics, surgery, and physiotherapy. The most severe option was to "break" my feet and then reconstruct them to include an arch and realign my legs. That didn't feel like a reasonable intervention, so I decreased my physical activity, focused on my spiritual pursuits, and hoped that one day I'd meet a healer who could help. Years later, after I'd begun to journey in the world of Native American spirituality and tradition, I asked my Lakota mentor and spiritual father, Wanagi Wachi, if he knew of any medicine in his culture that could help. That's how I ended up in that far-off place.

The time for the ceremony to begin was drawing near, and I was feeling isolated and unsure. I had no idea what to expect. I was torn between my disbelief and my desire for healing. I wanted to believe that somehow this healer could work a bit of magic and change my body, but everything I knew told me otherwise.

Just then, the lead assistant approached me. He kneeled closely, looked at me intensely, and said, "I don't care where you're from or what you believe. Tonight we all need to be of one mind for this healing to work and so that no one gets hurt. This is no time for fear or doubt. You asked for this, and now a lot of people are here to help."

"This man," he motioned toward the healer, "is risking his life for you. As long as the ceremony goes on, focus on your prayers, think positive thoughts, and trust that this will work. If you do so, everything will be fine." He left as abruptly as he came. Then everyone suddenly settled down and he took his seat. The healer moved to the middle of the room, sat on the altar space, and the lights were turned out. I was at a total loss.

The drumbeats and the singing began. The room had been prepared so that not the slightest bit of light could enter. It was pitch black. I heard songs and sounds that I'd never experienced before, and I felt an excitement and nervousness that was hard to contain. My mind raced to make sense of what was happening, but there was nothing familiar to grasp. At first, I heard the healer praying in the Lakota language: the tones and words were strange to me; but also beautiful, powerful, and comforting. Soon after, the healer fell silent. The drumming and singing continued for hours.

Deep into the ceremony, I heard the sound of a rattle shaking in the center of the room. I looked into the darkness to see if there was a sign of movement, but I couldn't see anything—not even my hand in front of my face. Suddenly I saw a flash—flashes of blue light were dancing around where the healer had been seated. I'd read about spirits appearing in ceremonies as blue lights but never thought it was literally true. Then the rattle began to glow. It flickered on and off and faded to black again.

The next thing I knew, the rattle was right in front of me as if it had flown from the healer's hand to me. I sensed he was there before me as well. I couldn't imagine how he had moved from the complex arrangement of objects without knocking things over, nor could I imagine how he had located me precisely in the absolutely blackened room.

The rattle immediately went to my body, as if attracted to the exact places I'd experienced pain. It didn't fumble or search—it was exact, touching me lightly but vigorously. Then the light began to flash again. I could tell what it was, but I felt like crying. Tears welled up; tremendous emotion surged. I wasn't scared or sad, but felt blessed and profoundly grateful. I didn't understand any of it, but somehow I felt that something or someone was present to help. It seemed that the world was much, much greater than anything I'd imagined.

Then the rattle moved. It danced around the room and stopped in seemingly specific places on specific people. It seemed that it was the tool of healing. This continued for some time, as I prayed and prayed for everyone in the room. I prayed for my healer and for myself, and for all that I didn't understand. And I gave thanks to whatever was present.

When it was over and the lights came on, I was relieved and yet sad that the dark cocoon of the ceremony was dissolving. People began to talk again. A few rituals followed, and late into the night the whole event was brought to a close. At that time, the healer called me over to him and shook my hand. "You'll be fine," he said with quiet confidence. "Here, take this." It was a piece of a root as wide as two fingers but no longer than my thumb.

"Every day you can grate some of this into a powder and make two cups of tea with it. Drink one cup and use the other to wash the parts that trouble you. Make sure that you pray as you do these things." I looked at the small root and worried that it wasn't enough. I wondered how a simple tea could change the structure of my bones and muscles, and eliminate the pain I was so used to. "Could I have a little more?" I asked.

He smiled and laughed. "You take this until it works. If you run out, give me a call and I'll mail you more."

It was only six weeks later that I'd stopped taking the medicine and gotten rid of my foot prostheses. I started exercising, hiking, and running again; and I've never had trouble since. I still have half of that root today. I can't explain why or how that ceremony worked, but it healed my body and changed my life. I remember every day with each step I take that true magic is not only possible, but it's more common than we think.

Looking back at that transformative experience, I now see how it was the product of spiritual practice. The healer's power was maintained by spiritual practice; the ceremony was preceded by preparations through spiritual practice; the healing ceremony is a spiritual practice; and when I left, I was instructed to follow a spiritual practice. At the time, much of this was overwhelming to me. Now I see the wisdom of the many ways we can activate the healing power of The Sacred.

Healing Power

"If you bring forth that which is within you, that which is within you will save you. If you do not bring forth that which is within you, that which is within you will destroy you."
— Jesus Christ, from the Gospel of Thomas, Nag Hammadi

"The weight of published evidence overwhelmingly confirms that our spiritual life influences our health. This can no longer be ignored."
— Jeff Levin, Ph.D., M.P.H.

When we study history, we find that most medical traditions around the world have incorporated spiritually based forms of diagnosis and treatment. In Eastern and Indigenous medicine, subtle energies and natural powers are integrated into the understanding of illness and medicine. Mystical states were known to produce healing results and even insight in the development of medicines. Only in the last 100 years has Spirit been quarantined from the medical community—and mostly in Western nations.

Before I became initiated as a Venda traditional healer in Africa, my mentor, Tshivengwa, spent a great deal of time impressing upon me the importance of herbal medicine and proper diagnosis. He had no resistance to Western medicine and taught me that different systems of medicine could work well together. "The true power of the herbs," Tshivengwa stressed, "is that they're from the earth. They still have their spirit. That spirit, that power in the plant, works on your spirit. I think you call it 'energy.' The plants are energy healers. Your body is energy. That's how you say it, correct?"

I agreed.

"This means," he went on, "that you can learn how to heal and what to heal from the plants themselves. Listen to their spirits and feel their energy—and you will understand. For me, it comes in dreams. I hear the plant, or I am visited by my ancestors. They tell me what medicine will help what patient, and sometimes where to find it. You see, there are many ways the Spirit is involved in healing: ceremony, prayer, dance, diagnosis (divination), in the plants, and in the dreams that teach us how to heal. There are many ways because it all comes from the one Spirit. We call it *Nwali* and the Ancestors. You'd call them God and the angels."

Nearly every Indigenous healer I've met over time has echoed these sentiments. They don't see these practices and techniques as magic; rather, many of them view spiritual practices as technologies that can be used to shape consciousness, energy, and the physical world. In many cultures today, the spiritual technologies of healing are kept alive and well. Unlike Western medicine, spiritual practices heal at the confluence of many factors and forces, all of which can't be controlled or predicted. We find spiritual healing practices to be a science in their design and a mystery in their outcomes and mechanisms. By definition, they defy logic and the ordinary senses.

The Center from Which All Meaning Flows

I'm still surprised and fascinated by the impact of spiritual practice on health. In addition to being a source of miraculous healing, we find that spiritual practice is also a health determinant. A great many physicians, such as the renowned Andrew Weil, M.D.; Bernie Siegel, M.D.; Christiane Northrup, M.D.; Larry Dossey, M.D.; and Rachel Naomi Remen, M.D., have all worked hard to stress this potential in their writing and work. Even in the roots of modern medicine, we find that some of the founding fathers such as William Osler, M.D., and the ancient Hippocrates saw that the spirituality of a person is critical to their health and healing.

Perhaps more than the capacity to cure, I've always been drawn to the necessity of spirituality in maintaining a healing relationship with the world. A healthy spirituality becomes an orientation point for all of our choices. One day I met a seasoned sailor, a man who used to race large sailboats in tours that crossed the globe. I asked him what it was like to be out at sea for weeks at a time when there's no land in sight. I suggested that today's advanced technology must make it easier to manage.

"The old custom of watching the stars is still as important to me as any GPS or digital tracking system. Some call it 'celestial navigation.' If you know the stars—how they line up and where you need to be in relationship to them—you really don't need to see the land. It doesn't matter if the ocean is rough or calm; the stars keep you steadily on course."

"What about during the day or during stormy times? Don't you get lost?" I asked.

"Think about it," he said. "At one time the stars are all we had to go by. Of course it works.

"It's never a perfect process; it's an adventure. You keep watch and set your course. You check every chance you can. Sometimes you find you've wandered off track, and other times you're still on course. When you can no longer see the stars, you eventually develop a sense, a gut feeling about where they would be and where you are. Other times, it's just a kind of faith until you can be sure again." He smiled wistfully, "I guess it's a lot like life. Can you imagine trying to navigate just by watching the waves around you? You have to look higher than that to find your way."

令 令 令

A simple story about the stars says so much about the power and importance of a spiritual life. It allows us to live by what matters most and not the moment-to-moment reactions and distractions that we're prone to. Spiritual experiences and practices can be like guiding stars, providing a kind of clarity and orientation by which we make our most crucial decisions. It impacts every aspect of our health, from our physical condition to our emotional well-being, relationships, and the way we use our time and treat ourselves. With each conclusion we come to along the way, we test, try, and recommit to the questions again, always checking our choices against our guiding light. The exploration unfolds and spiritual growth occurs: we begin to evolve our sense of who we are and what this life is about.

Ego-centeredness, misdirection, and limiting beliefs are like clouds that cover the stars that lead us. We can forget the truth behind the gray. But when we finally do see beyond the passing distractions and reorient ourselves, we transcend our circumstances and an evolution of the self occurs. We continue to check the sky with growing clarity and deviate less and less as we go. It's not about being perfect; it's about being clear and staying connected.

Much of the despair and disease I've encountered in my work in hospitals and my counseling and healing practice is rooted in life choices that create disharmony. When people honor their deepest sense of meaning, identity, and purpose, they tend to be resilient, vibrant, and ready to cope well. When people live according to expectations, roles, and the judgments of others, a feeling of disconnection and depression often emerges. The vital force of life responds to the harmony within us, and is diminished whenever there is a loss of love and balance.

As you understand and honor your innermost sense of self, it impacts your relationships, work, and connection to the mysteries of life. When you examine and evaluate the depth and nature of your spirituality, you'll begin to encounter aspects of yourself and the world around you that you may have forgotten or overlooked. Carl Jung was fascinated by this problem and talked about the "shadow" as an important dimension of healing. The shadow self is not the "negative" aspects of self, but those aspects that are denied, unaccepted, or disowned. When you accept and explore the aspects of yourself that you've hidden, forgotten, or denied, you gain access to new reserves of energy, clarity, and freedom.

At first, much of spirituality can look like psychological healing and "personal growth." This is a significant layer of the excavation and evolution because it's about revealing limiting thoughts and feelings. Everyone can also benefit from the chance to explore their preferences and attractions. Before you know yourself well, you may be attracted to superficial pleasures because they're easy, appealing, and enforced by society. If you continue to be open to questioning and exploring your true nature, those superficial needs and desires become less satisfying as you naturally turn further inward, connecting to your spiritual essence.

As your spiritual practice reveals the value of the intangible, you'll often be surprised that your experience of the world dramatically changes. Opening your heart with the presence of compassion and connection in your choices will begin to attune you to your subtler senses and perceptions. As you release judgment and expectations, you'll experience the power of being fully present and aware. This is the beginning of spiritual experience.

At times, you may encounter new dimensions of the world, such as the possibility of subtle energies, mysterious forces, or the sense that you're being guided or watched over by Divine beings. An openness to the unfolding self leads to an openness to fresh possibilities, and you'll witness your ability to effect change in the world.

Inner Peace and Emotional Well-Being

The evidence that spirituality is the foundation for a satisfying life and good physical health is something I've experienced and been taught again and again in nearly all of the non-Western spiritual and healing traditions I've encountered. Over the years, I've spent a great deal of time involved with Native American and Indigenous healers and communities and noticed that they scarcely make a distinction between their healing and spiritual traditions. I've also been involved in research examining the effectiveness of Native American–focused treatment programs in hospitals, prisons, and communities.

My brother, Lawrence Ellerby, Ph.D., is a clinical psychologist who has specialized in the treatment of violent offenders in correctional and community settings. He's now recognized as an international expert in forensic psychology and has attributed much of his success to the integration of spiritual themes and approaches in his clinical and community practice. Years ago, he and I were involved in a very interesting study in which I traveled throughout central Canada visiting prisons that had Indigenous (Native Canadian) culturally based treatment programs for Native offenders. The research project was to see whether or not therapy and rehabilitation programs that included Native spiritual practices were making a difference.

What we found in the study was that there is a dramatic difference between treatment programs that include spiritual practices (such as ceremonies, prayer, sacred music, community service, meditation, and ascetic practices) and those that don't. In fact, not only were Native inmates more likely to complete their treatment programs when spirituality was included, but they made greater progress and were less likely to reoffend. Consistently, spiritual practices helped the men make lasting changes by addressing key issues in their lives, such as dealing with anger and violence, addiction, and trauma.

To our surprise, we found that these programs were not only better for Native people, but also better for men of any culture who attended the programs. It didn't matter "whose" spirituality was a part of the program. If it was inclusive, introspective, and supportive, spirituality was a dominant factor in the most effective programs we saw—again and again. Looking at other programs, such as AA and even Weight Watchers, we hear that many people who've found success point to a spiritual quality in their change and transformation. A deeper sense of meaning, a clearer sense of identity, and a conscious connection to something Sacred seems to have a nearly universal healing effect.

One day during a visit with my dear friends and extended family in South Dakota, I told my mentor and spiritual father, Wanagi Wachi, about the results of our study. Knowing that integrating spirituality into the therapeutic process was the secret to his own success as a healer and nationally recognized addictions-program developer, I asked why he thought it worked.

It was a rare occasion when Wanagi Wachi would actually give me a straight answer without first driving me into silence, intuition, or confusion. This question seemed to interest him, and he replied.

"Maslow was a great Western psychologist, right?" he asked with sincerity.

I agreed. "He was a pioneer."

"You've heard of Maslow's hierarchy of needs?"

"Yes," I replied. "It has physical and biological needs at the bottom of a scale for human development and self-actualization at the top, right? You have to settle survival issues first, then get to accomplishments, and finally spiritual growth." I recalled my university courses in psychology.

"Yes. Maslow taught that people naturally look after certain needs in a sort of priority sequence. He theorized that first people require that their basic physical needs are met, such as food, shelter, and sleep. Then when they've had enough of that, they can worry about safety, order, and protection. After that's looked after, they turn more inward and seek belonging and love. Next, they can work toward achievement, esteem, and responsibility. Finally, they have the time to worry about their place in the universe—personal growth, spirituality, self-actualization, God."

"That's right," I added, "and I've seen some authors add levels, but the basic breakdown remains the same. It makes sense: how can people worry about spirituality if they don't know where their next meal is coming from or if their country is at war? Spirituality is kind of a luxury, according to this way of thinking."

"This is where the Indigenous mind and all the great spiritual teachers disagree with Maslow and the Western world." I was surprised to hear Wanagi Wachi's certainty but sensed the absurdity in the idea that spirituality is a luxury only for the rich and accomplished.

He added, "In our culture and way of healing, we flip this picture upside down. The reason why your research showed that healing programs that incorporate spirituality work better than those that don't is simply because we as humans are first and foremost *spiritual beings*. We are spiritual beings having a human experience—not the other way around.

"If we don't care for that fundamental dimension of who we are first, we'll struggle with all the others. If we don't have a strong sense of meaning; a healthy identity; and good relationships with the people, places, and powers surrounding us, then we'll always be out of balance. If you don't have that spiritual health, everything becomes difficult—not just healing, but thriving and enjoying life, no matter who you are. How can you know balance if you haven't found your 'center'? Why would you listen to your doctor if you don't view your body as sacred? Out of fear? Well, that won't last long; it just creates more problems.

"When you have spiritual health you can face anything; you can be conscious on the journey of life. When you don't have spiritual health, all those basic needs become difficult because you make decisions in reaction—not intention. It's a nice theory Maslow had, but it's backward. Energy and vitality are available to us when we live from the heart, not the mind. If we place the material world first, we'll always be confused."

I knew what Wanagi Wachi said was true, and I had seen it in so many settings. The process of spiritual growth is learning that the more attached we are to the "nonspiritual" aspects of life, such as survival, wealth, and social importance, the more we tend to suffer. All the spiritual traditions have cautioned us in the same way: never make your ego, control, or material comfort your life's priority. Our happiness is as conditional as the things we attach it to.

Most spiritual practices help us realize this. Many do so by removing our ability to focus on the body, safety, or ego accomplishments, for there can be no absolute certainty or control over those important but precarious dimensions of life. *When we create harmony between the truest sense of self that we know and our daily attitudes and actions, only then is our greatest potential for health and fulfillment activated.* Spiritual integrity and balance is so critical to mental and emotional health that its influence is found in most modern psychological therapies and in most innovations in psychology since Freud.

Good Medicine: Spirituality and Health

Hippocrates is often credited with being the father of modern medicine, although many of his timeless teachings are no longer central to medicine today. One of his beliefs was that physicians are only the facilitators of their patients' natural and supernatural powers to heal themselves. His statement, "Natural forces within us are the true healers of disease," points us to a lesson that the most advanced medical sciences are now beginning to rediscover: health and medicine aren't confined to the physical domain.

Over years of spiritual experience and study, I've come to see a healing force at work in many spiritual practices. I've also witnessed that all healing is ultimately derived from a Sacred Source: a source within each of us and greater than any one of us. When we live in connection to that essence within and beyond us, we access a force, an actual energy that can be harnessed and directed in our bodies and lives. This is a key to understanding the value and importance of mind-body medicine and the embrace of ancient ways of healing.

The idea that physical health is impacted by the congruence of our inner and outer worlds, as well as the subtle energies we direct with our intention, is becoming more broadly accepted in Western medicine. More than just a sense of meaning or philosophy, we find that a deep spiritual life *is* medicine to the body, sometimes evoking an auxiliary power to heal. The Sacred connects us to mechanisms and means to heal our hearts, minds, and bodies. Researchers David Larson, Ph.D., Harold Koenig, M.D., Daniel Benor, M.D., and Jeff Levin, Ph.D., have made great strides in documenting and communicating this reality.

Even in settings where such language and spiritual medicine aren't accepted, people still find ways to access these forces. A spiritual aspect of healing is innate. The modern "complementary and alternative health" movement demonstrates the natural human need for the integration of spirituality in health, healing, and coping.

In the U.S., for example, it was determined by the National Institutes of Health that when spiritually based therapies (such as prayer, yoga, and meditation) are included in the estimate, more than 60 percent of the population practices alternatives to mainstream medicine. When spiritually related medicines are left out, the number drops to less than half. Back in 1997, it was estimated that Americans spent nearly $47 billion on complementary medicines—many of which involved a spiritual element or perspective. Nearly half of this was spent out of their own pockets: people crave spirituality in their care and believe in its impact on their health. These numbers have only increased with time.

The medical community is seeing dramatic correlations between unresolved trauma and stress and long-term health conditions and chronic illnesses. As I mentioned, well-known physicians such as Christiane Northrup, M.D., Rachel Naomi Remen, M.D., Andrew Weil, M.D., Bernie Siegel, M.D., Dharma Singh Khalsa, M.D., Norman Shealy, M.D., and Dean Ornish, M.D., have long asserted and written that attitude, connection to a higher power, and self-image may be some of the most important health determinants, as much as or more so than genetics, environment, or diet. The astonishing and important research of microbiologist Bruce Lipton, Ph.D., and Candace Pert, Ph.D., has literally begun to prove the roots of this healing mechanism through modern laboratory experiments in neurology, chemistry, genetics, and biology.

Research shows that people who engage in regular spiritual practice and a mature spiritual life show a range of positive health outcomes. Jeff Levin, Ph.D., skillfully summarizes many of these benefits in his book *God, Faith, and Health*. The many documented positive benefits of a healthy spiritual life and practice include the following:

- ☸ Community support and promotion of a healthy lifestyle
- ☸ Social support, which reduces the impact of stress and isolation
- ☸ The physiological benefits of positive emotions (such as love, joy, and connection)
- ☸ Conscious choices in physical activity and lifestyle
- ☸ The influence of positive attitude (such as hope, optimism, and positive expectation)
- ☸ The healing influence of bioenergies activated through spiritual practices and spiritual states of consciousness
- ☸ The activation of psychosomatic healing mechanisms
- ☸ The activation of a nonlocal healing intelligence and energy (Higher Power/God)

Researchers like those whom I just mentioned, and many others, have gone to great lengths to document this evidence. Moreover, established medical programs such as the ones at Duke University, Harvard, Brown, Stanford, the University of Minnesota, and even the National Institutes of Health's National Center for Complementary and Alternative Medicine have gone to great lengths to examine and affirm the connection between health and spirituality. Among the many conditions that spiritual practice has been associated with helping are:

- ☸ High blood pressure
- ☸ Hypertension
- ☸ Cardiac arrhythmias
- ☸ Chronic pain
- ☸ Anxiety
- ☸ Insomnia
- ☸ Muscle tension
- ☸ Mild to moderate depression

- ☷ Infertility
- ☷ Erratic brain waves
- ☷ Postoperative anxiety
- ☷ Premenstrual syndrome
- ☷ Migraine and cluster headaches
- ☷ Low self-esteem
- ☷ Symptoms of cancer and acquired immunodeficiency syndrome (AIDS)
- ☷ Wound healing

Whether in a hospital setting, health resort, or private practice, it's been my experience that people who have a strong spiritual practice are better able to manage the challenges and difficult choices they face. They also possess an openness to a greater range of tools for healing, such as prayer, ceremony, sound healing techniques, and energy medicine. Today many complementary and conventional healers have built their careers on the premise that the healing journey must include a spiritual dimension for optimal effect.

Spiritual growth doesn't mean that you'll no longer get sick or that you're guaranteed to be cured of all disease. It does mean, however, that you can always find a way to heal. It doesn't promise that you won't have bad days or difficult emotions, or that you'll always get what you want. Old age, sickness, and death are a part of life for everyone—spirituality isn't a quick fix or magical escape. But it can teach you how to meet life's choices and challenges with clarity and intention. Spiritual maturity allows us to restore relationships, forgive the past, and live with an integrity that feeds the vitality of life.

Spiritual Essence of Healing

Bella's story is one I've heard over and over in the lives of so many people as the years have gone by. I met her when I worked in a hospital in Canada. Bella was married with three children and worked as a nurse on a unit I used to visit. I remember how she looked after everyone and the way she talked about her home life;

she seemed like "supermom." She never said no, and always seemed to be the one to support others. When we talked about her family, she said that her husband worked long hours and they didn't spend much time together. She handled most of the household chores. When he was home, he was playful with his children and loved to go golfing with friends. I never heard her talk about things he did for her or with her. I never knew Bella to have any hobbies, interests, or time for herself.

Years later after I'd moved away from Winnipeg, I heard that Bella's husband became very ill with cancer. Much as she always did, Bella stepped up and did everything she could to care for him. She continued to work but reduced her hours so that she could be her husband's primary caregiver. She continued to look after her children, as well as the friends and family she always seemed to be supporting. She didn't seem to "need" to work for her family's welfare, but I knew she was a dedicated person and never wanted to let anyone down. I wasn't surprised to hear of the burden she took on.

Sadly, her husband didn't live long after his diagnosis. After a year of very difficult treatments and progressive worsening, he passed, and Bella was left exhausted and grief stricken. A few months after the funeral, I ran into her at a store while visiting Winnipeg. Since we had a nice friendship and she knew I had experience in working with death and bereavement, we somehow fell into a conversation about her journey and about how she was really doing behind what she showed her friends. With me, Bella shared her feelings openly and expressed a lot of confusion, wondering if the process she was going through was somehow wrong or impaired.

"I guess I started to grieve before my husband died. They tell me that's normal," she began, "but the part I feel awful about is the sense of relief and freedom I'm experiencing!" I tried to assure her that such feelings are normal, especially after being a caregiver for some time.

"No, you don't understand," she retorted. "I mean that I pushed myself to my limit. I thought I was going to die, and when he finally did, something broke open inside me. A part of me died—the part that felt I had to do it all. Now I feel free of all of it: being a wife, being Mrs. Perfect, putting up with some of his friends I didn't like, going to events he wanted to and I didn't. I feel like the weight of so many expectations was lifted from me. It was amazing!

"But now that I'm free, I feel lost. I spent so much of my life being what he, his family, and his friends wanted me to be that I have no idea who I am or what I want. I've gained so much weight; I've lost my old, dear friends; and I just don't remember how to have fun. What's wrong with me!?"

Unfortunately, this is more common than one would think, as most live with such a sense of duty and burden in their lives. People allow themselves to *become* the roles and expectations that are thrust upon them and fail to realize they have choices; they can co-create the relationships in their lives. Yet out of a desire to be loved, liked, or accepted, they build a mask that reflects what everyone in their life requires, and who they long to be is lost. The influences of the outside world, childhood, and parents are so strong and penetrating that it's hard to think beyond what they've encoded and impressed upon us.

It wasn't until about three years later that I saw Bella again. I'd been away for school and travel and had returned for a family event. I saw her in one of the beautiful parks in Winnipeg. She was radiant and seemed like a new woman, and she was quick to call me over to talk.

"I'll tell you that it hasn't been easy. I do miss my husband still— we had so many things we enjoyed. The kids are only just starting to get over his loss. At the same time, it's been the most amazing period of my life. I spent the first two years working with a therapist. Wow, what a lot of junk I was carrying around unconsciously in so many ways! It helped me with my grief and also to understand how I got so lost in my relationships. Finally, I started to ask, 'What do *I* want? Who am I going to be?' I learned to say no and started to get involved in things that I enjoy: I took French lessons and became part of a reading group. We'd been reading books about spiritual topics and talking about what we learned.

"That's when it happened. We read a book about what modern physics and spiritual philosophies have in common, and it was like someone turned on the light! There's so much more to this world than just our little city, our little lives. I've become a Healing Touch practitioner and have taken all kinds of workshops about what they call 'energy medicine' and alternative healing. I do yoga twice a week and practice a form of meditation about five times a week. It's not for long, but it's something. It helps me not fall into those old traps and habits.

"Instead of living from what everyone wants of me or even what I only want for myself, I live for the higher good—but I'm a part of that balance. I serve the higher good in the way that I love, on my terms. I'm still active with my family and community, but it doesn't drain me anymore. Now I understand why you used to help people in the hospitals. When I found my Self, I found my health . . . and so much more."

"Yes," I replied, "you truly have begun the most amazing journey, and this is just the beginning!"

Bella's story reflects that of many people in today's world and demonstrates how a shift in identity is central to the path of healing and spiritual awakening.

The Most Practical Thing You Can Invest In: The Essence of Healing

Beyond Roles and Expectations

At the heart of all deep healing—physical or emotional—is the letting go of characteristics, qualities, and assumptions about who we are that don't serve our well-being. Some call this overcoming ego attachments and expectations. Although our families, friends, and society can be powerful forces in shaping and expecting certain roles from us, if those roles don't match our deeper selves they will in time create despair and even disease. The more we lack alignment between our personal truth and the way we live, the more we'll feel disconnection, loss of energy, and the feeling that "something is missing."

For a long time, Bella was living her life for others at the expense of herself. Perhaps because of the way her parents behaved or experiences she had at impressionable times, Bella had unconsciously accepted some assumptions about what a "good" wife, mother, and friend should be. She forgot, however, to ask herself who she wanted to be, or if there was a higher purpose or gift she had not yet revealed. All the years I knew her at work, she acted like something in her life was missing. And it was true— something *was* missing: her soul.

Soul-Centered Living

The soul isn't a simple aspect of who we are; it has a complex anatomy and many layers. The simplest way to describe the soul would be to call it the "true self": the preferences, talents/gifts, qualities, and characteristics that naturally bring us joy, vitality, and peace. When we live from the soul, we feel empowered, engaged, and vibrant. We access a natural power, an actual force that contributes to health and happiness.

As we expose and transcend our identification with false roles and expectations, we become free to explore and live from the soul. We find that we have a core self—a basic, innate identity with distinct characteristics. When Bella's husband died and she made radical changes in her life, she didn't become a recluse or a selfish, indulgent miser. She let go of the things that didn't feel right to her and embraced the ones that did. Her natural love of helping others was still expressed, yet in a way that created health for her and in a balanced way for others.

When people talk about "finding themselves," "being authentic," or "living in alignment," they're really talking about living from their soul. It's easy to know when the soul is engaged because a felt-sense of vitality increases. We feel a congruence and balance in our actions. Whether or not we're successful in achieving what we desire, we know that we're approaching it with intention and empowerment.

Learning to live from the soul is part of the healing gift of spiritual practice. Each type of spiritual experience helps us expose the false self and become more aware of the soul, the true self. Each spiritual practice that's selected *by* the soul will lead *to* the soul. If selected by others or imposed or expected, it may only affirm the false self that is debilitating and blinding.

Awakening to Spirit

As we become more aware of the soul and learn more about it, the deepest dimension of who we are begins to reveal itself. It may appear in spiritual experiences, subtle feelings, or a shift in perspective. When we move into the depth of spiritual growth and begin to cross the edges toward enlightenment, we realize that at the heart of our very own soul *is* the Sacred Source.

There are thousands of names for this place within us: pure consciousness, oneness, the ultimate field of being. Mystic teachers throughout history have agreed and converged on the same realization: God is within us. The Great Mystery and Sacred Power of this creation is something that has lived within us all along. Only in releasing the masks that hide us and honoring the soul we were blessed with, do we awaken to the Sacred Power that is the true essence of all things.

In our deepest self, we find a spirit that is profoundly impersonal yet unifies us with all people, all things. Within us lives the very soul of the Great Mystery of Life: *we are the Great Mystery of Life*. Ancient Hinduism has long focused on the expression "Atman [self] is Brahman [God]." This simply states that at the deepest core of who we are, we encounter the realization of our oneness with all things: we are a part of God. The innermost self is the outermost force. This doesn't mean that you are God, but it does mean that God is you! The words used to explain this vary from person to person, but the *experience* of awakening to this truth is universal.

All of the great spiritual practices have the power to help us reach this point of identity and transcendence in which we realize that we're a sacred being. They help us understand that every struggle is an opportunity to find a deeper quality of freedom. Every challenge brings a lesson and a step closer to realizing that there's a force within us that is eternal, indestructible, and beautiful beyond words. After such a realization, we are never the same again. The false self burns away in the light of the innermost spirit, and the soul begins to shine.

This is the territory of the mystic where the greatest pain can lead to the greatest freedom; the greatest comfort leads to the greatest despair. Here we navigate the paradoxes of life. We realize that all things are for our healing, including loss, sickness, and death. When we learn to perceive with the spiritual senses, our greatest tragedies are like angels, begging to set us free. This is the domain of the enlightened heart and mind. Healing is the only direction when we live in conscious awareness of our Sacred Source.

In the stillness
of that dark night,
I awakened
to a moment
that held all moments

There was a pure absence
a true presence
a freedom from being and becoming

Looking back now,
my body knew it as energy
my mind understood it as consciousness
my heart felt it was God
but my soul forever knows
nothing can contain
that which is
and gives life
to everything

— J.H. Ellerby

Chapter Three

THE MASTER PATHS

12 Roads to Spiritual Awakening

The Inner Pathway Leads Everywhere

The ancient pine forests of Vancouver Island radiate an invisible vibrancy that is easily felt. The large ferryboat that took me there moved steadily from the port in Washington State. Standing at the front of the boat and staring outward, I felt my heart leap with each diving gull. The world was alive and fresh with the sea air and deep green forests. No sooner had I dreamed the possibility of seeing a whale when three appeared together, breaking the surface gently and moving slowly like the rhythm of the earth itself. I was both excited and uncertain about my journey. I was traveling because I had the urge to go and nothing more.

During the year after high school when I took off to work and travel, I spent months in the national parks of the West focused on my spiritual studies, meditations, and contemplations. Before I left home for a few months of camping, a dear friend had given me the name and number of a man who she thought was "some sort of priest who works with Native people." He sounded interesting so I took his contact info with me. Months later when I arrived at his house, I didn't realize that he'd retired from that life years before. The phone call that brought me there was short and cryptic.

"Can I speak to Roy?" I asked carefully when the gruff male voice answered the phone.

"I expect you can," replied the voice, and then there was silence.

"Is Roy there?" I persisted.

"People call me Roy."

"I was given your name and number by a friend and neighbor of ours. She said we'd have a lot to talk about if we met. I'm not sure what she meant."

"Well, what do you want? You want to come and visit?"

"Sure. I have time, and it's only a two-day drive from where I am in Idaho."

"All right—we have a spare room. Come on up. I'll be home this week. Call when you're getting close, and I'll give you directions."

That was it. That was how I ended up at the home of a man I knew nothing about on beautiful Vancouver Island in British Columbia. I didn't learn until days after my arrival that Roy was an author and spiritual teacher. Although he denied his adherence to any tradition and asserted the infinite error of labeling anything in life, I'd describe him now as being very much like a wild Zen Master.

Roy cursed a great deal and was silent a great deal. When he spoke, he was loud and uninhibited. He was a wonderful, overpowering force, often funny and frequently rude. Before either of us really knew what was unfolding, I was invited to live for a short while with this man and his family. To pay for my room and board, I helped maintain and repair their turkey farm. The secret contract, however, was a spiritual one. The lesson was freedom from suffering and attachments of the mind. We never discussed this openly, but we both knew shortly after we met that this was the agenda.

I didn't realize that I was involved in a spiritual practice at the time, but a guru-like mentorship sprang forth. Roy was indirectly encouraging and instructing me in meditation and cultivating a meditative mind. He frequently questioned me about various topics throughout the day; and as I replied, he'd attack and expose the thoughts that were based on judgments, labels, and attachments. If I identified something as "good" or "bad," he'd challenge me. He'd say things like, "Do you really think that's true for everyone? How can a TV show be 'bad'? Is it evil? It can be poorly directed or poorly acted. You might not enjoy it, but can you really label it 'bad'? Someone liked it; someone made it. *Bad* suggests an absolute condition, a statement of essence and value. A TV show isn't 'bad.' Nothing is!"

You can imagine that just about every conversation had the potential to become volatile. The day we met he asked me to tell him about myself. When I mentioned something about my "spiritual path," he nearly fell off his chair laughing. "Path! What path? Show me a trail behind you! Do you really believe in the past? I bet you also believe that there's a future!" He laughed as if I were convinced of a science a hundred years out of date.

"There is only this moment! That's the only thing I know and can prove. How about you?" Our conversations often ended in silence and my frustration. I couldn't disagree with him, but at the same time, it felt like everything I thought was true was being eroded away.

After days of Roy's abrupt confrontations, I finally expressed my discomfort with his common attacks. He attacked me for that as well. "Why should you care what I think? Why do you want my approval? I'm not important—you just met me! If you hang your happiness on how I behave, you'll never be happy. You could leave, but then you'll hang your happiness on how someone else behaves. I'll bet you attach your happiness to every person you meet. Don't you see how conditional your life is? Your suffering is based on whether or not you get what you want. That is attachment—and that, my friend, is bullshit."

I was left raw and unsettled, but I couldn't help but feel that there was something true in his message. The method was harsh, but I decided to stay on with Roy and his family. Never one to deal well with conflict, I slowly retreated into silence. I began to be more cautious about not only what I was saying, but how much and what I was thinking.

I began to realize how much time I spent on thoughts of what I wanted or didn't want and how much energy I wasted on reactions and distractions. I was always reacting to the past or future and to how I wanted people to see me and think of me. Under it all was a desire for control.

Finally, I started to work toward just being comfortable focusing on the task at hand. If I ate, I just enjoyed the food. I wouldn't plan what I was going to do later; I stayed present to colors, tastes, and textures. If I was working in the barn, I stayed conscious of my breath and the experience of my body. Thoughts, worries, and daydreams still came to mind, but I slowly learned not to feed them or dwell on them. I began to notice more in each moment. There seemed to be a simple beauty in everything.

It was a difficult time, yet slowly I felt a change. My deep discomfort and fear of my Zen Master began to turn into compassionate indifference. Slowly, his countenance toward me also changed. Once he recognized the way my mind was settling down, he provided me with a number of books he'd written: short Zen-like commentaries on the mind, relationships, and the cost of having strong investments in value labels such as "good and bad" or "right and wrong."

I noticed that when I'd arrived, my mind was hungry. I wanted spiritual readings, practices, philosophies, and answers. By the time my mind had slowed down, I was interested but far less excited about reading or philosophizing. Life was good as it was, and I felt complete in a way I hadn't before. The constant striving was gone.

One day after finishing my chores in the barn, I took one of Roy's books and found a quiet spot beneath a tree to sit, read, and reflect. Although it was nearly two decades ago, I can recall the afternoon with absolute clarity. To my left, the sun was setting over the lush forest and rolling countryside. My hosts' quaint home was in front of me, far off from where I sat; and to my right, there were fruit trees and a path. Behind me at a distance were the livestock and farmyard. The world seemed gold and green—a dance of sunlight and nature. There was nowhere to be, and I had all the time I needed to spend as I chose.

I took my shoes off, crossed my legs, and leaned back against the tree to read. I don't recall exactly what I was reading, but most likely it was some paradoxical commentary on how people become trapped in their stories about the world. The ways we define ourselves and find self-importance can become the sources of our ego attachment and desire for control, which ultimately is the cause of our sorrow.

After reading only a page or two, I laid the book down, closed my eyes, and took a deep breath. When I opened them, I found myself overwhelmed by intense sensory stimulation. Sounds rushed in; lights seemed too bright; colors were vibrant; and the entire world began to spin around me as if I were in the center of a great drain, and all things were spinning and whirling into me.

One moment slipped into the next, and in a flash, I was lost in timeless space. I'd entered the direct experience of The Sacred: the Formless Spirit. My mind was blank—empty in a way I'd never known and couldn't describe. I sensed an incredible bliss that seemed to consume my awareness. Every sense of self dissolved into the experience of deep joy. In that moment, I was bliss. I don't know how long it lasted, but when the force began to diminish, something else took its place: I became alert and self-aware. My thoughts were few and came only when summoned; they didn't pour forth in a typical constant stream. Everything seemed to be moving slower, and every detail around me was more acute than I could have ever imagined.

A bird passed by in flight, and it was as if I could see the contours of its body, feel the crest of air it was riding on, and sense its delicate form and beating heart. The grass was pulsating; each blade was alive and reaching with ancient wisdom toward the sky. They'd been cut down again and again yet were resolved to return and grow. The house was an act of art and creative genius, and every detail showed the history of humanity. Everything seemed to be an unlikely and perfect invention and evolution: roofing tiles, doorways, and the miracles of windows—solid and transparent—all crafted by someone's hands.

Everything expressed its history, complexity, and story of interdependence. The cement walkway, the truck in the distance, the soil, the fruit trees, and the sky—they were all infinitely complex yet one system, one amazing symphony, one machine, and one life, connected and interconnected on some level.

I rose slowly as I watched this concert of color and design with total awe. The feeling of walking was liberating, as if I as doing it for the first time. I entered the house to hear a Vivaldi concerto playing in the living room. The notes of the violin seemed to hang in the air, as if I could feel them flowing from the speakers to my ears. I was hearing with my body. I was moving through the sound like water, and the spaces between the notes were as gorgeous as the notes themselves. This Divine experience continued for some time and gradually faded as the night went on.

஬ ஬ ஬

Sometimes the vivid images and senses are hard to recall, but the meaning and wisdom of that experience has never faded—it changed my life. I felt a quality of absolute certainty and clarity in that moment. The interconnection I perceived wasn't a simple metaphor or wishful thinking; it was a clear perception of spiritual and scientific truth. The very idea of interconnection and interdependence has never since been far from my mind. While I have moments of thoughtless action—and certainly lack awareness of the levels or depths of interconnection at times in my day-to-day life—I'm unable to fully extract myself from the awareness of this great web of life.

Kindness to others—people, plants, and animals—is only natural. Harm to one is harm to all. It's a complicated philosophy. When experienced, however, it's simple and easy to follow. When I make choices, I don't choose solely for myself; I choose for future generations of children and the vitality of the planet. Some would say that it sounds like a heavy responsibility. Instead, it feels like an honor, a privilege, and a power. Such an awareness is a gift, for the experience of absolute interconnection showed me that I can never be alone or insignificant. All people, all things, are mighty and meaningful in their relationship to everything else that exists.

People often reflect on stories like this one and pass them off as happy accidents. Some see them as pleasant aberrations in the brain's function, and others view them as blessings of grace or natural aptitude. Such explanations dismiss the possibility that these experiences can be cultivated and prepared for. Periods of luminous clarity and connection can be the result of accumulated moments of meditation, reflection, study, and mentorship.

Without my teacher and his instructive jokes and jabs, the manual labor, and the practice of observing my mind, how likely would it have been for me to simply fall into such an experience? Extraordinary awareness and the maturity of the soul are the fruits of spiritual growth. They bloom from the many branches of spiritual practice in our lives: the fewer branches, the less fruit. Some experiences may come as a blessing to those who do little, yet to maintain and learn from them, spiritual practice is necessary.

The Gift of the Ancient World: The Master Paths

If you were facing a major illness and had no treatment options left except something new that hadn't been proven to work, you might think it was a reasonable risk to take. If, however, you also learned of a remedy that had been used successfully for generations with few side effects and at a low cost, which treatment would you choose? In a similar way, I encourage you to explore the time-tested spiritual practices that everyone is heir to.

The 12 Master Path practices described in this book have roots that we can trace back anywhere from 5,000 to more than 20,000 years. Religion itself may be facing a crisis of legitimacy, relevance, and evolution today; nevertheless, the core spiritual practices that numerous religions have brought to us are still maintained around the world and can help us heal and awaken to The Sacred Spirit of Life.

The 12 Master Paths are:

1. Ceremony and Ritual
2. Sacred Movement
3. Sacred Sound and Music
4. Prayer
5. Meditation
6. Sacred Study
7. Devotion
8. Sacred Service
9. Guru Guidance: Master Teacher
10. Ascetic Practices
11. Death Practice
12. Life Path

When you choose modern practices, you may gain a lot in customization but lose much through a lack of mature mentoring, supportive resources, and communities, and an overdependence on individual teachers and innovators. However, ancient practices have generations of oral and written history to support you, including hundreds of commentaries and cautions. Ancient practices also have communities and codes that guide teachers and students alike. No system is perfect, but time has proven their blessing.

Part of the beauty of these living traditions is that they demonstrate a thread of continuity so that you may learn from past students and teachers, and they have the capacity to be applied in any age or stage of history. A natural evolution and adaptation occurs whenever they're applied. Everything that makes you unique can be brought to your practice. Start where you are.

Your ethnicity and religion are welcome. You may even dress your practice in words and colors to suit your heritage, but be open to change and to something new. Allow yourself to learn from experience and the development of your practice. Nonattachment to whom we think we are and how we think the world should be is an essential ingredient.

The purpose of a practice is transformation—*not* consistency, safety, or self-preservation. That isn't the intention you should bring to spiritual growth (or anything else in life). Choose a steady path from which to spring wildly into your beautiful, unfolding potential. It's about the power of the known path to free you *from* the known territory. Let your spiritual practice free you from your conditions and conditioning into a life of possibility, peace, and freedom.

Extraordinary Outcomes Require Extraordinary Steps

When we consider the road it takes for any accomplished person to move from their early stages of life to their later days of success, we realize that talent and opportunity is only a fraction of the story. Effort, endurance, talent, and dedication are required. Reflect on anything great you've achieved in life. Whether it was raising a child, starting a business, finishing school, or dealing with an illness or addiction, you know very well that such things don't always come easily. They take commitment, guidance, practice, trial, and the grace of timing and connection.

Consider those who've achieved success in their field of work or performance, and ask yourself, *How did they get there? What did it take?* When we think of extraordinary achievements by individuals who've become household names—such as Tiger Woods, Luciano Pavarotti, Oprah Winfrey, Bill Gates, and Mother Teresa—many people at first will try to dismiss their greatness by claiming: "She was born that way," "He's a natural," or "She has something that I don't."

On further reflection, we know that success requires practice. To be excellent at something takes hard work. Medical doctors engage in years of training, athletes endure hundreds of hours of practice, artists invest thousands of hours in trial and error, and Nobel Prize–winning scientists conduct more failed experiments than successful ones before they discover a valuable formula. All great things require deeply personal investments of time, energy, and effort. So why do we think spiritual health and development would be any other way? It isn't.

Few extraordinary things come easily, and spiritual awakening is no different. Even though some people may be born with natural aptitudes and tendencies that give them advantages over others, ultimately, if we want the fruits of spiritual awareness, then we must plant the seeds, till the soil, let nature take its course, and wait for the harvest that follows. More than physical, mental, or emotional success, the rewards of a healthy spiritual life are virtually unlimited: freedom, peace, balance, and clarity. A deeply spiritual life enhances the enjoyment and appreciation of all other types and levels of success. But the path is long, uncomfortable at times, and often filled with unexpected challenges.

This perspective isn't meant to scare people from the spiritual path but to prepare them for the realities ahead. Over the years, many of my clients have struggled to find a path or practice that works for them. One of the key impasses they've encountered is the discouragement they experience when their natural, haphazard approach to study and practice becomes difficult or requires discipline. They like to try practices but not commit to anything over time.

Many people succumb to the modern consumer logic that assumes that everything should come in a neat little package, instantly, and at a discounted price. By understanding the complexity of spiritual growth, the challenges become easier to manage. When we expect something to be easy and it isn't, it's natural to become frustrated. However, when we know that challenge is a part of what we're facing, the change in mind-set alone makes things easier. The investment of self that's required for spiritual practice and awakening also underscores the importance of having a well-suited practice that we can focus our efforts and intentions on.

If You Wait for the Perfect Path, You'll Wait Forever

Recently after a lecture I gave on spiritual practice, two women approached me together. These friends shared a common concern. "If spiritual practice is so important, I think we're in trouble!" one asserted.

"Why is that?" I asked. The first one to speak began by explaining how she'd read everything imaginable about spirituality and religion. From quantum physics to the history of religion and modern self-help icons, she had degrees' worth of book knowledge about the soul, God, and the Spiritual World.

"But," she exclaimed, "I still don't get it! It just seems more confusing now than ever. Who's right?"

Her friend was just as perplexed: "I'm worse off! I've been to more workshops and lectures than you can imagine. My local college has a comparative-religion speaker series, and I attend them all. If there's a conference nearby, I go. I've sat through hours of teachers and teachings, and I still don't know what they have that I don't!"

"Well, what practices have you tried in your personal life on an ongoing basis?" I asked.

"I think that's the problem," they both responded. "We've never really had a spiritual practice because we just can't figure it out. We can't seem to choose. Which one is best?"

"Ah, that's your obstacle! You're trying to 'figure it out.' Spirituality isn't about who or what you know or even *think,* nor is it based on any typical measurement or standard. It's about something much deeper—even deeper than our emotions. But you can't really understand it until you experience it. It's like love: we know it when we feel it, but we can't give it to someone else. We can only create conditions, serve as a role model, teach, inspire, and then leave it up to them. It's something they have to feel."

I continued to simplify matters. "If you keep waiting for the perfect practice, you'll never begin. Pay attention to what you feel, select a practice that helps you feel more connected than you do now, and stick to it for a while. Every seed needs time to sprout and take root. If you planted a seed and kept digging it up every day to see if it had grown, you'd kill it before it had a chance. This is the spiritual path: be patient, commit yourself, and trust. Let nature take its course."

One of the ladies looked a bit sad and remarked, "But that sounds so straightforward. I've been making it so complicated. You mean that what I'm looking for is not an answer but an experience?"

"Yes," I agreed, "it's that simple."

These women are like many others who are driven by the accumulation of information and sometimes mistake knowledge for wisdom. Spiritual seekers often fall into this trap, and for most, the exploration of beliefs and philosophies involves little emotional risk or personal discomfort. By studying ideas and theologies we may feel affirmed, intrigued, or educated. Yet we often come to the edge of a philosophy in the way we come to the edge of many things in this world: like audience members or spectators.

Many people today have become spiritual window-shoppers. They look at the beliefs and practices of others and fantasize about what they might become but rarely go into the store to make a purchase. When it comes to spiritual and personal growth, research is a good start, but experience will change your life.

We can't expect extraordinary changes in our lives unless we're prepared to see in an extraordinary way. Experience is whole-self, involving body, mind, heart, and soul. To study spiritual truth may feel good and affirming, but it doesn't always create lasting change. To *experience* spiritual truth is to experience the convergence of thought, feeling, and sensation in a transformative way. For those who seek lasting peace and living wisdom, awakening must become a deeply personal, intentional, and invested process.

Tradition vs. Diversity: "Am I Allowed to Choose My Path?"

Recently a friend took me to a Sunday service at his church. I noticed that some people were involved in the choir, some were involved in the ritual, and others were working with the children's group in the basement. Some had become involved in helping with service projects during the week; and others seemed intently focused inwardly, deep in meditation, as if they could have been anywhere.

This experience affirmed the natural diversity of humanity, which is timeless and still necessary. I also noticed that the people who weren't engaged in something that connected with their spiritual personality looked as if they were half asleep. Some were snoring! The diversity of expression and way of finding connection is common to humankind and knows no religious boundaries. No matter how insistent a tradition is on maintaining consistency, diversity will rise up—either within, or when people leave to find something that works better for them.

I look for these patterns in any religious or spiritual setting I attend and am amazed by the way they recur. My wife, Monica, is a Kundalini yoga teacher, and a while ago, she took me to a special Kundalini yoga retreat. This type of yoga is known for its intense focus on repetitive postures, breath work, and mantras (sacred chants) that create shifts in energy and consciousness. Some people who practice other yoga traditions have stereotypes about what type of person does Kundalini yoga and the kinds of devotees it attracts. I shared some of those assumptions until I learned more about the tradition.

Although I'd been to a number of retreats before, this one caught my attention. Throughout the day, there was a range of practices that showed a great deal of diversity. There were various sessions: in the early morning, we focused on postures and breath. Then the next session taught traditional devotional dance. In the afternoon, we sat for a lecture on spiritual teachings; and following that, we enjoyed a beautiful session of chanting and one on meditation. All this was in one tradition, in one day.

It was clear that some attendees were more invested in certain sessions than others, and the teachers themselves clearly had areas of strength and interest. This is the way it is anywhere you go. In my travels around the world, the story has always been the same. In African village ceremonies, there are healers, singers, dancers, speakers, cooks, and children's teachers. In Tibetan monasteries, I saw those whose focus was on scripture, some were devoted to chanting, some on prostrations, some on teaching, and some on sacred music. Churches, synagogues, mosques, and other places of worship host more diversity than you might expect.

Each practice has the ability to awaken us to the power of present-moment awareness and spiritual experience, though they do it in different ways. We as human beings need the diversity of numerous practices to ensure that we're able to access Divine light and wisdom in our lives. The same basic diversity is found in almost all religious and spiritual traditions. These variations aren't always celebrated equally and aren't necessarily common knowledge, but if we look, we'll find all or most of the 12 Master Paths within them. They're found in nearly every culture and reflect a common spectrum of spiritual styles and personalities.

If you contrast the Master Paths with the many practices found today, you'll see that most "innovations" and "new" practices are simply revisions and adaptations of these 12 essential forms of spiritual practice. What's most important is that your options are clear so that you can consciously choose a vehicle that will help you endure a long and wonderful journey. People seem to make the most spiritual progress—healing, maturation, and transformation—when they choose a path that honors their natural tendencies and preferences. If you don't have a path that truly reflects who you are, then how will you take it to its ultimate conclusion?

How Do You Decide? Your Spiritual Personality

In the Western world today, we live with the burden of abundance. We live with a surplus of information and opportunity, as well as an easy ability to be touched by the infinite range of human experiences. Technology such as newspapers, radio, television, and the Internet make ideas available in the blink of an eye. People become overwhelmed by the search for spiritual growth. Many feel swamped by the myriad paths, practices, and spiritual teachers in the world; others feel trapped in religious communities that no longer help them feel connected; and there are some who don't even know where to begin at all. The confusion sets in when people think they need to have the "right" path or philosophy in order to be successful spiritually.

But as I've already explained, spiritual success is profoundly personal, ever evolving, and comes from within. Your spiritual path is a unique expression of your unique soul. Therefore, the important question isn't "What's right?" but "What's right for me?" The reason why the world is full of so much spiritual and religious diversity is because it reflects the complexity of the human search: different things work for different people.

Everyone has their own "spiritual personality" that naturally draws them to one thing or another. Deeper than your "persona," all the roles, expectations, and preconceived ideas you've accepted from others are innate knowledge of what *you* find inspiring, restoring, and meaningful. Your spiritual personality reflects your "true self": your soul, your basic spiritual nature.

The only thing that defines the worth of your spiritual practice is whether or not it works for you. Does it help you become free in heart, mind, and spirit? It should truly connect you to the qualities you seek: love, trust, connection to Higher Power, and grace in the flow of life. There can be no hierarchy of spiritual practices even though it seems it would make the choice much easier.

There's no logical pattern to the way you personally might combine a variety of practices in your life. Today it's possible to find a guide, teacher, book or product that will help you make anything into a source of healing and spiritual growth. From exercise to mind-body computer programs; and from new self-help strategies to cinema, pet therapy, and chocolate—if you look hard enough, you can find someone who'll teach you how to transform anything into a spiritual practice.

Most traditions believe that psychology, genetics, and the nurturing of our environments are only layers, like clothing, that are worn by the true self or soul. These traditions believe that it's the soul that is the source of our spiritual personalities; it's the root of our preferences and healthy attractions. Spiritual personality is all about where we uniquely find a sense of connection, peace, and healing.

Some people love to sing, some love to pray, some love sacred movement, and some find connection in art or science. There is truly something for everyone. When people are unaware of their spiritual personality, it's easy to feel confused when the things they're attracted to don't match what they've been told to love by family members and friends. We can be made to feel wrong for choosing a practice that is strange to our family or community. Remember that those who impose expectations on others often fail to recognize the diversity of practice that's natural to all people and communities.

For some readers, choosing and committing to one or more of the 12 Master Paths may feel like a risk or an adventure, and for others, this is simply a time to reevaluate their current practice. Is it time to add a new layer? Is it challenging you enough? Are you still growing? Is there something new you could explore to create the change you seek? The stories in this book will help you reflect on your spiritual journey: where you've been, what's possible, and where you're going.

Spiritual Personality: Four Orientations

Each human being is a complex expression of four main dimensions: body (physical), mind (mental), heart (emotional), and soul (spiritual). Each of us generally has a tendency to favor or orient our lives around one of these four dimensions. There is no better or worse, healthy or unhealthy; there are only different preferences. Our spiritual personality may reflect our aptitudes and talents or our present-moment needs. At different stages of our lives, we tend toward one of these four spiritual biases.

You may also notice that there are distinct tendencies in how people relate to the world. Some people are "thinkers" and like to live in the world of thoughts and the mind. Some are highly emotional and easily feel empathy and connection to others. Others live in their bodies: their appearance, physical health, and pleasure of movement all dominate their choices. And others are naturally oriented to the soul: the questions of ultimate meaning and a sense of a higher power develop naturally from a young age and become a preoccupation and lens through which all choices and actions are examined.

Typically from these biases our spiritual attractions are formed. People who are body oriented are attracted to things like yoga, walking meditations, and Tai Chi—all movement based. People who are mind oriented are attracted to reading, lectures, audio CDs, and discussions—all intellectual pursuits. People who are heart oriented are attracted to acts of service, devotional practices, or relationships with gurus and communities—all are emotive and relational. People who are soul oriented typically seek to experience the reduction of the other domains through actions such as fasting, isolation, or rigorous renunciation of one kind or another—all seeking the experience of the raw spirit. These people want to move beyond emotional, mental, or physical encounters into what might be described as "soul to Spirit" contact. Usually, this is expressing either an extreme form of devotion or an extreme desire for enlightenment—the full awakening of consciousness to the eternal nature of being.

Pay attention to your natural pulls and longing. No path is wrong; no path is right. The only thing that makes a path unhealthy is the motivation behind it. If your spiritual practice is feeding your ego or a bias to an extreme or actually becomes a barrier to your maturation, it's time for a major change. Don't let fear or peer pressure decide for you, either. Following your spiritual personality isn't the same as doing what's easy or comfortable. Once you've committed, the work begins. No matter how much you love your practice, there will be times of challenge; if not, it isn't a healthy path for you. Always be careful of the ego, and be willing to try something outside your area of strength and preference.

The 12 Master Paths can also be organized and understood according to the four spiritual personalities. Depending on the primary dimension of the self that a practice is rooted in, it will fall into one of the following four categories:

- Body-Centered Practice
- Mind-Centered Practice
- Heart-Centered Practice
- Soul-Centered Practice

All practices have the potential to lead a person to fully awaken spiritually. History has shown that mystics have been born of each and every one of these pathways. If applied with a healthy intention, they can lead to lasting change and transformation. Knowing the general orientation of the 12 Master Paths will help you select the practice that will offer you the greatest power and potential.

The 12 Master Paths can be organized as follows:

Body-Centered

- Ceremony and Ritual
- Sacred Movement
- Sacred Sound and Music

Heart-Centered

- Devotion
- Sacred Service
- Guru Guidance: Master Teacher

Mind-Centered

- Prayer
- Meditation
- Sacred Study

Soul-Centered

- Ascetic Practices
- Death Practice
- Life Path

Take Your Pick

Rather than step-by-step instructions, the following four Parts (II–V) introduce you to the essence of each practice as it's experienced. By encountering these practices from the inside, you'll naturally understand the mechanics and "how to." As you review the stories and overviews of the 12 Master Paths in the chapters, pay attention to your response to each story and description. You'll notice that some will repel you, and others will excite you. The ones that excite you may be just what you need to try. Be aware that people tend to have strong reactions to spiritual practices that don't suit them. This doesn't mean they're unworthy; it's only a matter of preference and spirituality personality. A spiritual practice that runs counter to someone's nature may elicit responses as strong as disgust and resistance.

To learn about your own biases and preferences, notice how you feel as you read the stories and descriptions of each. Observe how your body reacts and what stimulates thought and creativity. Ask yourself, *Am I making value judgments based on my past experiences? Do I have assumptions about which is "better" or more sophisticated? Is society influencing my beliefs?* Observe your reactions, keep an open mind, and give your full attention to each. There can be no harm or betrayal of your faith if you find what works for you.

A few of these paths are practiced in isolation, but most can complement one another or even be integrated. In my life, I've used each and every practice at one point or another. I've done some for decades and others only for short periods of time. You'll most likely find at least two or more practices to combine and blend to move you along your journey toward peace and true awakening.

Fear Is the Barrier

Approach the world of spiritual practice with trust and an open heart. Don't be afraid of spiritual experiences. Strange sensations of energy, a feeling of deep love, vulnerability, connectedness, and a loss of ego and control are all aspects of spiritual experience that test and try people's limits. Such profound and healing encounters can trigger fear and resistance. People doubt what they don't know, resist what they don't understand, and cling to what's familiar. It's a longing for safety that sacrifices freedom and growth. Some even fear for their mental and physical health when they begin to have pronounced spiritual experiences.

These concerns are not hollow. We've all seen examples of people who seem very committed to a religion or spiritual practice; and the outcome is only distraction, a new source of control, or worse, a rational for the judgment of others. These, however, are not examples of effective applications of spiritual practices nor are they accurate expressions of what spiritual experience teaches.

A healthy spiritual practice is both the mechanics *and* a certain mind-set about the practice. These elements—combined with guidance, grace, and dedication—are necessary to liberate the human spirit. Without an open mind and heart, without a sincere desire to learn, grow, and discover, any spiritual practice can become a *barrier* to growth.

Much of what scares people about spirituality is its demand to move beyond absolute trust in science and the five ordinary senses. The Spiritual World largely remains beyond the scope of material science, but that isn't a "problem"—it is simply its nature. In his magnificent book *The Little Prince,* Antoine de Saint-Exupéry wrote: "It is only with the heart that one can see rightly; what is essential is invisible to the eye."

Joseph Campbell, the great historian of mythology and religion, affirmed this by pointing out that nearly every culture in the world holds foundational stories of sacred heroes whose only salvation comes from facing their deepest fears and risking the life that is familiar in favor of a willingness to explore the unknown. Often, we must sever the ties to what we know and believe in order to be reborn and revived.

It is this dimension of the spiritual journey that remains the greatest barrier: fear. Anywhere that fear lives, the Spirit withdraws—including in groups, in families, or in ourselves. Where fear grows, love is diminished and the qualities of The Sacred are forgotten. People become paralyzed by the fear of the unknown, of being rejected, of not being in control, and of the discomfort they might face as they surrender who they've come to believe they are.

A healthy spiritual practice will cause you to become aware of your limits *and* your opportunities to heal and grow. This ensures that it won't always be easy, but it will always be worthwhile. My own journey has also come with many difficult crossroads, including loneliness, surprises, the recognition of old wounds, hard choices, and the need to make many sacrifices. But it has also blessed me with the most rewarding gifts and an abundant sense of personal power, happiness, and freedom.

In a circle of stones
We turn toward the sky
Our hearts become the drum
Songs sung by our ancestors
Become sunlight dancing around us

We turn ourselves
Into prayers
We hold our hearts
Candles flickering in the wind
Hold on
Burn just a little longer
We have come through such a dark dark night

Call to the Patient Earth
Call the Divine Light
Everything wants this Mercy
All things want this Grace
We touch the ground
and surrender who we once were
In exchange for hope
And a world reborn.

— J. H. Ellerby

SPIRITUAL TRAVELER TIPS:
IMPORTANT GUIDANCE AS YOU BEGIN TO
EXPLORE THE PRACTICES IN THIS BOOK

Natural Power: Nature and Spirituality

It's difficult not to consider the deep relationship people have to nature and wilderness as a spiritual path. Many of the experiences of The Sacred that I describe in this book take place in nature or in practices that are closely connected to the natural world. Nature, however, is not a path in itself. The paths and practices are specific behaviors, actions, and attitudes that converge in a consistent formation. Nature is greater than any path, practice, or experience. Nature *is* The Sacred and can be a powerful part of nearly any path.

All of the 12 Master Paths can be practiced *in* nature, and I recommend that you find ways to involve this in your exploration. In my own life, the natural world has been my greatest spiritual teacher and healer. It's a direct expression of The Sacred and takes its form, pattern, and spiritual qualities directly from its Creator. Involving nature in your practice is a sure way to accelerate your development.

Involving nature can be as simple as meditating on a flower or walking in a park. If you have little or no experience in the natural world, you may not choose to explore this as a spiritual source of inspiration right away, or you may want to ask a friend to help you explore the majestic wilderness in a way that's safe.

Safety and Instruction

Any practice that could have a measure of risk to body or mind should be supervised and coached until you've reached a level of competency. In addition, anything that involves specific techniques (such as meditation or yoga) should be done with guidance until you feel confident. Books and DVDs are a nice supplement to instruction, but they aren't a replacement for an instructor who can observe your progress and development.

In a similar respect, if you're having spiritual experiences that feel overwhelming, emotionally demanding, or difficult to manage and integrate, seek a spiritual counselor or therapist with knowledge of spiritual practice. Difficult times are to be expected, and most people can benefit from good advice and the ability to discuss their experiences with a professional.

If you're unsure about whether or not you need mental-health support, you should seek it. You may start by going to a spiritual mentor whom you can trust (such as a chaplain, rabbi, or an advanced yoga teacher) and asking for his or her opinion and guidance. Be aware that *not* all religious leaders will respect a spiritual practice or understand spiritual experiences. Some will discourage any practice that they don't understand or haven't experienced. Don't be confused by their fear. Choose your spiritual adviser wisely.

You may want to ask prospective spiritual advisers to tell you about their own spiritual journey first. Learn about their credentials, mentors, and what practices have shaped their lives. Ask why they do the work they do and how they like to best work with people. You can learn a lot by asking questions, so take your time and listen to your intuition. No matter how many degrees or credentials a person has, if you have a "bad feeling," you should seek another opinion or go elsewhere. (For more information, consult the Resources at the end of this book.)

Daily, Weekly, and Seasonally

Most spiritual practices should have a *daily* component, and this can be complemented by a weekly group process or community experience. Further deepening and advancement should be done seasonally, such as once or twice a year, in which you immerse yourself in an environment of training and study.

Naturally, there are exceptions. Some practices are typically done in groups, including yoga and certain forms of meditation. And some ascetic practices are impractical or impossible to do on a regular basis. Use your intuition and best judgment. If you can't do it all, something is better than nothing. Don't forget that what you put into your practice, you will get out of your practice.

Home and Community

Don't be afraid to move beyond your comfort zone and invest time in your practice or to associate yourself with a community. You'll be glad you did. Maintaining a practice on your own takes an extreme amount of self-discipline, but a community of fellow seekers can be a great and fun support.

Find a balance between creating the time and space for your practice at home and having a group you can access or attend as necessary. Spiritual fellowship is an important way to keep a healthy perspective on your attitude and progress. Too much isolation can sometimes lead to a loss of self-awareness.

The Mystic Mind-set: Attitudes That Will Help You Transform Your Practice

Whether you have a teacher, a community, or a practice on your own, the following eight attitudes are companions to any spiritual path and practice. They are fundamental to avoid getting caught in routine, rules, and dogma. Applying these perspectives will help you access the deepest wisdom and healing in any spiritual practice and at any stage of your development.

When your spiritual tradition or practice ceases to help you become more self-aware and spiritually connected, revisit this list before changing paths. Know that sometimes a new attitude isn't enough; it's natural to need a change in your practice from time to time.

1. **Compassion: No Harm.** Be kind, empowering, patient, and forgiving to yourself and others as you carry out your practice. Let love be your compass, helping you make all decisions.

Compassion seeks the highest good—not making everyone happy.

2. **Optimism: No Fear.** Always ask yourself, *What can I learn from this moment? What am I grateful for?* Never let go of hope and the infinite field of possibility. Don't let fear change your mind, as it's only a sign that there's something to learn, pay attention to, or heal. Look for lessons in everything.

3. **Observation: No Judgment.** Self-awareness is key. Observe yourself during your practice, and don't criticize or judge your experience. Judgment of others is a distraction and an impediment, and it also creates an energy that blocks healing and growth.

4. **Contemplation: No Striving.** With each new experience in your practice, take time to reflect deeply on what it means, what it reveals, and what it teaches. Learn to listen to your innermost thoughts and feelings. Take the time to let your experiences, intentions, and lessons sit within you. Insight can't be forced.

5. **Dedication: No Procrastination.** Stay committed and willing. On some days, enduring discomfort will be all that you can manage. Focus and dedication are necessary. Remember to make your practice regular and consistent when possible and appropriate. Rest and renewal is necessary sometimes, as it's also a part of the path. Avoidance and procrastination diminish the power of the soul.

6. **Humor: No Ego.** Have fun! Don't be afraid to laugh at yourself or even your deepest beliefs.

Humor feeds a healthy practice and will keep you balanced and centered. Learn to appreciate playfulness, creativity, and the absurdity of life.

7. **Surrender: No Attachment.** Let go of constant questioning and controlling. Let your unique process unfold with your full participation. Give yourself fully to your practice without expectations. Have inspirations and intentions, but hold them lightly with flexibility and openness. Expect the unexpected, and be willing to let a higher order take over. Remember, you aren't in charge. Let The Sacred reveal its magic.

8. **Intention: No Doubt.** Your intention isn't a goal to be fixated on but a deep clarity and longing for what it is you seek. If you can be clear, dedicated, and intent on your goal—such as union with a higher power, communication with God, or knowledge of the hidden wisdom of the universe—you'll attract the lessons, teachers, and experiences you need. Intention is not just a picture, but a deep, heartfelt feeling. It comes from the force within your soul. Let your intention focus your attention and strengthen your energy.

PART II

Body-Centered Practices

In this moment, the world dances with me
And time stands still
In this place, everything glows
With an inner fire

I close my eyes for a moment,
Enter the familiar motion
Like an embrace
Open my heart, and suddenly
Everything has meaning again

Compassion and Wisdom
Ripen before me and I drink the nectar
This is more than hope,
More than wishful thinking
This sacred act is
The fulfillment of 10,000 dreams

I move so deeply
Into this body, into this breath,
This simple act is a doorway
Something within me dissolves
I know everything I have is Yours
Even the idea that I have an existence without You
Vanishes

Here I release the questions,
Here I give up the search
Here I give in to You and
The perfection of this moment
Takes me deeper and deeper
Into a Love I can scarcely understand
Much less hold on to

But I will return
And reach out to You
Again and again.

— J. H. Ellerby

Chapter Four

THE PATH OF CEREMONY AND RITUAL

Evoking the Sacred

Many years ago as a teenager, I was introduced to a simple Native American ritual that changed my life. A Canadian Ojibwa healer taught me the practice. Frank was a "well-seasoned" man who had seen the highs and lows of life in extremes before he settled on a path dedicated to helping, healing, and honoring his ancestors' traditions.

"In this world," he instructed, "the Creator has given us everything we need: food, shelter, and clothing. If we know how to live in harmony with the world around us, all of these things will come to us. But we must live with respect because there's an energy, a Spirit, within each thing. Everything has power. It can help us or hurt us. Each has its own way. Just as we were given ways to feed our bodies, we were also given ways to feed our spirit, and ways to make communication with The Spirit That Watches Over All. You may not know it yet, but you can interact with that power. We do so with ceremony, with ritual. It's our sacred technology.

"Some plants, for example, are for medicine, some for food, and some are especially for helping us open the pathways between the worlds. I'm not talking about drugs, either. We're given spiritual medicines, such as sage, sweetgrass, cedar, and red willow, to purify our bodies and minds and strengthen our prayers. The plant itself has an energy that's powerful and helpful by just holding it or keeping it near you.

"Each plant has a special purpose, a distinct nature; some attract Good Spirits, and some release negative ones. All of the sacred plants can be used to cleanse the spirit, the body, the mind, and the heart when we want to center ourselves in prayer and meditation. White people call what we do with the plants 'smudging.' You can even find these plants in stores today. But if you understand their power, you'll learn to go pick it yourself, dry it properly, and be sure that every step is done with respect. When people buy 'medicine' in stores, they forget that they're absorbing all the energy that went into it. You can't always trust where such things come from. If you take these things lightly, you shouldn't be involved with them.

"When we approach a moment of prayer—connection with a Higher Power—we approach it with respect, reverence, and always gratitude. In our way, we create a ceremony—you might say a ritual—when we want to make a prayer. The way we use these sacred plants in a prayer ritual is to take the dried leaves of one, or a combination, and then burn them briefly. Light them with a match or lighter, and just when it catches fire, let the flame die. You might wave it in the air or fan it with a feather to help put the fire out. Then the plant will smolder like the incense you see in some churches.

"It's the smoke from a sacred plant that you wash yourself with. We don't smoke it like a cigarette—it's not for breathing in, and it isn't a drug. We use the energy of that sacred plant to cleanse us. Through that medicine we are purified, the mind is quieted, and we call the attention of the Spirit World. This is a powerful act to help you pray for pure heart, body, mind, and spirit. It's a ritual I do every day."

I listened, absorbing every word the way a desert takes in water. It all made sense. "Is that it?" I asked. "It's so simple, but it makes sense."

"Yes," he replied. "It is that simple, and there are two other elements I never forget: gratitude and intention. If you just burn the plants because I told you to, you won't feel their power. You have to use that smudge with the intention to be clear and purified, and show gratitude. Feel and express your gratitude. I offer tobacco every day."

"Tobacco? You mean you smoke a cigarette?"

"No, I mean that I physically offer something sacred to God and the Spirit World. In our culture, our ancestors have taught us that the original tobacco we grew generations ago was precious to us, and the spirits welcome it as a sign of gratitude. It's what the spirits have asked for in exchange for their help and attention. Maybe in your culture it's something else.

"I met a man from Japan, and he places a little rice and fruit in a bowl to thank his ancestors and the spirits. I know that the Navajo use corn pollen as an offering. It's about finding an action and a small gift that helps you say thank you and acknowledge the presence of the Spiritual World. The offering is left outside, or in a sacred place in your home, and then eventually released into nature. You don't just throw it out. Try it sometime. When you pray, make an offering."

Since that day, I've started almost all of my days with this simple ritual that Frank taught me so long ago. I go to a quiet place that reminds me of or connects me with a feeling of The Sacred, I purify my body and mind with a smudge, and I take some time to clear my mind and set my intentions. I keep a little container of an offering, such as loose tobacco, uncooked rice, or even raw wheat kernels since that's what Jewish people in my culture used hundreds of years ago.

When I finish my prayers, I either place a pinch of the offering on the ground (beside a tree, for example), or I use a special bowl and collect it for a week and then take it outside. It is a spiritual practice I wouldn't want to live without. For me, my morning prayers and meditations wouldn't be the same without that ceremony. If I don't take the time to wash my soul and make an offering to The Sacred, I don't feel as if I've started my day right.

Building a Bridge: Ceremony and Ritual

A ceremony can be as complex as a Native American Sun Dance, a Japanese Tea Ceremony, or a Catholic Mass; or it can be as simple as a daily pattern of offering, purification, and prayerful behavior similar to the one I just described. The words *ceremony* and *ritual* have lost their importance for many people, yet their power remains available to everyone. Along with physical objects, places, symbols, and patterns, ceremony helps us engage The Sacred, allowing us to participate in the Spiritual World through conscious uses of time, space, motivation, action, sound, and symbol. With ceremony, we create a bridge to The Sacred, embodying its qualities here on Earth.

When combined with proper intention and symbolic action, we have the ability to create an integration of body (action), heart (emotion), mind (intent), and soul (intuition and awareness of The Sacred). During a meaningful ceremony or ritual, we experience the deepening of three central relationships: with ourselves, our community, and The Sacred. With symbolic objects that signify our most precious values and understanding of The Sacred, we energetically interact with the Spiritual World. In such a moment, our connection and interdependence on all things becomes palpable and more real.

Sacred Time and Space

Ceremony and ritual allow us to alter time and space to create breaks in our routine and ways of thinking and feeling. The Jewish ritual observance of the Sabbath begins on Friday night at sundown. In a beautiful and simple ceremony, we acknowledge the blessings we've received throughout the week and the gratitude we feel for whatever health and shelter we have. The ceremony also marks a transition into sacred space and time.

Before the *Shabbat* (Sabbath) ceremony, we're engrossed in the daily routines of work, school, and family. Our minds are easily distracted, and God can drift from our thoughts. After the *Shabbat* evening ceremony, we're in a contemplative time and turn our attention to God and family. We rest from work and commerce and the complexity of the technological world. Our thoughts and attitudes are more reflective, and we remember our sacred origin. Without this ritual, the drama of life races on without stop. There would be no "time out" from the hurried pace of life.

Every culture on the planet has always used ceremony and ritual to help mark special times in our days, weeks, and years. Ceremonies are used not only to mark the seasons but to participate in their passing. Ritual and ceremony is often about bringing us into alignment with the world around us and acknowledging the changes in the natural cycles of the world. We stop to reflect on the past season and embrace the necessary attitude for the coming one.

Rites of Passage

Rites of passage are ceremonies that help us create or manage transition in our life. The Christian Confirmation, Jewish Bar and Bat Mitzvah, Hindu Sacred Thread Ceremony, and Indigenous Vision Quests are all examples of "coming of age" ceremonies. In cultures where they mark the passage through significant stages in life, we see a healthy self-awareness about the changes and expectations people face as they age.

In cultures where such rituals are lost, we see youth who are overwhelmed by confusion, a sense of entitlement, or despondency about their roles in the world. Without rituals to honor the beauty of life transitions, we forget the power of each stage. People begin to fear aging, experience midlife crises, and struggle to grieve the past. Ceremony is about reorientation *in* and *with* The Sacred; without it, we experience disorientation and disconnection.

Ceremonies themselves can be taken for granted and their meanings lost. In most, the symbols, actions, and songs that might be integral are only the visible element. The most important aspect of any ceremony lies in the people participating—that is, their clarity of motivation, unity of intent, and willingness to engage a higher order of being. The value of the physicality of ceremony lies in its ability to focus and direct the mind and heart. When people lose that awareness, rituals become hollow and ceremonies become boring or even frustrating. When you find yourself in that kind of situation, search for your own meaning in the symbols and words that are present. Ask yourself if you *must* continue in that way or if maybe there are new ceremonies or rituals that will assist you. Perhaps you need to try a new path altogether.

Healing Ceremonies

Modern science has barely begun to understand the extraordinary impact that ceremonies can have on people. The science of placebo effect and mind-body mechanisms barely begins to touch upon the phenomena that may be encountered in ceremonies. Deep psychological change, emotional release, physical healing, and radically altered states of consciousness are all possible outcomes in a ceremony that invokes the healing force of the soul and Universal Spirit.

An essential paradox that is essential to the effect of ceremonies that heal and transform lies in their embrace of both mystery and concrete frameworks that provide sense, focus, and meaning for the participants. In his groundbreaking research uniting modern physics and ancient cultures, Gregg Braden shows how traditions have long taught that when emotion and mental clarity are matched in a healing intention, radical change in biology and environment are possible.

Primarily in the Indigenous world, I've seen this formula at work with my own eyes. I have watched and known people to be healed of addictions, cancer, multiple sclerosis, and other extreme conditions through ceremony. The outcome is never guaranteed, which makes ceremony an unlikely conventional medicine. On the other hand, there is an ever-present capacity to create lasting emotional healing, inner peace, and transformative spiritual states of awareness.

It's Only Natural

The ceremonies that have been the most powerful to me are either simple, such as the ritual of daily smudging and offering, or profoundly complex, taking me dramatically out of my typical mind-set. The best example I can think of is the ceremonial steam bath. In Native American traditions, the English name for these ceremonies is "Sweat Lodge." I've experienced ceremonial steam baths and Sweat Lodges across Canada and the United States, as well as in Mexico, Swaziland, South Africa, and Zimbabwe. Steam baths have been used in many countries and cultures as a means to purify the body, mind, and spirit. There is a great range of differences, yet some common elements also exist.

The Native American Lodges, for example, typically involve a small dome-shaped structure made of arched branches that are covered with heavy canvas tarps. This sphere-like tent becomes the womb of the earth, the home of the ceremony, where participants crawl in to pray, meditate, and sing. In the center of the Lodge is a hollowed-out pit where rocks that have been heated on a sacred fire outside are placed.

Once the door to the Lodge is closed, the circle of people are plunged into complete darkness. The ceremonial leader guides the journey of the heart and soul, pouring water on the hot rocks and managing the flow of the ritual, which can last for hours. The space is physically small, yet to be in the Lodge is to be aware of the totality of the universe and humanity's precious and vulnerable place within it. The rawness of the connection to heat, steam, earth, and air brings participants into acute awareness of their dependence on the natural world while also turning their senses to the spiritual. Impossible things can occur within a Sweat Lodge.

I'm honored to have been trained and "ordained" to run Lodges in a few traditions. Out of respect for cultural integrity, however, I don't run specific Native American ceremonies outside Native communities or without the supervision of a Native elder. I've also been blessed to have received a new ceremony, which is called the "Spirit Lodge"—an interfaith ceremony that draws on the many steam-bath traditions of the world. Spirit Lodge leaders follow a specific ceremony and ritual that also requires them to honor their own cultural heritage and spiritual training.

What has been the most amazing about conducting these ceremonies and mentoring people to become leaders in them has been the profound and natural response so many people have to ritual and ceremony. Although it may be foreign, strange, and challenging to some who attend for the first time, the impact is often beyond words. The experience moves people out of the familiar and heightens the awareness of the heart and spiritual senses.

It isn't ideal for everyone, but those who come willingly will encounter an experience of The Sacred that transcends their everyday reality. Regardless of culture or religion, people find the permission and pathways to release control and consider the spiritual dimension of life and themselves. Healing tears, connection, renewal, and letting go are all common in the Spirit Lodge.

This has shown me again and again how innate the response is to ceremony and ritual. I'm humbled by each ceremony I lead or participate in. Whether performing a wedding, baby blessing, prayer circle, funeral, or Spirit Lodge, I know that I'm a small part in what touches people's lives. When we create a space with love, deep meaning, and the clear intent to heal, the power and presence of The Sacred is more than anyone can explain or deny. In the practice of ceremony and ritual, we create a bridge to the world of Spirit and are awakened by the force that flows through.

Chapter Five

THE PATH OF SACRED MOVEMENT

The Unexpected Yogi

Rishikesh is a small town in northern India that's famous for its many ashrams and abundance of gurus, *sadhus* (wandering holy men), and yogis. While in India, I set out for that captivating place with a serious intent to find a supreme yoga teacher with whom I could study for a few weeks. At the time I was particularly interested in the body-centered practice of yoga, a focus that Westerners often call "asana yoga" or "hatha yoga." Hatha, or physical yoga, is only one of many dimensions of the history and practice of any yogic path. The physical postures and poses, called *asanas*, were developed in order to assist spiritual seekers in the pursuit of enlightenment. These physical postures and poses are integrated into most forms of yoga, but not all.

Physical yoga practices were designed to refine concentration, prepare the body for meditation, and awaken the vital energies of the self. Despite its supplementary nature in Hindu tradition, asana (posture) yoga has become the focus of Western attention above all other aspects.

To begin my search, I spent days walking the streets, passing temples and watching the crowds of devotees. Ashrams (spiritual communities) and hermitages are abundant in Rishikesh, and I felt sure I'd find a wise old yogi or yogini (a female yoga master) to teach me to master my body and mind. As I became more familiar with the setting, I began to talk to many of the travelers and seekers I met along the way and asked them if they knew of any great yoga teachers. As I did, a strange thing kept happening.

To my surprise, I received the same answer again and again: "Yes, you should look for Pierre!" I was a bit taken aback by the name "Pierre" because it sounded so very French! I was hoping for a yogi with an exotic name, dark skin, and Indian heritage; but the amount of recommendations to seek out Pierre for guidance was overwhelming.

There I was in the ancient heart of India, in the yoga capital of the world, and the only teacher I could get a good reference for was a guy from Paris! This wasn't what I expected, but as with many things on the spiritual path, some of the greatest experiences begin in unlikely ways.

Trusting the coincidence of recommendations, I decided to track down Pierre. I found out that he was staying in the northern town of Dharamsala in order to escape the summer heat. So off I went in search of him. I survived the long bus ride and immediately began to look for my new French yogi. Fortunately, I easily located him and his daily classes, which took place atop a residence for Buddhist monks in the heart of Dharamsala.

Pierre was an excellent teacher, after all. He was trained in the Shivananda tradition and seemed impeccable in his manner, instruction, and knowledge. He had also been initiated and ordained as a Tai monk and had trained with the renowned master Achan Chah. Pierre wasn't an old, weathered pandit, but a slender Frenchman who was an acclaimed master of yoga.

Within the week, I connected with a few of his regular students, and we discussed our desire to practice daily with Pierre until we left Dharamsala. One of the students knew the mysterious teacher and arranged for us to meet him to express our intentions. He was kind and supportive and offered to begin a 40-day *sadhana* (practice), which involved our commitment to attend his class at least once a day for 40 days.

So every evening for the next 40 days, we met Pierre and a showing of transient and semiregular students who made up the rest of the class. Pierre only instructed during sunup or sundown, following the tradition of his guru who taught that the active energies of the daylight hours were too chaotic for deep yoga practice. I committed to attending the rooftop classes at dusk. Each day we looked out over the town and valley from our high studio as the fading light washed the land with magnificent hues of orange, pink, and red.

As the sun sank, I felt my soul descend deeper and deeper into an inner stillness. I felt the effects of the postures, which eventually became a seamless part of the rhythm of the day. After I made it through the first 21 days, I discovered that there was also a sunrise practice that I was missing because I was studying at the local Buddhist monastery in the mornings. Having brought other commitments to an end, some of us decided to attend that class as well whenever we could. For most of the remaining days, I attended Pierre's yoga classes at dawn and dusk. The process, the feelings, and the peace were so deep, so beautiful, that it created a thirst for more.

I'd never before engaged in a physical practice so diligently or with such dedication, and the experience was extraordinary. I found myself slowly progressing through stages of change. It began with a time of discomfort, confusion, and awkwardness. I recall mixing up Pierre's instructions, confusing my right and left sides, feeling unsteady, and not being able to complete many of the poses. I was often unmotivated or felt a sense of doubt and frustration, but all I could do was forgive myself, concentrate on the practice, and persist.

In time, however, I found myself moving into the poses with greater and greater ease as I learned the patterns, posture, and alignment. My mind began to grow quiet as my attention became rooted in my muscles and bones. My body started to crave the sessions, and motivation came with ease. Things I could never perceive in my body at the beginning became glaringly important by the end. My senses and physical awareness became more and more sensitive.

More than anything, I noticed an incredible sense of peace that would overcome me midway through each session. It was as if I were floating and only semi-awake to what I was doing, yet somehow alert, astute, and attentive. My body became flexible; my mind became quiet and easy to observe throughout the day; and my emotions turned to a kind of happiness that was a sort of high, which lasted like a song always in the back of my mind.

Pierre was a great teacher after all, and for the first time I truly understood the value of physical yoga. I'd *studied* it in my university courses on religion, and I'd dropped in on many different types of classes over the years. But it wasn't until I committed to a true practice that I experienced and understood the mental, emotional, and physical benefits of regular yoga practice.

The Wisdom of the Body

I'd grown up assuming that the body was a barrier to spirituality—not a pathway. I felt that I'd always heard Western spiritual leaders talking about the body as a distraction, something to be overcome or denied. I'd been taught in school that the only way of "knowing" something was through words, logic, and the mind. These were the cultural assumptions I took for granted. A spiritual practice that's rooted in movement taught me quite the contrary.

Sacred movement includes physical postures and movements such as those found in Tai Chi, Chi Gong, walking meditations, various forms of yoga, Jewish ophanim, and ceremonial dance. Common to nearly all traditions, this practice involves the intentional focus on the body in patterned movement to shift awareness from the wandering mind to the sensations and wisdom of the body. In a sacred-movement practice, your body will show you not only *where* you hold tension, but sometimes *why*. In your own body, you can find an imprint of your inner world.

Your life story is recorded in the body, and a sacred-movement practice allows you to hear it. In your impediments of movement, you learn about your impediments of fear, control, and resistance. The body is in many ways a metaphor for the way you live your life, so it's important to learn to be more aware of how you move. Some people stoop with the weight of life's burdens, and others lean forward, preoccupied with the future. Do you hold your shoulders high with tension, or clothe yourself in order to hide your form? Do you walk with your head up or lowered? What does the way you move say about you? Do you feel balance, grace, or intention? What has shown up over the years?

Paying close and attentive attention to the body and its experience is a sure way to come into the present moment. It reveals not only your own nature, but also an abiding peace in the world. Make peace with your own body and you will make peace in your life.

Dancing with the Soul

Roberta is a woman I met years ago at a conference about Native American approaches to healing. When I saw her at the beginning of the weekend, she was pale, walked with a cane, and seemed to be in constant pain. As one of the organizers, I had the chance to connect with her a number of times and ask about her condition. Roberta called herself "crippled" and attributed her condition to a combination of aging, genetics, and an accident she'd had a few years previously.

She said, "I've never been the same since. I knew I'd never be the same the day of the car accident. I can't play with my grandchildren, and I can't do things for my kids. It's like everything is being taken from me—it's the story of my life."

I watched as the inspiring talks and moving sessions began to create a shift in her mood. Toward the end of Saturday, the second day, I approached her. She didn't look happy, but there was something a bit different about her. I asked how she was feeling.

"Well," she said with a big sigh, "I guess I have a lot to think about. I'm beginning to realize that I have to take some responsibility for my choices and body. I've been so negative all my life, and when this happened, I can now see that it just gave me an excuse to dive into my own sorrow and self-pity. Things aren't great, but maybe they aren't that bad, either. I'm just not sure what my next step is. I want to heal this leg of mine . . . I want to get my energy back."

"Have you thought of coming to the dance tonight?" I offered. "We hold a dance on the second night so people can get out of their heads and blow off some of the heaviness of this gathering. We need balance, right?"

"Me? Dance? Not likely!" She held up her cane.

"Why not?" I challenged. "I thought you wanted to break free from those old thoughts and feelings? Besides, you can just watch and get an idea of what to look forward to."

"Maybe," she said with a slight turn in her mood.

Later that night I was at the community dance. It was a simple event held in a Girl Scouts' meeting hall with entertainment by a local DJ. The room was darkened, lights flashed from the DJ's station, and the middle of the room was emptied for the dance floor. The walls were lined with folding tables and chairs. The evening began slow with the typical interplay you might find at a wedding. The young people huddled in a corner away from the adults, and the younger boys and girls teased each other. Occasionally a small group would dance in a circle when the music was just right. The adults were slower to start but then took over the floor.

It was a night of the "oldies but goodies"; and the presenters, organizers, and participants all mixed and mingled in a silly spirit that relieved the tension of the day's sessions on trauma, suicide, and grief. Everyone was ready for a break. Soon we all forgot our shyness and caution and gave in to a playful mood. That's when I noticed Roberta sitting in the corner. She'd come to the dance!

Finding a friend of hers, I asked if she'd try to persuade Roberta to get on the dance floor—no matter what. A small group of us watched as Roberta resisted and fussed. We then began waving and begging foolishly. Finally, she came limping with her cane to the edge of our circle. One of the male presenters, a psychologist, immediately went over to her and started to make her laugh. Next thing we knew, she was moving a bit more, and soon she was dancing with her whole body. Her face lit up and was flush with color.

I lost track of Roberta a number of times that night, but by the end we caught up with each other. She was smiling and covered in sweat. "I haven't had this much fun in years," she said. "This is the beginning of my new life. I'm going to dance my way to health!"

One year later on the first day of the very same annual gathering, I felt a firm tap on my shoulder. I turned around to see Roberta, her arms open wide for a hug—no cane in her hand.

"I've been to energy healers, I've changed my diet, and I've been focusing on the positive. I try to dance all I can. It's my new exercise and now I know where my mind is at. I've learned to *feel* my body and not fear it. This old thing isn't perfect, but it will still do the job!"

Dancing changed Roberta's life. I've seen her several times since then over the years, and her progress has been steady. She is now the first on the dance floor and the last to sit down.

The connection between the body, mind, heart, and soul is so close that simple changes in the way we carry ourselves create new feelings and awareness. New experiences of our physical form inspire a recognition of what we can change and what we can work to accept. It can even change our lives. Roberta's dancing changed her way of thinking; it connected her to a part of herself that's timeless and joyful.

Embody Your Self

As we tune in to the body's rhythms, potential, and limits, we awaken to the sacredness of who we are as people. We discover that we've been given a beautiful gift: a body in which to move our souls throughout this life. Sacred movement isn't about perfection, appearance, or physical beauty; it's about the incredible power of the body to bring our awareness fully into the present where we face what is in the moment.

Yoga with a focus on postures and conscious-patterned movement has been met in the Western world with an overwhelming success that has spread like a wildfire. People of all walks of life and all levels of motivation have tried and committed to a regular yoga practice. At the heart of the reason for the incredible spread of yoga in the West is something much more than stronger, more flexible, and leaner bodies. What keeps so many people connected to their yoga practice is the way it makes them *feel* during and after a session. For most, the worries of life fade from attention; the busy mind grows quiet; and there is a reconnection with a place within the self that is not about *doing* anything reactive—rather, it is about *being* intentional.

A sacred-movement practice could be something unstructured, such as regular dance; however, the intent would have to be clear and more than recreational. Sacred-movement practices are typically performed in groups, and most are best supported by study with a teacher at some point. Watching DVDs is an excellent way to maintain a practice but isn't a substitute for proper coaching and community. Part of the power of sacred movement is learning to be more self-aware and more comfortable with what we are becoming aware of. If we hide out at home, we run the risk of isolating ourselves from the very feedback and challenges that cause a sacred-movement practice to be so meaningful.

Once a practice is established, the "where" and "when" become less important. When the mind knows how to surrender to the body and relax into the spiritual senses, the gift of sacred movement takes us beyond self-healing and into a deep awareness of The Sacred.

Chapter Six

THE PATH OF SACRED
SOUND AND MUSIC

Songs of the Spirit

The Venda of South Africa live in a precious land. The earth is soft and a deep rust color that makes you want to touch it, and the huge baobab trees preside over the area like guardians from another world. The region is high and rocky in places but not too far from the wise, green Limpopo River, which has made this place home forever. The winding roads are still more like footpaths, and people are always walking everywhere. Their smiles are deep and shining like the blue African sky that looks down upon it all.

Years ago, I took a trip with my wife, Monica, to see my teacher Tshivengwa in his home village in northeastern South Africa. It was Monica's first time there; and as an herbalist, Kundalini yoga teacher, and seasoned student of Indigenous medicine, she was quickly accepted and respected by my mentors. On that trip, we were also hosting friends who'd wanted to witness the power of African healing, culture, and wildlife. Together, we decided to experience the work of a number of healers, as well as the songs and dances of my home community in Venda.

Every day was filled with the gentle rhythms of the villages. Far from the major highways, there were only dusty dirt roads, a few cars, and people traveling mostly on foot. Some workers rode on donkey-driven carts. Women carried large loads of wood and containers of water balanced on top of their heads, while at the same time carefully holding babies or other supplies in their hands. The sound of grazing goats and proud roosters often played in the distance. Life had a simple pace, and we loved it.

One morning we set out with our teacher in the well-worn "minivan" that carried us from place to place. Beneath the expansive sky, down the rugged dirt roads that crawled through the mighty baobab trees, we made our way as we often did in search of Sacred Places, old healers, and plant medicines.

Without prompting, Tshivengwa turned to me with a suspicious grin and said, "Tonight you will understand why we sing to the ancestors. You will see why they love our tune." Then he turned in silence and didn't say another word about what he meant for the rest of the day. Tshivengwa's English was very good, but his expressions were frequently difficult to interpret. All I could do was try to figure out what he was referring to.

The day seemed to be more relaxed than others, as if Tshivengwa—who often charged about like a bull elephant—was trying to save our energy and give us a break from our usually full days of learning. At one point, we stopped by a local supply shop. A typical village store, it was simple, and built out of corrugated tin. There was no modern commercial shelving, and no color schemes or uniforms to entice customers. It was just a simple room with goods to be sold, and, of course, a series of large coolers provided by Coca-Cola to stock their products. I was baffled by the quantity of drinks he bought, and it seemed there were other supplies that were wrapped up and difficult to discern.

We got home to our lodgings in Tshivengwa's camp at dusk. The sky slowly drained of light as a blanket of deep purples and navy blues settled over the village. The camp was a small fenced-in compound with five round structures that might be called "huts" by an American. The walls were made of clay and cow dung, and the roofs were thatched. Locally, these simple dwellings were known as *rondavels,* and they all seemed about the same size, approximately 15 feet across.

Tshivengwa ushered us into the rondavel where we always ate. At one point, Monica got up to get something from the one we slept in and came back with a strange look on her face, as if she'd seen something that she couldn't understand. "Go to our room," she said, "and look around as you go. Something is going on."

I went out into the night. The sky was now completely dark, and a few lamps barely lit the space between the small buildings. There was a strange, unfamiliar feeling in the air. A woman in traditional Venda attire whom I'd never seen before came out of the darkness and hurried across my path. I was startled but not surprised. Tshivengwa often had members of the community in his home who had come seeking healing.

At that moment, a door opened into one of the spare rondavels. In the dim glow of a lantern within, I saw what seemed like a sea of dark faces and bodies low to the ground. The door quickly closed. It was a very mysterious scene. I went straight back to the room where we were finishing dinner as excitement and anxiety stirred within me.

Tshivengwa had been absent from the meal and seemed busy. We waited and talked about the day, but our minds were wandering. It was clear that under cover of the night something was unfolding, but we couldn't guess what it was. "What were those people doing? Are we going to find out?" The ceremonies we'd previously encountered had all taken place outside. There were no community members gathered in the front yard, and none of the normal signs of an event was present.

Then Tshivengwa came for us and announced, "You must ready yourself for the night. Clean up and prepare for our ceremony. We will sing through the night." After a few more instructions, we headed out to get ready and found a small group of old women standing around a fire that had been lit. We greeted each other in Venda: *"Madekwana."* They giggled to hear our foreign accents and pronunciations but were pleased by our efforts. Then we were led to the rondavel that had been so mysteriously kept shut. We entered and a new lamp was lit. That's when we saw the room clearly.

The round clay room was full of middle-aged and older women, who were wearing traditional dress and sitting on the floor. Holding large rattles, they seemed to occupy nearly every inch available. There was no furniture—only a single open space in the middle of the room and a small place where we were being seated to the left of three huge wooden drums.

The feeling was awkward. We didn't know what was about to happen. We didn't know these women, and they didn't know who we were. It was as if we'd interrupted a very private conversation. After some final commotion and rearranging of bodies, Tshivengwa came in and started to speak.

"Last year you asked how we call the Spirits, and I told you about a very old ceremony. Few communities still practice this way. The Christians among us wish it weren't so. We practice in secret, under the night's dark cover. These women have been initiated in the old way—they have 'the Spirit.' Not everyone can do this, but tonight you will see." With that, he moved to the far side of the room by the door, and the ceremony began with a brief and furious shake of the rattles. The women made calls and sounds, something like a mixture of a cry of praise and one for help.

There was loud praying spoken in Venda by a few who appeared to be leaders. The drum then sounded, deep and loud. It filled the room, vibrating within us, and the clay wall resonated behind my back. Gradually, the pace of the drums increased and became regulated in a strange and powerful rhythm. The women began to sing and shake their rattles in unison. More than 25 rattles, sharp and treble in their sounds, rang out.

We were overwhelmed at first. All of the sounds seemed foreign and were in patterns and tones that none of us had ever heard before. I tried to watch in order to figure out what was going on, looking for signs I could interpret. But the rattles surged and the drumming continued, and my thoughts seemed to be dissolving as quickly as I could gather them. Before I knew it, I was humming along, moving my body in my seat on the floor. The sound was overtaking me. It felt more uncomfortable to resist the music than to let myself be moved by it—the only thing left was to dive in.

The sequence of events that followed is difficult to recall, and some of it is too secret to repeat. We were given rattles and encouraged to play along, and even to sing as best we could. Not long into the ceremony, an old woman stood up and moved to the middle of the tightly packed room. There in the small clearing, she closed her eyes for a moment, and the music changed. Suddenly the drummers broke into a new and vigorous beat. Despite the confined space, she burst into explosive action and dance in a manner I'd never seen before. Her feet stepped and jumped in ways I couldn't count or follow.

One at a time, each of the women took turns dancing in the center of the room. All the while, the space resonated with singing, drumming, and the rattles. This went on for hours before there was a rest. The breaks were brief, and the ceremony continued through-out the night. At the participants' urging and coaxing, we, too, had all danced by the end. The pulse and rhythm had totally overcome our self-consciousness, liberating our spirits and energizing our bodies. After sunrise, there was a break where we rested and were fed. We were all exhausted yet exhilarated.

The world seemed still: my body felt light, and my mind was clear. When I stepped out into the day, the blinding light of the African morning sun was like a deep embrace of the most Divine love. Everyone felt it, as if every cell within had been renewed, restored, and revived. It was as if the vibration of the beat, the rattles, and the drums had shaken off a film of static energy from every cell in our bodies. Each of us in our own way felt more pres-ent, aware, and alive than we could remember. The interconnection of everything felt apparent; the peace within was palpable. All of our worries and troubles were washed away in the rush of rhythm. Something in the sounds—the healing, stirring pulses and waves of music—changed us that night in a most indelible way.

Good Vibrations

There are few people in the world who don't enjoy music. There are millions of styles and sounds, and millions of ways of making music. The melody of voices, the hum of traffic, songs on the radio, the symphony of nature's sounds, and the pattern of our steps are all forms of music. Our very birth and formation unfolds to the pulsing rhythm of our mother's heartbeat. The human soul responds to sound faster than the mind can recognize or explain. Music penetrates the subconscious, communicates directly with the body, and activates the soul.

Like the Venda of Africa, all traditions have used sound and music to turn people's attention to The Sacred. Chimes, bells, drums, hypnotic chants, choirs, orchestras, clapping hands, and droning tones are used to quiet the mind and evoke deep emotion in the heart. Music infused with meaning, intent, and a healing vibration will touch people no matter what their culture or beliefs.

As we danced and shook our rattles throughout the night in the Venda ceremony, it didn't matter that we couldn't understand the words. We felt the sincerity and energy of the heart. It hit us like a wave and carried us beyond ourselves.

In my private healing practice, I employ a technique called "shamanic journey work." I use a drum and large crystal toning bowls that make deep resonant sounds that people can feel in their bodies. In my work at Canyon Ranch Health Resort, I combine these elements with a "neuroacoustic" sound bed—a soft platform, which is made of sound chambers and speakers. Specially formulated music is played, and the bed directs specific sound frequencies to regions of the nervous system in order to stimulate relaxation and a healing response. With sound as a support, I'm able to quickly shift and transport people's awareness in a way that meditation or hypnosis alone rarely can.

All of these sound elements distract and soothe the analytical mind and stimulate the intuitive, creative mind. People don't have to believe in this method for it to work its healing magic. The spiritual senses are heightened as the body responds to the enchanting mood and vibration. Through this use of sound, we can access deep spiritual experiences of all types. A little breath work and guidance on my part and the inner wisdom of the "client" takes over. The healing power comes from within. Accessing information, attaining insights, and releasing energy blocks become natural in a field of healing sound.

Science is keen to understand the interface between the subtle energetic frequencies of sound and the vibration and health of the cells of our bodies. Meanwhile, spiritual traditions continue to use the sacred sound technologies with thousands of years of their own evidence. In the Hindu temple, Spirit Lodge, Sweat Lodge, mosque, synagogue, and church, we find that sounds and songs anchor our attention, establish sacred space, and help us express our devotion and gratitude to the Spiritual World. Music permeates the world, and sacred sound permeates the spiritual practices of the ages. Sacred sound isn't just a complement to ceremonies and healing practices, however; it is a practice in itself.

Shifting Mind and Mood

I've known healers and spiritual teachers the world over whose primary vehicle for accessing the domains of the Spirit are based in sacred sound. For instance, shamans drum themselves into a trance so that they may contact the Spirit World, monks chant until they reach a state of deep meditation where they may encounter the Invisible Spirit of Consciousness, and gospel singers feel the presence and love of Christ during their devotional praises. All of these are ways to let sound be a vehicle to the Spirit.

A wonderful example of sacred sound is *kirtan,* an East Indian tradition of chanting the names of God. Kirtan is practiced in many regions of India and in numerous traditions, including the Hindu, Tamal, and Sikh cultures. Many years ago I was first introduced to this practice as many others were in the Western world: I was at a yoga studio and someone was playing a CD by Krishna Das. Krishna Das is the spiritual name of an American-born devotee of Neem Karoli Baba, a Hindu guru. While studying with him in

India, the American musician was introduced to this ancient style of devotional chanting. For Krishna Das, after years of exploring various spiritual practices, kirtan became central to his spiritual path and his interpretation of it became his gift to the world. Similar stories are told of other amazing American kirtan singers, including Jai Uttal, Wah!, and Snatam Kaur.

Kirtan is not so much about singing as it is about expressing love and devotion to the Divine. It's a way of turning inward and creating harmony in the body, mind, and soul. Songs are generally "call and response," accompanied by simple instrumentality. A single song can last anywhere from seven minutes to seven hours! Melodies and words are simple and repetitive. They can also be understood as *mantras,* sacred words designed to free the mind. Singing kirtan, however, is nothing like chanting a mantra. It's based in classical Indian music in sound and feel, and is frequently arousing and animated.

The emphasis in kirtan is placed on heartfelt feeling and enthusiasm more than on precision or entertainment. The words are literally combinations of the many names of God. In Sanskrit or Hindi, for example, you might sing the words *Sita* and *Ram,* evoking the feminine and masculine aspects of God. In Gurmukhi or Punjabi, you might sing *Sat Nam* as part of a kirtan, which can be translated as: "Truth is my identity, and I call upon the eternal Truth that resides in all of us." The words all tend to be simple in sound and complex in meaning, pointing the mind to the multifaceted and infinite nature of The Sacred.

Soon after I heard my first kirtan song, I sought out a recording and listened to it over and over. It was so easy to sing along, and knowing that I was singing the Divine into my self and the world was uplifting and inspiring. Over the years, my wife and I have become more and more involved in devotional singing. We've trained with a few different teachers, including the brilliant Jai Uttal. We've chanted in many community and yoga gatherings. When my wife was pregnant, we practiced nearly every day, chanting songs of love and devotion to our growing baby. When stressed out, we chant to quiet the mind; when celebrating, we chant to rejoice. Chanting has enabled us to create harmony together.

No Talent Required

There isn't an effective way to express the power of sacred sound without citing actual experience as a reference. I'm frequently moved to tears because the feeling of love and connection is so intense. Even among people who've never chanted before, when permission and safety are provided, incredible things can happen. I recall one time when two dear friends of mine who lead kirtan classes came to visit the Canyon Ranch location in the Berkshires of Massachusetts. We'd planned to run a simple one-hour session for guests as a bit of a test to see if an audience of generally conservative people who knew nothing of this ancient practice would respond well to it.

The postings were simple, and the session was scheduled to be the last one in the evening. The night came, and the room filled quickly. People of all ages and backgrounds, men and women alike, showed up. My friends Lynn and Ned, who were the instructors, began the session simply with some breathing exercises and humming to help people get comfortable making sounds and release self-consciousness. I sat in the front row, eyes closed. As one of the coordinators of the event, I was nervous and didn't know what to expect. In a well-established and highly credible environment like a Canyon Ranch health resort, some might not have seen the value or need for a kirtan event.

But Ned took the next risk and leapt forward. "Let's begin with something simple. After we sing, you just repeat it back as best as you can. Imagine that you're singing from your soul—not for your neighbor or us."

The chant began. Ned played his harmonium as Lynn accompanied him beautifully on guitar. When the time came for the group response, I felt a moment of tension but then a rush of energy as my heart exploded open and I was hit by the unexpected force of the entire room joining in together—no hesitation, utter sincerity, and total willingness. The evening poured forward from that moment in a steady flow.

The chanting was a dance between the leaders and the group. There was a sense of freedom from the ordinary, having the ability to experience the simple joy of the resonant self, and the love of something greater. There was little explanation, little rational reason for what we shared, but it somehow all made sense. As our session came to a close, some guests headed back to their rooms for the night, and others longed for more so we sang for another half hour. By the end, there were both tears and smiles, and several people wanted to know how they could practice kirtan every week at home.

Like other sacred paths, sacred sound is something that must be experienced. You can rarely assume what it will be like until you allow yourself to let go and surrender to it. This is an aspect of the Divine nature of sound. It transcends logic and is inexplicable, yet as real as anything you can know. When you seek sacred music as your path, you only need to listen, paying attention to your heart and body. The right sacred-sound practice is easy to discern because it's impossible to ignore.

It is common knowledge and widely accepted in the medical community that music can ease pain, calm agitation, enhance brain function, and serve countless other health-promoting functions. More so, we have all had moments when a song lifted our spirits: giving hope, easing sorrow, or raising our courage. Music is drawing us toward our souls more often than we know it. The path of sacred sound embraces this human drive in a natural and immediate way.

Is there a song that lifts your spirit? What if you started your day, every day for a week, walking around your block listening to that song or singing it in the shower? Have you ever wanted to join your church choir or thought to seek out a healer who uses sound in their work? If so, take a step, take a risk. Take the time to explore the world of sound healing in your local music store, or explore the work of authors like Don Campbell, Christine Stevens, Brad Keeney, and Jonathan Goldman. Song and sound, rhythm and melody—they are ordinary, common, and ever present. They are also transcendent, transformative, and transporting. Simply paying more attention to the music of life will draw you toward awakening, the way the call of a song bird turns your eyes toward the heavens.

PART III

Mind-Centered Practices

I sit watching my thoughts
Like endless birds in an endless sky
I wait for an end to the storm of wings
An end to the stream of flickering movements
Breath after breath
I begin to sink beneath it all
Slowly the waters rise around me
Soon the sky turns to dusk
Colors bleed and blur together as one
The birds are fewer now
They are almost gone

Night pours in
It is growing more and more difficult
To hear the feathers overhead
The breath deepens and
I am flooded by the vastness
By the thick, dark night
A current comes over me
There is only stillness now, only peace
The intensity comes and goes with each wave
I let go and float in the clear space within
Rising and falling
Drifting
In the spacious moments
Between breaths
And the dim shadows of awareness
These moments are the seeds of life
I follow them into the blissful and shocking emptiness
Where I absorb them
One by one

—J. H. Ellerby

Chapter Seven

THE PATH OF PRAYER

Soul Speaking: Beginning to Pray

Hawaii is known as a spectacular destination for recreation, sun, and surf. For many, however, it is truly a land for re-*creation* of the self. The energy of the dark lava rocks and lush vegetation is radiant. The Indigenous people of Hawaii are as beautiful and vibrant as the surging surf, azure skies, and waterfalls that adorn the islands. The first time I visited Kauai triggered another formative period in my life. I was 15 years old, and my brother and sister, who are both older than I am, didn't join my parents and me on this vacation.

While my parents were checking in to our hotel, I wandered over to the tourist information desk. An "all American"-looking man greeted me and asked if he could help me. I was keen and naïve enough that I simply asked, "Is there a place I could learn more about traditional Hawaiian spirituality? Not just culture and history, but spirituality."

There was a long pause and a surprised look. He replied slowly, "Well, you're the first person who's ever asked me that. And it just so happens that this is your lucky day." He excused himself and went into a back room.

Now *I* was the surprised one.

From around the corner, a large, older Hawaiian Native woman appeared. She stopped in the doorway and stared at me.

"How can I help you?" she asked with a strange intensity.

I felt as if she were looking right through me, and I repeated my question. Walking right up to me, she looked down from her large stature and through her glasses, which were falling down toward the tip of her nose. "Are you sure?"

It seemed like a strange question, and I assured her I was. I began to explain my longtime interest in spiritual matters and my search for growth and awakening. She never stopped staring at me. After a long pause, she shook my hand and said, "I'm Lani. If you come again tomorrow morning, there are some things I can show you. Make sure you have some time if you're serious."

That next morning, Lani sat me down to make a lei. At first we worked in silence, but then she asked me questions about my life and interests. Finally, as we finished, she told me that I had to learn how to pray and work with "energy" if I wanted to go any further. I had no idea what she was talking about at first, but as she began to explain, I felt as if she was simply reminding me of things I already knew.

What followed was ten days of the most astonishing apprenticeship. It opened new worlds for me, truly changing me forever. Fortunately, my parents were used to my spiritual interests and thirst for knowledge and experience. They'd met Lani and trusted that I'd be safe in her care, although I can't imagine that they had any idea where it would all lead. Lani taught me extraordinary things: feeling energy in people and the land, changing weather with the power of thought, the nature of telepathy; and the greater powers of her ancestors and the great kahunas of Hawaii. Although each of these lessons challenged my worldview and showed me things that I hadn't previously imagined, the most important teachings were simple. At the very foundation of it all was a lesson in prayer.

One day we were on an area of land near the ocean. The windy sky was full of enormous billowing clouds. The filtered sun came and went, casting a terrific light show across the vast sea. As we walked and talked together, I hung on every word Lani offered.

"Do you know how to pray?" she asked.

I told her about attending synagogue on religious holidays, and that during the services we conducted at home on Pesach (Passover), we read prayers that were laid out for us by our ancestors. I explained that I also prayed in school: we said grace before meals as well as the Lord's Prayer every morning in an all-student assembly.

I thought I understood prayer, but when I thought about it, I realized that it was always something that someone else had to supply for me. I often felt an overwhelming connection with a Sacred Spirit in all things; and I saw the natural world as its voice and spent my time observing, listening, and receiving the messages that would unfold around me. Yet it had never fully occurred to me that I could simply *talk* to that Sacred Spirit myself. Until then I had only been an observer, a passenger.

"I follow my traditional Hawaiian ways, and I'm also a Christian," she explained. "On both of these paths, we have prayers that we say for special occasions, services, and ceremonies. We have special prayers for the sick, prayers for the earth, prayers for the sun, and prayers for certain birds and types of rocks. Some prayers we say, some we sing, some we repeat with others, and some we say silently to ourselves.

"The real prayer, however, doesn't come from here," she said, pointing to her head. "It's not about memorization or 'doing it right.' The true power of prayer starts here." She pointed to my heart.

"A prayer begins as a feeling—a true, deep feeling—that activates the energy of your body and your mind. That feeling is like a beacon in the universe, and God will find you by it. That feeling is the voice of your spirit. What is truly in your heart of hearts, the Spirit World will always hear.

"When you communicate from that place—in words out loud or in deep and sincere thought—it is a prayer. It can be anything that comes from your soul: a wish, a thanksgiving, or an intention for yourself. This world is alive and listening to you: your prayers, your actions, your energy. The Creator God, the One True Power, hears every prayer from the heart. Prayer is one of the greatest powers in the world. I'll show you some things this week that you'll find amazing—powers within yourself and the world. Prayer will be the key.

"When you seek anything, you must be clear in your prayers. Be humble, grateful, and aware of the Great Spirit that is always listening. Pray thanks when you wake up. Pray thanks when you eat. Pray thanks for a beautiful day. When the day isn't beautiful, pray thanks that you have a place to come in from the storm. Then give thanks for the rain that feeds the land. Pray when you arrive in a new place and when you leave an old one. When you need help, ask for it. Let God be your friend—talk with God. How else will God and the angels know what you intend?"

I was both excited and stunned at the same time. "Why would God want to hear from me? There are people who need more or could use more help. Wouldn't it be better to stay out of the way?"

"Don't be shy! How can you hide from God? Don't think you're bothering God with your prayers. God isn't a human parent whom you can wear down over time with incessant needs and pestering. God doesn't have a single set of eyes or a back to turn on people." Lani laughed and said, "We're talking about the one Infinite Power of the Universe! God is just a name. We say 'He' or 'She,' but we know in our souls that God is beyond sex or gender.

"The hard part at first isn't in finding the words, the reason, the time, or the place; it's learning to listen to your soul. Trust your soul. Your trust is knowing that your deepest prayers start beyond words—they're feelings deep within you and they matter. Boy, do they matter!"

Her words felt like the truth, like something I already knew but had forgotten. Time had stopped. The wind moved around me as if it were holding me in place, wanting me to receive every word. I could hear the water against the shore, and somehow there was a longing in the tumult of its song. All the elements of nature gathered around as if listening, as if eager. It's impossible to explain, but it felt as if the very Earth wanted me to understand this simple truth. This wasn't a moment when the world dissolved; rather, it became vibrant. And this wasn't an occasion when the Great Spirit of Life dissolved all things; instead, all things shone with the Great Spirit of Life. Every element seemed to have its own voice and power. The world and all things in it felt alive and full of wisdom.

The sun came out just then and cast a fan of streaming golden rays on the ocean. A door was now open: prayer! I had been afraid for so long, but now it seemed so right. Since then, I've never lived a day without prayer.

Divine Words, Sacred Thoughts

We are born to communicate. Words and thoughts fill our lives and relationships. We communicate constantly through words, actions, body language, and even energy. Our relationships are built on communication, and our identity is shaped by it. More often than not, our communication is as much about what we need to say as it is about what others need to hear. We communicate in order to be clear about what we want and need. And we do so to establish bonds of trust, gratitude, and love. In our relationships, we also communicate to understand ourselves and our partners. As we express our thoughts and feelings, we're able to assess what seems right and what doesn't. So, too, with a Higher Power, with The Sacred, we discover ourselves and build a relationship as we pray.

Deeper than this, our prayers connect us with the capacity and potential in ourselves that can move spirit and energy and influence the world. Praying shapes thoughts, clarifies intent, energizes affirmations, and strengthens resolve and optimism. As we become clearer in our prayers, we become clearer in who we are, and our whole being begins to radiate the energy we seek. True prayer helps us become what we are praying for. As best-selling author Gregg Braden reminds us: "Don't pray *for* peace, as if it will always exist in the future. *Pray peace.* Feel and be its energy *now*."

As we experience the true power of prayer, we understand that each thought is a prayer, sending a signal throughout the body and to the universe about who we are and what we want to draw toward us. Prayer as a path and practice refines the mind and helps us take accountability for what we create, while learning to surrender our desire to control the things we never could. This is at the heart of the well-known "Serenity Prayer," which was originally written for use in a sermon in the 1930s by Reinhold Niebuhr.

> *God grant me the serenity to accept the things I cannot change,*
> *Courage to change the things I can,*
> *And the wisdom to know the difference.*

A prayer can be patterned, repetitious, spontaneous, culturally bound, or read from a text. The critical point is to ensure a whole-self connection with feeling and intent. This is why I encourage people to pray as if speaking—that is, as if they're having a direct conversation with God.

We have to let God or "The Universe" be our friend, our beloved, our grandma or grandpa. We need to talk to The Sacred in our heart and mind. Many people feel shy or awkward about such an idea as if an omnipotent Spirit can only witness some of our thoughts. But we're always connected to the Greater Spirit, whether we communicate or not. Like a telephone to a higher power, prayer makes the message loud and clear, but the line is always open and the connection is always live. The choice to use it is ours.

Daily Prayer

My Lakota teacher Wanagi Wachi used to stress the importance of daily prayer. One night after an *Inipi* (a Lakota Sweat Lodge ceremony), we were cleaning up the ritual area beneath a radiant full moon. It had been a particularly long ceremony, as a lot of people had come with heavy hearts and busy minds. After loading his pickup truck with the last of the supplies we had to take home, he paused to take a deep breath. Looking to *hanwi,* the silver sun of the night sky, he pointed something out to me.

"You heard the way people prayed when they got into that ceremony tonight? Long, deep, heartfelt prayers. You hear people pray for every aspect of their life. They pray for everything in the world. It's all good. It is good for them. I've heard people like this at church, funerals, and weddings. Anytime people feel safe and entitled to pray, they really go for it.

"They do so because they don't take the time to pray every day. They think God is only in certain places, or they don't trust in their ability to pray without a spiritual leader present. Others think you have to believe in God to pray. None of those things are necessary, though. They just keep us from a natural relationship that we all have with *Wakantanka,* the Sacred Mystery of this world that's beyond the mind.

"Because they're so disconnected, when they finally get to a ceremony, it's a bit like a child who has been away from their parent for a long time. They want so badly to catch up, to express and explain so many things. They feel the lack of relationship and want to reestablish the bond. They need it, and it's good that they have done so. It reminds us that if we had a closer relationship with our Creator and took the time to pray every day, we'd already have a strong relationship there.

"If we let prayer be a part of our daily experience, we wouldn't need to fill God in on every detail because we'd know that our Creator is always with us. We'd know that we've already expressed our intentions. We'd know that prayer is not just once a week or even once a day. It is ongoing. Our connection would be strong, and we could have extra attention and energy for others instead of always having to play catch-up with our Higher Power. Keep your relationship with the Creator strong through prayer, and you won't have to rebuild it all the time."

Wanagi Wachi reminds us that it's easy to think of The Sacred as something conditional. Like little children who cover their eyes and believe that an object in front of them has disappeared simply because they can no longer see it, many of us act like children in our relationship with the Divine. Some of us think that The Sacred is present only when our attention is focused upon it, and then we forget about it when we feel undecided or preoccupied.

Talk to God

If it's ever present, then it's always there. The Sacred is real and listening. Honoring the ever-present Divine through regular prayer is a way of living close to the edge of spiritual experience while cultivating the strength of our spiritual senses. Our dear Shona African friend and spiritual teacher, Kandemwa, also stresses this point. Once or twice a year I'm fortunate to have some private time with him; sometimes we visit him while in Zimbabwe, and other times we see him at events and gatherings in North America.

Kandemwa often teaches about the importance of regular prayer and sometimes alarms people with his passion and intensity. I once heard him address an interfaith group, and he said, "We must be grateful for all the houses of prayer in this world, no matter what the tradition. Anyplace we can be close with the Great Spirit is a good place. Anyplace we can talk with that Spirit is a great place.

"And, my brothers and sisters, I hope that one day we'll have no need for those places. I look forward to the day when we don't feel we have to wait until special times to pray. And I look forward to the day when we no longer need special places to pray. I look forward to the day when we see that we are sacred and that the Great Spirit is anywhere we stand. Every home is a church, every man is a rabbi, and every woman is a guru. You are already as connected to the Spirit as you will ever be—don't let anyone get in the way of that."

The great Native American mystic Black Elk foretold these sentiments in the early 1900s when he said, "The first peace, which is the most important, is that which comes within the souls of [people] when they realize their relationship, their oneness, with the universe and all its powers, and when they realize that at the center of the universe dwells Wakan Tanka [the Great Spirit], and that this center is really everywhere; it is within each of us."

Real Magic

It's true that prayer can elicit healing, and it can change events and lives, but this occurs only with the deep resonance of the heart behind it and the recognition of the One True Source of Power. Again, we can reflect on the words of Gregg Braden, who's known for his research into the bridge between science and spirituality. In his book *Secrets of the Lost Mode of Prayer,* he says:

> As modern science continues to validate a relationship between our inner thoughts, feelings, and dreams with the outer world that surrounds us, we open the door to a powerful bridge that links the world of our prayers with that of our experience. In light of such research, what is the potential of applying such subtle principles of prayer to an outcome of collective healing, global peace, and graceful transition through the challenges that await us in the new millennium?

Braden reminds us that prayer is a practice requiring responsibility and caution. Larry Dossey, M.D., wrote an entire book called *Be Careful What You Pray For.* I've witnessed many prayers come true—some with miraculous results. I've even had many of my own prayers come true with amazing accuracy. The trap occurs when we introduce the ego and its desire to control and avoid situations in life. Not all prayers are answered in the way we expect, and we aren't always able to manage the immense weight of a prayer that has come true.

Prayer as a spiritual path isn't about getting what you want, but about learning to love and bless the world as it is. It's about coming into right relationship with The Sacred and surrendering to a higher order in life. Even scientific studies have shown that the most potent prayer remains *Thy will be done.* Your greatest prayers manifest when you learn to align yourself with the will and flow of The Sacred.

Prayer as a spiritual practice *is* a spiritual experience. When prayer is your spiritual practice, you learn to think from the heart and deepen your sense of gratitude, intention, and surrender. When prayer is your practice, you may set regular times in your day for prayers of formal and informal types. Most important, you realize that you are co-creating your life with the Divine Energies of this world. Let your mind be in conscious contact with The Sacred throughout each and every day.

Chapter Eight

THE PATH OF
MEDITATION

A Wild Ride to a Quiet Place

When I arrived in Dharamsala, in northern India, I was exhausted from the long and rough bus ride. Home to the exiled traditional Tibetan spiritual and political leadership, Dharamsala is known for its most renowned inhabitant: Tenzin Gyatso, also known as the 14th Dalai Lama. Since 1959, tens of thousands of Tibetans have fled persecution and taken refuge in this mountain foothill town, also known as McCloud Ganj. Tibetan shops, businesses, and Buddhist-related arts and crafts line the narrow streets.

Gathering my backpack, maps, and my wits, I was immediately struck by how distinct the village seemed. The fresh mountain air, ever-present reminders of the Buddha, Tibetan smiles, and traditional dress all seemed to combine to create a feeling that I had not yet experienced in India. Hungry and tired, I set out immediately in search of food and lodging. While wandering the narrow streets,

I passed prayer wheels and monks in saffron robes. Weaving my way through beggars and merchants, I found a café called Rangzen, which eventually became a frequent stop for me. The owner said that its name meant "freedom" or "independence" in Tibetan.

It was at that café, in the first hour after I arrived, that I happened to run into an American traveler who told me that the next morning His Holiness The Dalai Lama would be greeting visitors. "Everyone had to submit their passports and get screened by security to get on the list," my fellow traveler told me, "but maybe if you go really early before anything opens you'll get in."

The next day much before sunrise, I set out for Tsuglag Khang, the central temple of the Tibetan Buddhist monastic community. Inhaling the cool morning air deeply into my lungs, I worked to release any worry about whether or not my quest would be successful. I simply placed my attention on the slowing shifting colors of dawn and the strange and wonderful fragrances that played on the wind. As I walked down the steep hill path to the temple, I imagined that I was sinking into the energy of the monastery, as if there were a cloud of peace and ancient memory surrounding the immediate area.

When I arrived at the front gates, they were locked and there was little sign of activity. A lone monk was sweeping the courtyard in the distance, and shadows moved slowly in the corridors that I could see. The sun's first light revealed something of interest: to my right, there seemed to be a pathway leading around the side of the temple, and people—monks and Tibetan laypeople alike—emerged one or two at a time. There was no pattern that I could discern; they seemed to be going for a walk, or maybe they were leaving an early morning service of some kind. I walked over to see what was going on. Trying to be unassuming, I continued down the path, which began to curve around the temple.

Soon I noticed that every person I passed appeared to be deep in prayer or meditation. They were spinning prayer wheels, reciting mantras, and walking with measured steps. There were variations, but few. The other thing I noticed was that I was the only non-Tibetan and the only one who was moving counterclockwise around the temple. Just then it hit me—I was in the wrong place, going the wrong way!

Feeling like a foolish tourist, I quickly stepped to the side where I found a set of old stone benches. I tried to look purposeful despite my awkwardness. Breathing deeply into my belly, I attempted to release my self-judgment, so I sat down and simply focused on my breath, slowing the cycle of embarrassment and striving within. I reminded myself to "be present" and let go of all the self-doubting thoughts and feelings that were surfacing.

"Good place," said a voice with a thick accent. I opened my eyes to find an old Tibetan monk sitting on a bench beside me. He gestured across the path at the beautiful view of trees and a valley, and repeated, "Good place." I agreed. We then struck up a somewhat stunted but meaningful conversation.

Through his broken English, the weathered monk asked me about my reason for traveling and my work at home. I mentioned my spiritual service and study, and he seem greatly engaged. When he inquired more directly about how I'd ended up on the Prayer Path, I explained that I was hoping to meet the Dalai Lama.

His eyes lit up. "Come," he stood up and gestured. "This is your path?" I wasn't sure if he was referring to the Prayer Path we were on or the spiritual path that is my life.

"Yes," I replied. "This is my path."

The old monk guided me quickly toward the temple and an alternate entrance to the main gate. We moved into the monastic quarters and my heart quickened. Now in full morning light, I could see the beautiful faces of the monks of all ages who acknowledged him with respect as we passed. The younger monks showed some distance, and a few other older monks stopped and spoke with him briefly.

I could only discern the word *geshe* as part of his title. A geshe is an academic title similar to a professor. There are many levels of geshe, and the highest ones can take decades of study to achieve. Extensive knowledge of virtually all aspects of Buddhist wisdom, scripture, practice, and history are mastered by the great teachers. This monk, whom I'll simply call Lharampa Geshe (which is actually the title of the most esteemed degree awarded) was clearly a senior teacher whom others seemed to revere and consult with. Everywhere we went, he seemed the elder to the others.

Lharampa Geshe took me to his room and study, which at the most was about six by ten feet. It consisted of a simple bed, small shelves with books, and ancient scrolls and texts. There were also a few wooden boxes that must have contained his personal effects. The room was modestly decorated, mostly yellow with some deep reds. Every cloth and rug was a tribute to the tradition; the sacred symbols offered splashes of colors to the eye. He sat me down, poured me a cup of yak-butter tea, asked for my passport, and left.

When he returned, he was smiling. He gave me back my passport and said, "No problem." Then he presented me with a white silk scarf and explained that I was to give it to the Dalai Lama. He also demonstrated specific motions and things I should say upon meeting him. Finally, he said, "Afterward, you come find me."

That day I did meet the Dalai Lama, although it was very brief. It was a remarkable moment in my life, but it was just the beginning of a remarkable relationship with the senior monk who took me to meet His Holiness. The story of my meeting with this monk unfolded into a hundred stories. When I returned to Lharampa Geshe, he spontaneously assumed the role of my instructor, without question, conversation, or even my asking. He insisted that I go to daily meditation and prayer with the monks. In the afternoons, I was to attend the Tibetan institute farther down the hill, where classes were taught to monks and visiting English students.

Impossibly Simple

At first all of this was overwhelming. My "teacher" didn't speak much English and had basically assigned me to an experiential practice without explanation. I really wasn't sure what his intention was for me, but the afternoon classes were interesting for the most part. I learned a little about the history and a lot about the complicated philosophies of Tibetan Buddhists.

As a Jewish person, some of the complexity in Buddhist scriptures reminded me of the Talmud, an ancient Jewish text of rabbinical commentary about the Torah, Jewish law, and customs. Every concept and belief had layers of meaning and extrapolation. Out of every teaching flowed an endless number of interpretations, perspectives, and articulations.

It seemed that most of the Western students had more background in Tibetan studies than I did, and most were Buddhist converts or graduate students. Many of the terms and titles were foreign to me. My commitment to the studies was not total, and I often missed sessions. However, I didn't falter on the morning assignment for that month.

Every morning just after sunrise, I'd go to the sanctuary of the main temple where rank after rank of shaved heads and red-robed monks sat in formation on three sides of a square. All rows faced inward toward the center and front of the square where a small council of high Lamas (and at times, Lharampa Geshe) sat. I've since seen pictures of the Dalai Lama sitting in the center seat, but he wasn't there during the month I visited.

Each day there were monks who played ancient instruments, including gongs and long horns. For hours they chanted, meditated, and prayed. In low hypnotic tones and repetitive verses, the morning sessions went on without rest. I was seated in an outer area with the younger monks. None spoke English to me, and I had no clear explanation as to what was going on.

During the time I was there, I never saw another Western face or anyone wearing street clothes like myself. It felt like an honor, and strangely, at times, like a curse. I recall the first and last instruction from Lharampa Geshe when he led me to the assembly of monks: "You sit: no mind, no thinking. Just breathe. Feel quiet inside. You don't need to understand this and that—chanting and prayer. Just sit and listen to the Quiet Inside." He smiled and said, "Practice. Every day, practice. Breathe, watch, let go."

I'd studied meditation before and had read books, attended classes, and was even at a point in my life where I was leading people in short meditations. However, this was a whole new level, a whole new awareness. I'd never considered meditation as a path for me and was more interested in ceremony and prayer. This was more than I'd bargained for. In total, it was about a month of meditation, sitting every day for hours.

Much of the time was horrid. I experienced boredom, a sore backside and body, wandering thoughts, and surprising emotions that would boil up unexpectedly and sporadically. I was sitting in the most magnificent place of reverence—among the most dedicated and advanced students—but none of that mattered when my mind wandered or when I grew bored. I moved my body very little, but inside I was like a caged bull, wildly thrashing about trying to find freedom from an impenetrable jail: my mind.

The first few days were wonderful. I was full of pride, basking in the gift that fate had brought me and riding the emotions of honor and privilege. I was captivated by moments of "truth and beauty" and experienced frequent periods of calm. My eyes were closed, yet the energy of the large group and the sacred sounds were permeating my awareness. It wasn't long, however, before the pride began to wear off and the impatience, cramping, and frustration began to set in.

The most astounding things came to mind as I sat there. It was as if I had all the time in the world to either cultivate a *quiet* mind or indulge every facet of my *wandering* mind. I reviewed memories long forgotten; fantasized; made plans; created worlds in my head; explored whole lifetimes; and thought of old friends, past girlfriends, school, favorite places, aspirations, and failures. It was amazing how my thoughts could help me escape the moment. Sometimes I allowed my eyes to open, and I'd watch the monks surrounding me and make up stories about each of them. Everything I could possibly think of, I thought of . . . and the thoughts kept coming!

Some days I felt like I'd be crushed by the weight of my own thoughts. They stifled and enclosed me, like an endless sea of questions. Although I was supposed to be focused upon my breath, the frustration of trying to breathe consciously while softening my thoughts and quieting my mind choked the life out of me on some days. It felt like the hardest thing I'd ever done.

When I went to see Lharampa Geshe, he didn't inquire about my happiness or even whether I understood the lessons of the afternoon.

He asked if I was still going to morning meditation, just wanting to know if I was sticking to the practice. Occasionally, he'd ask random questions about English metaphors for the mind or the cycles of suffering, which I seemed to answer to his satisfaction. My time with him was brief, but my time in the temple was endless.

Then one day something new began to happen. The space between my wandering thoughts seemed to get longer. It was almost like falling asleep while awake. I'd have the sudden awareness that I'd been sitting without thoughts or feelings. The moment I realized this, however, the thoughts would flood back in. I watched for the edge of stillness that came at the ends of each exhale and inhale. My breath provided little windows through which I could crawl back into those moments of silence.

My mind would become still like a pool of water, and each thought that appeared was as a stone cast upon the surface. The ripples moved out endlessly but then subsided, and soon the surface returned to its calm once again. I was aware of the world around me, yet I was no longer telling stories about it. I was aware of my body's sensation, yet I was no longer attached to the idea of change or immediate comfort.

At some point I'd given up the idea that I'd ever be "good" at meditating. I'd simply made the commitment to finish a certain period of time as best I could while refining my breath awareness and concentration. Soon after this shift in attitude, I realized that the changes had begun. It was as if I'd strengthened a muscle of concentration: I had will and focus with commitment, yet no expectation.

I followed my breath: in through the nose, down into my abdomen, and then out long and slow through my mostly closed mouth. I knew that there were more sophisticated breathing techniques, but this was all I could concentrate on or remember. This short path of breath from the inhale to the exhale was still one of the longest and wildest journeys I've ever encountered, and most of it took place while sitting perfectly still.

Through Silence into Awareness

When I talked to fellow travelers about my experience in the Buddhist monastery, I realized that many of them had come to India to study meditation. None was in the monastery where I was, but they were in a hundred other places studying with Buddhist, Hindu, and Western teachers. They were studying Vipassana (insight) meditation; Tantric meditation; Tibetan, Zen, and yogic styles; and many other forms. I met one Christian fellow who was seasoned in something called Centering Prayer, a Christian form of meditation.

Their programs ranged in setup and commitment, and were mostly more formal than what I was involved in. The Vipassana programs, for example, took a minimum of ten days and most of the day was spent in seated meditation. The diet for practitioners was restricted, and time was spent in silence. I was shocked by the diversity and intensity of meditation practices. The training was typically rigorous, yet most seekers persisted because the outcomes could be so profound.

Meditation is universal and practiced by followers of religions as diverse as Judaism, Islam, Taoism, Sikhism, Christianity, and Baha'i. Like most of the great Master Paths, meditation has a home in all traditions and cultures. The forms can vary dramatically and may or may not include visualization, specific physical poses or props, breathing patterns, and the use of sound. Some forms are practiced in solitude and others take place within a community. You don't need to travel to India to find the remarkable diversity of meditative practices. Do some research where you live and you'll discover a range of meditation practices being cultivated— sometimes in unlikely places.

In today's world of stress management and health obsessions, meditation has become a fascination for many people. Its long-proven health benefits attract students of all types. As a spiritual path, however, meditation is anything but an escape. I've encountered many people who struggle with this. In fact, in several places where I've worked that include meditation sessions, practitioners would come to me with complaints about their instructors, such as: "They won't let me lie down! They won't let me leave early. Why are they so strict?"

"Meditation," I often explain, "is not only about relaxation— that is a side effect. Meditation is about working consciously with your awareness. It's about expanding awareness while moving beyond thought and mental distraction. It's about being totally present." Thinking back to my time in the monastery, a significant portion of my practice was anything but relaxing. Few spiritual practices are designed to keep people comfortable or to be an equal opportunity for all. Not everyone will embrace or be attracted to meditation. It's a steep and challenging practice that requires courage and compassion for the self.

From the Narrow to the Infinite

At its heart, the path of meditation seeks the realization of the impermanence of life and the formlessness of Spirit. In meditation we become conscious of the illusions that the mind creates and the ego feeds on. Most meditative practices are about the use of the mind's ability to concentrate and overcome the tendency to wander uncontrollably into worry, fear, projection, and random thoughts. This is typically done through extreme focus and concentration, or extreme mindfulness and relaxed observation. The object is to bring the mind from a place of active random thinking to a single, pointed awareness that is receptive but passive.

Meditation can involve concentration on the breath alone; on love and gratitude; on an object like a candle's flame; on a repeating word, such as the name of God; on simply observing the passing sensations and present-moment experience without analysis or judgment; or even on the stillness and silence between thoughts, causing the emptiness of thought to expand. Specific meditation schools are generally very precise, and having a teacher or guide for a period seems essential. Some instructors and forms of meditation are rigid and austere in their technique. They might stress perfect posture, long hours of sitting, and early-morning regimes.

Other teachers and forms of meditation are much gentler, stressing comfort, convenience, and compassion.

It's also helpful to recognize that some people use the term *meditation* more generally to refer to a quality of attention that can be brought to a moment. In this respect, *anything* can be a meditation or create a meditative state if one practices complete present-moment attention and fully absorbed, undistracted awareness. In addition, the word *meditation* is also used by many people to characterize relaxation practices that calm the mind and promote inner peace.

Naturally, anything that brings peace to our lives and the world is hard to find fault with. The goal of meditation as a practice is to learn to consciously travel the domains of The Sacred and the purity of consciousness. The common direction of meditation is where we encounter the release of all attachments, and we see beyond thoughts and feelings. In the shedding of the senses, meditation brings us to the depths of the self, the depths of The Sacred. In some meditation traditions, any phenomena short of Pure Consciousness are considered only distractions along the way.

Of course, meditation masters must seek a balance between striving for the release of all sense attachment and perception and the release of the desire for anything to happen other than what presents itself. There's an implicit trust that when all preoccupation with the world of duality and complexity in our lives ceases, the deeper nature of reality is encountered naturally.

The impact of meditation can be life changing. The side effects of self-discipline, compassion, and even mastery over the spiritual senses can be profound. Still, we must remember that the caveat on any Master Path is to not let the path become a goal, obsession, or source of pride and ego. Meditation is a powerful practice that should be approached with respect and guidance.

As a final story in this chapter, I want to include an example of how a meditative mind—one that is clear and open—can also access awareness of spiritual realities that are rich in content and meaning. Most Eastern traditions caution meditation students not to become caught up in the fantastic realms of the Spiritual World, which may spontaneously reveal themselves in a meditative moment. On the other hand, Indigenous traditions and the prophets, shamans, mystics, and visionaries of the world have long used the meditative skill to purposely access deeper dimensions of intuition and cosmic wisdom. Like the other paths, this practice has common uses and diverse intents that may be applied in many ways and may produce surprising experiences, as I found out one day in the temples of Teotihuacán, Mexico.

Swallowed by the Spirit

While meditation is associated with Eastern traditions and austerities, it's important to note that meditative states are a part of nearly every spiritual practice. Even in the settings and traditions that we least associate it with, the meditative mind becomes a central vehicle.

During my first trip to Mexico, I stayed with my friend Quetzal, a Mayan shaman. (A shaman is a healer whose primary mode of healing involves direct communication with the world of Spirits and Natural Spiritual Powers.) For Quetzal—like all of the Indigenous shamans I knew—his gift to heal and connect with the Spirit World wasn't chosen or taught. It was an ability directly given to him through dreams, supernatural events, and natural talents. Quetzal's mission was to bridge the modern world with the wisdom of the past for the healing of the future, and his style of teaching and helping reflected the ancient roots of his ancestors.

Shortly after I arrived, Quetzal said that there was a place (Teotihuacán) I needed to visit in order to truly connect with and understand his ancestors. Only when my spirit was acknowledged by the spirits of his ancestors could we continue our time together attending ceremonies and meeting other shamans. Following his direction, I made a special trip to Teotihuacán with his sister, Gia, a gifted spiritual healer and intuitive.

Teotihuacán is an astonishing and enormous ancient place of ceremonial pyramids, temples, and community living areas. Not far from Mexico City, the entire settlement is organized and laid out according to sacred geometry, astrological patterns, and intricate spiritual formulas and teachings. The site of great spiritual ceremonies and pilgrimages for centuries, it's been the subject of intense historical and anthropological study.

"I'll show you how we approach this holy place as a Mayan, not as a tourist," Gia asserted. "If you know how to see, how to feel, you will know the secrets of this place." We stopped before entering the site, prayed, placed a simple offering of tobacco on the earth, and set our intentions clearly in our hearts. Our intent was to be open to whatever healing channels of awareness might help us encounter the depths of this amazing and powerful place, and to enter with respect for the ancestors.

Near the beginning of our journey into the sacred structures, we entered a special temple, not one of the mighty pyramids, but another place. It was canyonlike, and I immediately felt a sense of "energy" as we entered. It was as if there was a subtle hum or vibration I could feel in my body. We found a place to sit that felt comfortable, safe, and centered. I noticed the ancient carvings and sculptures and felt their deep significance even though I didn't understand their meanings.

Once settled, Gia reached into her bag and pulled out a few ritual objects and set them between us. She instructed me to close my eyes and breathe deeply as if into my heart. I was to imagine my heart as a beautiful light radiating and expanding with each inhale. At the same time, I was to release all active thoughts and simply pay attention to whatever might come to me. As I focused on the task I was given, Gia sang a prayer song that I didn't know or understand, and then we both fell silent.

After an indistinguishable time, something changed. Suddenly I began to see images even though my eyes were closed. They became so vibrant that I could see and feel them as if they were real. A great snake, as thick as a bus and longer than I could see, appeared clearly in my mind. It had a ring of rainbow-colored feathers around its neck. Its scales were also dark, and as it moved, the light revealed a dull but distinct rainbow hue, similar to what one would see in a soap bubble.

I watched as it moved with ease and power through a dense jungle. It dove into the land, as if the earth were water. It traveled enormous distances in moments. I followed its journey as it roamed the ancient lands of central America. Moving from temple to temple, it dove into the earth again. This time when it surfaced, it shot straight up into the sky and flew. It circled right above us.

Although my eyes remained closed, it felt as if I were watching something that was actually taking place at that very moment. In an instant, the great snake plummeted to the earth, jaws open, and it consumed me in one sweeping movement. My mind went dark as I felt more than I saw. Now I was in the heart of this mighty being; yet somehow, I was the heart of the land and could feel the people, spirits, and sacred places all inside me. It was as if Mexico—its people, its history, and its guiding spirits—were swimming within me. Suddenly my awareness shifted again, and I was observing the earth as if I was in outer space. I watched as the earth became a brilliant ball of shining white light. Then everything became still.

By this time, Gia had begun to pray out loud. I opened my eyes and my attention turned to her. Tears were rolling down her cheeks. I couldn't understand her fast-paced Spanish, and her strong emotions made it even harder to follow. Then her disposition shifted, and her words became less passionate and softer. Strong, like the delivery of an important message, but gentle, as if the message were precious. I sat and absorbed the moment—surprised, but profoundly moved.

When Gia came to her normal awareness, I was ready and waiting to hear what had happened and eager to tell her about what had happened to me. She asked me to describe what I had seen first, since it seemed to have catalyzed what had happened to her. I told her about the enormous snake and all that I'd seen.

She was so intent, so serious, and then smiled, saying, "That was Quetzalcoatl, one of our most powerful gods! This place we are in is his temple, where the ancient people came to communicate with him. You've seen him and have been received by him." By that point, I had gone from surprised to speechless.

வ வ வ

Meditation has the capacity to shift your attention and awareness into your subtle senses. Some traditions seek to go beyond these encounters of the Spirit World, and others seek to open the psychic mind in order to access information and energy that may carry insight to help and heal. If your interest is in what can be called "shamanic meditation" and the development of intuition and spiritual senses, it will be important to apply the mystic mindset and resist the temptation to become caught up in the drama that also lives in the Spirit World.

Meditation is one of the most universal and long-celebrated spiritual practices. In many ways, the gifts and skills of meditation can be applied to all the Master Paths. The central function of coming fully into a present-moment, nonjudgmental awareness can be critical to a healthful journey on any spiritual path. In the meditative mind, we open to a self-awareness that empowers and liberates. Through meditation we move from identifying with our thoughts to a position of soul-awareness, in which thoughts and habits become the subjects of observation, freeing us to make conscious choices.

The irony to beware of lies in the inner worlds that meditation may reveal. While meditation intends to liberate from the cycles and suffering of the world, it is not intended as an escape. Whether you encounter spirits and angels, or calm spacious awareness during meditation, be sure to learn from your experiences and carry the blessings into your daily life and relationships. Meditation requires a fine balance, for it can be an easy source of pride or distraction. Overcome these temptations, and you'll find that a steady meditation practice will serve you in every aspect of your life.

Chapter Nine

THE PATH OF
SACRED STUDY

Words Beyond Words

Breathless from climbing the steep and rough-hewn trail that led up the mountainlike plateau, we stopped to survey our destination. It was sunrise, and light was now flooding over the ancient Judaean desert of southern Israel. Like honey, the morning sun poured a slow golden light across the stony land, washing over the crumbling walls of the legendary settlement before us: Masada.

I'd learned about Masada as a child. For a few years, I attended a Jewish Sunday school where students were taught the Hebrew language and the traditions, songs, and history of the Jewish people. Masada was a difficult story to relate to as a child. The events that made it famous took place around 70 C.E. during a time when the Romans invaded Jerusalem, destroyed the second temple, and took political control of the region.

That difficult time saw the end of a great uprising by the Jewish people, who were fighting for independence. And even as the

Roman Empire settled into their rule, many still worked to find ways to remain empowered. Small groups rose up who were deeply committed to the survival of the Jewish faith and state, and they continued to resist the foreign ruling power.

One large band of these rebellious freedom fighters fled to a fortress settlement atop a high desert plateau. (In the years prior to this, King Herod had secured the fortress as a stronghold for himself.) This determined group overthrew the garrison and occupied the walled settlement in order to reclaim their independence and preserve the Jewish heritage. The people modified the settlement—known now as Masada—and it became a village. A synagogue was built among other important features, and for more than three years this was their mountain home while they fended off the Roman army that continued to attack them.

After numerous failed attempts to invade the fortress, the Romans lay siege to Masada and surrounded the base of the plateau. The inhabitants were trapped in their home. It was expected that after months of restricted movement, the people would eventually starve or give up, yet somehow, they endured.

Finally, the Romans built an enormous ramp up the side of the plateau, intent on unleashing their full military force against the Jewish resisters. As the invasion became imminent, the besieged people made a decision that has marked the memory of nations ever since. Rather than live as slaves and prostitutes for the Romans, they decided to take their own lives and die as free people.

When the Roman army finally broke the walls and entered Masada, they found more than 900 dead men, women, and children. To circumvent the Jewish prohibition against suicide, the men took the lives of the women and children, and then killed one another. Such an act of defiance and devotion astounds the modern mind.

Regardless of the many views on this historic episode, Masada has become a symbol of Jewish freedom, spiritual devotion, and the desire for sovereignty. These thoughts went through my mind as we hiked up to the plateau in order to conduct my Bar Mitzvah. Having this ceremony in Masada, held in the synagogue that was nearly 2,000 years old, was a blessing and evoked an incredible sense of ancestry and connection.

In the early morning light, we slowly entered the ruins of the ancient synagogue that had been built by the hands of those determined souls. The mood was quiet. There was something mysterious and amazing about the place. Only parts of the walls remained, as well as an area to sit. The rabbi began to give instructions as we prepared for my Bar Mitzvah ceremony.

A Bar Mitzvah is a spiritual rite of passage, often viewed as a coming-of-age ceremony for Jewish boys. Young girls participate in something similar called a Bat Mitzvah. The Bar Mitzvah, which means "son of the commandments," is a time when a boy becomes accountable and responsible for his religious and spiritual life. At this point, he's expected to live by the commandments of his tradition and act as a member of his congregation. It takes place at a pivotal time in adolescent development, similar to the Confirmation ceremony in Christian traditions, the Sacred Thread ceremony in Hinduism, and the Vision Quest in many Native American communities.

Today, many people in America and Canada throw big parties for hundreds of family members and friends immediately following the special service that takes place in the synagogue. But when it was time for my Bar Mitzvah, my older brother and sister were backpacking through southern Europe together. So my parents thought that it would be the trip of a lifetime if we flew to Israel and met my siblings to celebrate my Bar Mitzvah atop Masada.

The ceremony was magical. Beneath the blue sky, the old rabbi sang the prayers and guided us through the necessary steps and stages. At the heart of the ceremony was my first true reading from the Sefer Torah. (It's often called the Hebrew Bible, but it's actually the first five books of the Old Testament. The word *Torah* means "teaching" or "law" and refers to the first five books of Moses.)

In most synagogues, the Sefer Torah forms the centerpiece of the sacred space. Written on scrolls of thin lamb skin or parchment, it's kept in a revered place called an "ark." The ark is carefully constructed, guarded, and tended to. The privilege and ability to read and study directly from the Sefer Torah is considered a tremendous honor and the duty of young people as they come of age.

On that special day, I was struck by the awesome power of the place and the beauty of family. I felt the profound sense of connection that is fed by traditions carried out with love. More so, I couldn't help but find my attention fixated on the Torah itself. I'd begun preparations for the reading of the Torah months in advance. I, like many Jewish children, had lessons in Hebrew and instructions from a rabbi and Hebrew tutor to help me prepare for the various elements involved in the ceremony and the actual experience of *reading* from the Torah.

The Gift of Learning

Everyone involved in my training seemed enamored with the words, letters, and language. One day while I had a session with a rabbi who was helping me prepare for some of the ritual elements of the ceremony, he asked, "How are your studies coming along?"

Not thinking much of the question, I replied, "Good, I guess."

"You aren't excited about it?"

I thought about my words carefully. "Well, I guess it's all right, but I don't think I'm going to read much Hebrew after this. It's a lot of work just to read something I don't understand."

The rabbi smiled. "I see how it must be from your perspective, but there's something you should understand. This isn't just trying to learn another language. You are learning how to read the most sacred teachings that we've been given as a people. This is sacred study—not homework. The teachings are a blessing, and the ability to learn and study them, to even have the opportunity to do so, is also a blessing.

"Once you learn, you'll be able to read it on your own with no one helping you. You'll be able to sit and read, just as people read thousands of years ago. In the words of the Torah, there's so much more than stories and rules. There is a living power!"

I think he was starting to lose me at that point—power in a book? I hadn't yet encountered a spiritual text that held any real meaning for me. (My life-changing discovery of Eastern spiritual texts that I mentioned earlier hadn't yet happened, and this idea was a stretch for me at the time.)

"Think of it this way," he explained. "God did not write this scroll with His hand. A long time ago, God communicated to wise men and women directly. He put ideas in their minds and feelings in their hearts. These people tried to express those ideas and feelings through the teachings and stories in the Torah.

"It's as if you saw something amazing outside and wanted to paint a picture of it. You might not paint it exactly the way it looks, for only the real thing is exact. Not even a photo is a perfect reproduction. But you'd paint as best as you could, using colors and shapes in a way that helped people not only recognize what you saw, but understand how you felt about it.

"So first there was God, then energy placed inside a person, and then a feeling. Then came a thought and the ability to record it—all with love, care, and devotion to the gift being shared. Every Torah is written by hand, and each is an exact copy of the one before it—a link all the way back to the very first. Every Torah is sacred. If you study the Torah every day, as I have, you'll find that you learn more than how to pronounce words. You understand what they mean, and even more so, one day you will *feel* the meaning alive inside you.

"It's more than the literal words; there's energy, a life force that has been captured and maintained through the dedicated study and preservation by rabbis and scholars for generations and generations. You will simply *know* what it all means, and it will help you for the rest of your life! That's why people would rather die than be forbidden from their blessed Torah—the love for the Torah and the life it gives us is that great.

"When you stand at Masada, you're standing in the power of the Torah. At the heart of the struggle of the Jewish people who fled to Masada was the passion to maintain their right to read, study, pray, and live with these sacred teachings at the center of their lives. These are more than words, my dear boy, much more than words.

"Now, how do you feel about your studies?"

I was a bit in awe after that lesson. It was still hard to relate to, but it somehow made sense. It was becoming clear that I wasn't *just* doing this process to make my parents happy or to jump through a cultural hoop. If I took the process seriously, perhaps I could, for just a moment, know what the first author felt when God was alive in his or her life. I kept those thoughts with me on our journey to Israel, and I felt their truth as I stood atop Masada. I felt the precious role of the scholars who had passed the ancient ways from one to the next.

Only a day or two after my Bar Mitzvah, we went to a place in Jerusalem called the Church of the Holy Sepulcher, which was built on what's commonly believed to be Golgotha, the hill where Jesus Christ was crucified. This same location is also said to be the site of the tomb where Jesus was buried and the location where he resurrected. The area is inhabited and maintained primarily by coexisting communities of Greek Orthodox, Armenian, Roman Catholic, Copt, Ethiopian, and Syrian Orthodox Christian denominations.

As our guide explained some of the practices of each of the Christian groups, I began to realize the existence of the Master Paths for the first time. Each tradition seemed to have similar elements, including sacred music, movement, ritual, prayer, meditation, and study! These Western traditions saw study as much more than academics or record keeping. Sacred study was a path to God.

Our guide went on to describe the study of scripture and commentary as one of the most central practices to the Christian traditions at the Holy Sepulcher. As I learned of the deep reverence in which monks recopied the gospels and handwrote the Bible, I remembered what the rabbi told me about scripture and study in my own tradition. Here, too, were people dedicating their lives to the study of scriptures, poring over each word, nuance, and intention with deep love. Through this process, these people had encountered an experience of The Sacred that was so deep and profound that they decided to dedicate their lives to studying the ancient scriptures.

There in Jerusalem it seemed that the path of sacred study was alive and well. I witnessed it in the Christian monasteries, the *yeshivas* (rabbinical schools), and in the training of *Imams* in Islam. Theology itself, which has become an academic degree, was originally a sacred path of awakening. Over time as I've studied and traveled, I've found this amazing relationship with scholarship and study almost everywhere. And in my graduate work, I found that study was a sacred act for many of the scholars and professors I encountered.

I've met Indigenous elders who dedicated their lives to studying the leather scrolls and stone carvings of their communities. In addition, Indigenous Earth-based traditions are oral traditions without the scripture or sacred texts that we're accustomed to; however, many do have other forms of scripture and study. Images on bark scrolls, petroglyphs, hieroglyphs, and pictographs, as well as sacred stories, are passed down verbatim from one generation of story keeper to another. They all reflect forms of sacred study in which the discipline of the mind can serve as a means to open the heart and soul.

The Tibetan teacher I studied with in India had a room full of sacred texts; and he mostly taught his students from those long, thin binders containing ancient script. Even those who teach the importance of overcoming the mind—like many traditional Buddhist teachers—also study the history and teachings of the various masters throughout time. You don't need to look far to find an example.

The Energy of Ideas

The Western world is dominated by the influence of the intellect. The skill of the mind has become highly prized: memorization of facts, application of logic, and mastery of information and knowledge. Books, computers, IQ tests, and university degrees have created a scale of intelligence that rarely relates much to the wisdom of maturity. Growing up, my father had a friend and co-worker, Mr. Room, who read volumes each week. Whenever I visited my dad at work, I'd see piles of books from the library on his desk.

As I grew older, I noticed that no matter what I was interested in, Mr. Room knew something about it. He was a walking encyclopedia. I also noticed, however, that he had little experience in the things he talked about. He could tell you many things about Hong Kong, for example, but he'd never been there. He knew much about opera but rarely, if ever, attended one. He was aware of strange foods and fascinating people, but he never had the taste or touch of either. This raised a sense of caution in me about the "learned." Information isn't the same as understanding, and knowledge isn't the same as wisdom.

Nevertheless, of all the paths I've traveled, I can't forget the importance of sacred study. It was the ancient Hindu texts that first let me know that I wasn't alone in my experience of The Sacred. It was the writings of the American transcendentalists Emerson and Thoreau who implored me to go deeper into my love of wilderness mysticism. And it was the great and challenging thinkers such as Nietzsche, Alan Watts, Ken Wilber, and Ram Dass who inspired me to find new ways of explaining the world. After more than 12 years of earning degrees, ordinations, and certificates, I can't deny what the gift of study can offer people on a spiritual path.

One mentor who helped me become aware of the heart that lives within the cold pages and ideas of academics was Beverly Lanzetta, Ph.D., my first comparative-religion professor in my undergraduate years. She required that we not only read the texts about the history of religions, but that we also read the poetry, mystics, and firsthand accounts from every tradition. She showed us how the mind *could* lead to the heart and soul. We kept journals of how our reading impacted us in thought and feeling and were asked to contemplate and reflect, not to simply memorize and repeat.

I learned that the world is full of scholars who believe in the capacity of study to open the heart and mature the mind. Dr. Lanzetta's mentor, Ewert Cousins, Ph.D., was one such person. His writings about the possibility for people to enter into the consciousness of each other through study, dialogue, and openhearted awareness inspired me. I was honored many years later when he became my doctoral adviser.

The Ego Loves the Mind

In my doctoral program at the Graduate Theological Foundation, I encountered a great honor and lesson. Dr. Cousins had recommended that I complete my final defense (where students present and answer questions about their thesis in order to obtain a doctoral degree) before a committee of the foundation's adjunct Oxford faculty members. This request was granted and I traveled to Oxford, England, the "city of dreaming spires," where for more than 800 years, study has been a sacred and privileged institution.

Fortunately, my defense went well, and the committee was both engaging and appreciative of my work. After the very positive deliberation was passed on to me, I was invited to attend a special end-of-term dinner for college alumni, staff, and students. I felt charged by the thrill of the day's success, and I knew that I was fortunate that my committee was made up of people who understood both the letter and spirit of study. After a long and complicated graduate program, I experienced a sense of vindication, pride, and relief.

I arrived a bit early, so while waiting for my sponsor, I watched the students and alumni arrive. In Oxford fashion, they checked their raincoats and then donned their black scholastic robes. I recognized that there were slightly different styles and lengths, which indicated different stages of accomplishment and education.

Then I noticed a tall middle-aged man getting upset with the coat-check staff.

"This is not mine!" He waved a black robe in the young woman's face. "I put it down right here. Are you telling me that you didn't move it? Where did it go?" He was raising his voice and looking around accusingly. "It probably belongs to a graduate student," he said with disgust.

I decided to leave the scene to look for my host and see if I could find anyone wearing a poorly fitting robe. When I turned the corner, I started laughing. There was a small group of young men, talking and visiting casually with each other. One man, who wasn't very tall to begin with, was wearing a robe that hung to the floor and a bit beyond. It looked silly and was clearly not the right fit. I approached and gently informed him that he must have grabbed the wrong robe at the coat check.

His friends laughed, and the young man became pale with fear. "Oh, thank you," he said. "I have to sort this out right away."

He grabbed my arm and pulled me aside. "Some people around here take these things very seriously. I love it here, but you can't imagine the hierarchy and judgment. I've seen it in many places. Where there is honor, there is arrogance. Where there are awards, there is competition. I used to attend an Ivy League school in the U.S., and it's no different. It's the reason why I left. In my previous college, there was so much comparison and antagonism, I began to wonder if I was really learning anything of value if it came at the cost of my humanity. I'm fitting in here now, so I don't want to rock the boat. I guess we all make some sacrifices."

It was a sobering moment. Just when I was beginning to well up with my own pride of achievement, I recognized that it's only one path of knowledge that's no better or worse than the next. The exchange was extreme and fleeting, but the message was lasting. Like any path, we can lose the power and intent of study to the hunger of the ego and the habit of pride.

It reminded me that the path of sacred study is one that must be approached with care, for within it lies a great trap. The world of intellect can easily be taken over by the ego. The false sense that all things of worth can be measured may become pervasive and a barrier to true learning and development. Instead of learning how to think and how to enter the wisdom of what's being studied, many fall into a competitive and judgmental mode where the heart and soul shut down. This is no longer sacred study.

I've seen this same dynamic in modern seekers. You don't have to be enrolled in higher education to be committed to a path of sacred study or to let the ego feed off of the intellect. Any deep engagement of the mind in learning about the self and The Sacred may lead to profound experiences and realizations. Weekend workshops, dedicated reading, listening voraciously to audio recordings, and research into history and related subjects can all be a part of a self-directed path of sacred study. These same things can add up to a lot of distraction and procrastination.

Similarly, sacred texts can become deified and worshipped with greater reverence than The Sacred Source itself. The path of sacred study can lead to trouble when the word and letter become more important than the Spirit Within. There's a common teaching among the world's traditions that the word gives birth to ideas, inspiration, and belief. Yet we must recall that there's something deeper than the created world of ideas and material things. There's a Sacred Source that gave birth to the word itself! In the end, all things are but an expression of The Sacred that transcends study.

Most people who claim to search for spiritual growth in books just go from one book to the next, hoping that the simple act of reading will do the trick. Listening to the same messages over and over can help but only to a point. The famous father of the self-help world, Wayne Dyer, Ph.D., offers us an incredible modern example of the path of sacred study.

A Good Example

After a series of synchronicities, Dyer found himself irresistibly drawn to study the ancient Taoist text called the Tao Te Ching. Written around the 6th century B.C.E., it's made up of 81 verses or chapters. Each one is simple and poetic and less than a page long. Each passage, however, is dense in wisdom and unsurpassed in clarity. It's widely known as one of the world's most incredible spiritual texts.

When Dyer made the commitment to studying the Tao as a sacred practice, he didn't just read it once or twice. He read it multiple times and even read numerous editions and translations. He studied its origin and committed himself to fully embracing the text with his whole presence and undivided attention.

Each day for 81 days, he would dedicate himself to a single verse. When he reached the end, he repeated the process. After more than a solid year of studying, writing, reading, and talking about the Tao, he not only felt as if he understood the text, but as if it were speaking to him—as if the author, Lao-tzu, were communicating directly with him. He described the feeling of entering into the consciousness of the text in his book *Change Your Thoughts— Change Your Life*. This is a perfect example of the path of sacred study.

Oprah Winfrey and spiritual teacher Eckhart Tolle also provide a great and ironic example of sacred study. Eckhart Tolle wrote two very good books about the power of present-moment awareness and the meditative mind's role in spiritual awakening, *The Power of Now* and *A New Earth*. Oprah enjoyed the books and their message so much that she wanted to share it with the world. In an unprecedented forum, she created an international Internet-based study program to examine the contents of the book with its author. Millions of people participated in some way, reading the book, attending study groups, completing a workbook, and listening to the dialogues that were broadcasted live and for free online.

Although the books were really about the paths of meditation and the "life path," the path that Oprah chose to teach was one of sacred study. Using the intellect, lessons, and learning, she and Eckhart Tolle led many participants to a deeper spiritual awareness.

ॐ ॐ ॐ

If reflection, contemplation, dedication, and application are objectively integrated, the path of sacred study can be transformative. Perceiving our own limits and biases can be extremely difficult. Without complete devotion to a study, it's necessary to work with a mentor, class, or other people who are involved in similar studies. This can help take the experience to a further level and ensure that the process of awakening remains at the core of intention and direction.

PART IV

Heart-Centered Practices

I hear their cry
And move toward the grasping heart
It often begins with fear

I step into a darkness
A fragile unknowing
I am lost in it

Everything I do seems small
But something pulls me forward
Though I resist facing the truth before me

I see it there, without apology or shame
In the moment when I look
Into the face of it all,

I catch a glimpse of the pain and hunger
Suddenly it is mine, more real than I can bear
And I will do anything I can to help

Reaching out, I am not sure anymore who I am trying to save
In the center of it all lives an Infinite Spirit
And it has swallowed me whole

A simple touch and we know
That "each other" is all we have
To get through

And I need you
more than you will ever understand
We are nothing without each other.

No matter how estranged
No matter how foreign
No matter how many

When souls connect
Only One remains

This is what you taught me
This is how the brokenness heals
And helps us to be whole

— J. H. Ellerby

Chapter Ten

THE PATH
OF DEVOTION

For the Love of God

We were on the road to Malinalco, Mexico, when we came upon clusters of people of all ages walking along the highway. It was surprising and mysterious to me. As we passed families, groups, and individuals, I felt as if I were looking through the car window into a world I couldn't begin to comprehend.

Some of the people carried crosses, some carried flowers, and others carried bags of food and water. The people seemed intent, and the mood appeared committed but also content. Their dark faces were made more beautiful in contrast to the freshly laundered clothing they were wearing, as if dressed for a special occasion.

"Where are they going?" I asked. It had been miles since the last town, and it was a very small one. "Where could they have all come from? Why?"

"Have you not seen people making a pilgrimage before?" my guide Raphael asked me. We were on our way to meet an Aztec healer,

Alejandro. I'd heard that he was considered to be a great healer, and was known for his traditional training and passion for his culture. I was traveling with his friend and mine, Raphael, a gentle Spanish-Mexican man who'd become deeply involved in Mexican Indigenous cultures years ago. Like me, he had long been attracted to the ancient ways of the First People.

My love of the natural world drew me to ceremonies that were held on the open land, accented by natural elements and powers. For me, nature is Sacred and had always been the highest expression of God that I could relate to in the physical world. I was excited to explore the ancient Aztec rituals and temples with Alejandro. Until we arrived at our destination, however, the stream of people, with their flowers and crosses, perplexed me and held my attention. I couldn't imagine what they were doing.

Sensing my bewilderment, Raphael explained. "They are on the road to Chalma, a sacred place where there's a cave with a very special altar. It's the second-most popular site for pilgrimages in Mexico. Hundreds of years ago, Native people would go there to honor and request help from Ozteotl."

Ozteotl was called many things: some tribes called him "the Dark Lord of the Cave," some saw him as a jaguar spirit, and others related him to the God of War. In any case, he was said to have great healing ability, and people visited this large stone in the cave in order to connect with his power to help and heal them. There's even a sacred spring of natural water there, and it, too, is said to be holy.

Historical accounts tell us that about 500 years ago, the Spanish came to the site and condemned the sacred practices, and they sought to convert the local people to Catholicism. There are many versions of what happened next. Most say that three days later when the Spanish missionaries returned, the black stone of Ozteotl was broken on the cave floor, and in its place on the altar was a dark stone cross with the image of Christ upon it. No one knew how it got there, and even the local priests were astounded. Many said it was a miracle.

Since that time, the cave has been dedicated to St. Michael and is now known as a place where people travel to be in the presence of God through miracles and experiences of the Divine. Pilgrims come as an act of devotion, and they make the journey on foot to show their deep love and commitment to God. Nothing and no one is more important to them. They want to prove their faith. If they're asking for miracles, they want to demonstrate their sincerity. They want God to know what's in their hearts.

At the time, I didn't understand the devotional path, and it made me uncomfortable. In the Western society of my upbringing, the emotional adoration of something "invisible" was hard to relate to. I found myself resisting and asked Raphael, "Do you mean it's similar to individuals who are in love saying to their beloved, 'I'd walk a hundred miles on broken glass if only you'd be mine'? Or the way people will stand in line for three days to buy concert tickets to see their favorite rock group?"

Raphael smirked. "Well, in some ways, yes—it is like that. I think those people say and do those things because they've found a connection to a force that helps them feel loved and understood. I've been to rock concerts like that! Everyone sings along as if the songs were about their own lives. They like to be understood and heard, experiencing a state of devotion. I think that the devotion itself feels good for them.

"The experience is similar for these pilgrims. Unlike adoring a rock star, the force that they're in love with has the power to work miracles in their lives. Their beloved offers grace and peace. I've traveled with the pilgrims in the past, and even some people in my family have gone on this trek. Thousands make the journey every year. Their worship comes from the heart, and they want to show it. They want to *feel* it. For you and me, we feel God in nature. We're comfortable with a faceless God who is expressed in the physical world as a force beyond ideas and words."

I agreed, and listened intently.

"For these people, God has a face, a body, and a name. Even the saints have personalities, form, and preferences. These people feel and need a personal relationship to God. They call upon Jesus by name. They honor Mother Mary by name, and they pray to the saints for help by name. They show their love and devotion and feel rewarded for it. Many of them even have altars and shrines in their homes.

"Love of God is their path. They're not unsophisticated or fool-ish. I know great professors, scientists, lawyers, doctors, and other highly educated people who worship in this way. They connect to The Sacred through love. It's no better or worse than what we are attracted to on mountaintops and in the call of the eagle."

The road eventually diverged from the trail of pilgrims, and we spent the rest of the time in silence. Something struck me deeply about what Raphael had said and what I'd seen. Images of the people, young and old, flickered through my mind. This Christian expression in Mexico reminded me of all the stories of devotion I'd heard and underestimated.

As I reflected on it, I realized that "devotion" as a spiritual prac-tice was everywhere. I remembered that in my studies of yoga, it was often taught that the word *yoga* means to be "yoked with" or "joined with" the Divine. Yoga itself has many expressions: there's hatha or asana yoga, which I mentioned is focused on the postures that many Westerners are familiar with; *jnana* yoga, which focuses on the mind like sacred study; karma yoga, which focuses on sacred service of others and the world; and *Bhakti* or devotional yoga, which is based on the adoration of a personal image of God. This is what Raphael was talking about.

Adoring the Divine

As my practice and experience have evolved in my life since that day, I've developed a very different relationship to the path of devotion. As my experience of The Sacred has deepened, I've felt compelled to relate to God—The Supreme Force and Divine Mystery—also as a friend and beloved. It somehow feels incomplete to restrict my connection to The Sacred to only my mind or body. It's difficult to focus the feeling of love *for* something if it has no personal dimension. To think of God as Pure Consciousness may be accurate, but it's awkward. The great Sufi spiritual teacher Hazrat Inayat Khan once said, "Mysticism without devotion is like uncooked food; it can never be assimilated."

How else do we direct the deep sense of gratitude and appreciation that we feel for our lives and the daily gifts we receive? Whether it's a choice or a natural shift in awareness due to spiritual experience, love of The Sacred will eventually emerge. The path of devotion is one way to begin that journey into the heart. We either turn to the face of God we already know, or we choose an expression that stirs us deeply within.

Not all traditions have a Spirit World dimension of God nor do they have a face for the Creator that can be painted or addressed. Unlike the Christians' worship of Jesus, the Buddhists' worship of the Buddha, and the many Hindu expressions of The Sacred, other traditions, such as Judaism, Islam, and Indigenous cultures, stress personal relationships to God because the Divine is invisible. They don't confine God to a body or image but maintain a personal language in order to feel a connection. To engage the deep sense of adoration and intimacy that is the hallmark of the path of devotion, it's necessary to hold an image or feeling of The Sacred that is finite and can be conceived in time and space.

Faith, trust, optimism, and connection all flow from a healthy personal relationship to The Sacred as a Divine Being. Love carries an energy that helps us activate our "soul sight." This deeply affectionate relationship emerges naturally as we experience The Sacred. Concepts, theories, and ideas fall away. We find that only love songs and poems can truly share the blissful union we feel with the Divine.

When reading the poetic writings of mystics spanning across cultures, we find that no matter what their spiritual practice, the path of devotion eventually becomes a core element. Kabir, Lalla, St. Teresa, Mirabai, Ramakrishna, and Hildegard of Bingen are just a few names of hundreds who had fallen in love with The Sacred. Many of history's great mystics, at some point or on some level, have had to use the path of devotion to truly immerse themselves in the passionate relationship to their experience of God.

🕉 🕉 🕉

While I was in India, I was invited to eat with the family of a shopkeeper named Raj whom I'd become friendly with. At his home, his mother and sisters kept a sacred shrine to Shiva. They tended to it daily, adorning it with flowers; talking and praying before it; and making offerings of incense, candy, and fruit. It was my strong suspicion, based on the conversations I was able to have with my friend Raj, that they believed the ancient Hindu precept that all expressions of God are mere aspects of a Divine "bliss consciousness" that transcends face and form. Nevertheless, they chose to engage in a deep and personal relationship with Shiva, one of the Divine masks of God.

Over time, I've also come to understand and embrace the devotional path in many ways. The love and blessings I've received along my spiritual path elicit extraordinary gratitude, reverence, and respect that I can only express in simple terms. I dialogue with The Sacred, I bow before The Sacred, and I offer my daily gratitude and affection for The Sacred—even though I know that The Ultimate Divine Power is beyond any "personality" that I may choose to address. I need the outlet as a vehicle to engage and express my heart in my relationship with God. The devotional practice may reduce God to a term, a being, and a persona, but when we worship with consciousness and intention, our devotion will continue to open us to the Infinite Light behind the face and name.

Fear Loves to Hide

For much of my life, I struggled with the path of devotion because I saw how many people use it as an escape. Rather than becoming a gateway to explore their identity and the nature of The Sacred, many people accept an image of God as a sort of psychological replacement for human relationships and possibly to fill a sense that something is missing or lacking in them. The path of devotion can easily become an escape from life, rather than an embrace of life.

When I used to work in hospitals as a spiritual counselor, I often heard patients say, "God will take care of it all." Sometimes this was a truly openhearted statement of trust and optimism. In other cases, however, this wasn't a statement of faith, but a displaced apathy. Sadly, I saw many people refuse to learn about their condition or involve their families in planning because they were so sure that God would rescue them from their problems.

I always tried to be respectful of people's devotion, but sometimes it betrayed even the aid of God. Rather than creating the positive conditions for a miracle or embracing the clear emotion of confidence, they acted and spoke from fear, using faith as a shield to protect them from having to share their feelings or face reality. Unfortunately, the beautiful path of devotion can become a dark shadow to hide in.

Most of us have heard the story about the pious man whose town was flooded and in grave danger. His family begged him to help them pack the car to escape, but he refused, saying, "I love God, and God loves me. I've been faithful and devoted, and I trust that he'll save me from harm." Soon the roads were washed out, and there was no way for them to escape; fortunately, a large army truck passed their home, and the driver offered to take them to safety. The father refused again, placing his faith in God. His family fled with all they could salvage.

The flood water continued to rise rapidly, and the first floor of the house was consumed in the rushing flow. As he ran to the second floor for shelter, a rescue boat came to the window, pleading to take him to safety.

"No," he said and repeated his conviction. "I love God, and God loves me. I've been faithful and devoted, and I trust that he'll save me from harm." The boat left and the town was empty of people or rescue vehicles. And the storm raged on.

Finally, the waters filled the second floor of the man's house, and he had to climb onto the roof for safety. He prayed and prayed for help. Just then a police helicopter flew over and threw down a ladder. The rescue workers shouted out to him to grab it. But his faith was certain. "No!" he shouted. "I love God, and God loves me. I've been faithful and devoted, and I trust that he'll save me from harm!" The helicopter finally left without him. The waters rose higher, and a great wave devoured the man, killing him.

The next thing he knew, the man realized he was in heaven, and there shining before him was God.

"Dear God!" he exclaimed, choking back his despair. "How could you have done this to me? I've been devoted all my life. I thought you would save me!"

God replied, "What do you expect from me? I sent you an army truck, a rescue boat, and a police helicopter! Don't you trust me enough to accept my help?"

This popular story illustrates that perhaps God does hear our prayers and answers them but not always in the ways we expect. Devotion doesn't mean being helpless or blind to the events of the world. A healing relationship with The Sacred emerges when we remain engaged in creation and are open to growing, learning, and changing. The path of devotion is about being awake to the continual presence of God, with love, trust, and surrender. In most cases, *surrender* means releasing our expectations and turning toward the Divine will. It does *not* mean that God will do everything for us.

With All Your Heart

One of the world's most powerful examples of devotion lives in the story of Jesus Christ. Many view Jesus as God incarnate: God with a face, a name, a history, and the ability to hear and feel us. As such, Jesus is loved and adored by millions who direct their heartfelt attention to him on the path of devotion. It is important to also note that Jesus himself walked the path of devotion, among others.

In Mark 12:29–30, Jesus states that the most important commandment is to "love the Lord your God with all your heart and with all your soul and with all your mind and with all your strength." This is simply a restatement of the Hebrew text in Deuteronomy 6:5. While the world may forever debate his words, one might take note of his attention to the path of devotion and the primary importance he placed, not on people's adoration of himself, but on the love of the Divine Creator and Sacred Source. Through this path, Jesus felt so united with God that he could only speak of him as his father. He trusted in God implicitly and beyond doubt.

He loved God above all, and as such, found his calling to serve God's children—God's creation—without discrimination.

The historical examples of the path of devotion are endless and often overwhelming in their intensity. Yet the path of devotion doesn't need to be scary, self-deprecating, or one of social disconnection. The path of devotion is partly about what we do, but mostly about how we do it.

As a practice, some people have a shrine to their beloved Divine in their home. Every morning they might pray to their beloved Divine, light a candle, and burn incense as an offering. Others show their devotion by frequently going to a house of worship; and some commit their lives to honoring their love of God by joining religious orders such as monasteries, ashrams, and nunneries. Many people simply remain in dialogue with God throughout the day, listening for guidance and striving to honor God's will.

On the path of devotion, we ultimately feel as if we have fallen "in love" with God. All actions, thoughts, and feelings circle around a preoccupation with the Divine. Our life becomes an offering; all things remind us of our sacred passion. We long to be held and touched by our beloved, and we are pained by anything that keeps us at a distance.

The force of our longing drives our practices and fills our attention. Love becomes the fuel of our awakening. The essence of the path of devotion lives in the capacity of the loving heart to shatter the persona of life and the egotistic mind. When the surrender is true and conscious, the path of devotion opens our lives to become a channel of sacred will and wisdom. We merge in love with our beloved, and life itself becomes the great offering.

Chapter Eleven

THE PATH OF
SACRED SERVICE

From the Darkness Comes a Light

The elevator moved slowly to the fourth floor. It was big enough for the wheelchairs and hospital beds that came in and out all day. Since my visits were in the evening hours, however, I was often the only one aboard. I stared at the outdated wood veneer and faded chrome handrails. The dingy floor and doors showed decades of wear and tear, and the occasional moans of the gears reminded me of its history—once shiny, promising, and new.

I always said a prayer as I rode up to the spinal-cord injury and amputee unit at the rehabilitation hospital. I wanted to be prepared for an evening of visiting, and bittersweet surprises that might be waiting. When the elevator doors opened, I could feel myself entering a new world.

It was quiet at night—strangely quiet—and the halls were sterile, white, aged. The day was done, and there was a different mood emerging as patients settled in for rest and the staff retreated for the day. A new rhythm emerged: the distant sound of a television, the occasional sharp tone from a computer monitor, the soft ring of a phone in the nursing station.

Staff members were friendly, attentive, and kind; and patients were typically subdued, mostly contemplative, depressed, or tired from the day's physical therapy. They were there because of something serious—something life altering. Sadly, a surprising number of people on this unit of dramatic and extreme injuries and illnesses were under 35 years of age.

Perhaps the inner-city location played a role or the fact that patients from the surrounding rural region were funneled there for the comprehensive services offered at this site. The unit contained an amazing cross section of society: old, young, diabetics, accident survivors, surgery casualties, and a disproportionate presence of Native American and low-income people filled the beds.

Many lived in this rehabilitation hospital for several months; few were there for relatively short stints. Because of the long stays and complicated circumstances, it was an ideal and often challenging place to provide spiritual counseling and emotional support. As part of my chaplaincy training, I'd selected this unit to do volunteer work because I needed to accumulate hours of practice, but more so from a deeper need to give back—a desire to serve a community of people who seemed to have little support.

The unit manager was a wonderful and ambitious woman who wanted more for her patients, but the hospital's budget restricted psychosocial care to a minimum. It was my pleasure to offer extra hours. When I began, I felt a sense of valiant pride. I had a secret ambition to be "the one to go the extra mile" in order to help the "less fortunate." I recall my first visit. Only hours after I began my work, it became clear that I'd greatly underestimated my task. I'd also underestimated the costs . . . and the rewards.

During my first week of visits, I met Vera, a Native American woman who changed my life. She was from a small Cree Nation community in central Manitoba, Canada; and she was dangerously overweight. Vera was in her mid-60s, but she appeared much older, as she clearly bore the ill effects of a life full of challenge, loss, and chronic health problems. I examined her medical chart and created an image of her in my mind, but when I entered her room, I was shocked.

It took me months before I could fully grasp the overwhelming reality of a body that was truly in decay and deterioration. This was the beginning of that adjustment. Vera's complexion was ashen, she looked exhausted, her size was of concern, and the empty space in the bed where her right leg used to be was a sign of worse things to come. There was a faint sickly odor in the dark room, which was scarcely illuminated by a reading light beside her bed. The other bed in the room was empty. The winter night outside was cold and black.

I was a bit nervous as I entered the room and introduced myself. I asked simple questions about her well-being and mood. Vera struck me as a kind of medical iceberg, in that even to the untrained eye, it was obvious that any conditions identified were only a visible fraction of an immense complexity at work in her body and life.

I sensed myself already pulling away from her emotionally, and somewhere in the back of my mind, I could feel my heroic intentions diminishing. Rationalizations about why I probably shouldn't spend much time with this patient slowly surfaced. They attempted to hide my growing discomfort.

To my surprise, Vera responded to my presence and was far less reserved than many of the other Native American people I'd worked with in hospital settings. At first she was quiet and just stared at me, and as I ran out of pleasantries, we gazed at each other awkwardly. Vera looked away, and I felt that I'd overstayed my welcome. I immediately thought about leaving, but then she reached out.

"It's nice you came. I'm very lonely here," she said in a faint voice with a Cree accent. She cleared her throat a lot.

"No one comes to see me. My kids live and work back home, and it's so far away that none of them can make the trip. They have their own problems to deal with anyway. My eldest boy used to live in the city here. He would have come to see me, but he was killed two years ago in an accident." She paused and closed her eyes as if to swallow the pain of the memory.

"My husband is gone, too. He died of diabetes. It's been five years." She paused again. Pointing to the empty space in her bed beneath the sheets where her right leg was removed, she continued. "That's why they took this: diabetes. They want to take the other one now.

"How will I get around? Back home on the reservation, most of our streets are still unpaved. There's just dirt. When it rains, you can't get a wheelchair through the mud. But I can't stay here either—it's too lonely in the city. My husband didn't want surgery. He was a fisherman all his life and always worked so hard. He only came to the city once—to the hospital. But he never returned. When he found out how sick he was, he drank himself to death. I never drank. I went to church almost every day to pray for him. I tried to get him to go with me, but I guess we never did get along."

She paused as her breathing became strained. "I always went to church, since I was little. I think he hated that about me. It made him feel guilty about his drinking, so he used to beat me up. I couldn't stop going though because it was the only place I felt safe.

"He was always drinking, always angry. And it just got worse at the end. I guess I knew it would be like that, but I'd always hoped it would turn out differently."

There was such sadness in her eyes, and I was at a complete loss for words. The immensity of her pain was more than I could bear. Most patients take their time to share such intimate details about their lives. In the hospital where the majority of my visits were unannounced and unrequested, people usually needed time to build a sense of rapport and connection. Then they'd eventually begin to open up more. Vera was different.

I was thinking about all those visits with patients, always wishing they'd share sooner. I never realized, however, that the timing was really to *my* benefit. I was unprepared for the sudden and intense nature of Vera's story, and it left me reeling. Up to that point in my training, I'd helped people face many of life's traumas and setbacks. But it was still all new to me, and this was too much and too honest—abuse, loss, illness, poverty, isolation. Then I remembered my commitment: service would be my gift, my path.

So I pulled a chair over to her bed, and we quietly sat together. Vera stared at the ceiling. I recalled a practice that I thought might help me feel better, if not her as well. I closed my eyes for a moment and imagined my heart as a large, glowing pink rosebud. Then I took some slow, deep breaths into my belly and imagined it opening into a radiant bloom. I said a little prayer asking for her healing and comfort and visualized a soft white light shining out from my heart to hers. I pictured a beautiful light of healing surrounding her.

Vera turned to me and smiled as I opened my eyes. Her eyes were bright, and she said, "Thank you. Can we say the Lord's Prayer together?" I was caught off guard. It was as if she felt the "energy" I was sending.

"Of course," I replied, and we began reciting, "Our Father who art in heaven . . ."

We held hands as Vera led the prayer, her voice growing stronger with each word. When we came to the end, I paused and she continued praying for healing for her grandchildren, children, and community. She prayed for her husband's peace in the Spirit, and for the ability to forgive him. She prayed for me and the "hard work of the heart" that I was doing. She prayed for all the people in the hospital—staff and patients. Finally, she prayed for herself. I was moved by the sincerity and generosity of her wishes for me, a stranger. I felt myself choke up with emotion.

"I haven't been able to pray since I got here," she said. "I felt like maybe my life was a failure and that God was disappointed in me. This place can feel so empty. No Spirit. But you came, and I can feel that you care. You want to do what's right. It makes me feel like *I am* worth something. People do care, don't they? God didn't forget about me. You're the proof!"

My hopes of being a hero dissolved in a wave of deep humility. I was embarrassed for the ways I'd judged Vera in my mind when I had first arrived. I felt her unconditional acceptance despite just having met me. I found myself aware of an awakening in her—and in me, as well. As her mood changed, I saw a twinkle in her eye. I felt a sweetness in her voice and presence. As she spoke of her gratitude for my company, I felt myself falling under the spell of compassion that was growing between us.

As I gazed at Vera, I saw images of her at different ages floating through my mind. I saw her as a young mother, a beautiful child, and as an active member of her community. I saw story after story flow through me—a gentle stream of thoughts and feelings.

"Vera," I said, putting my hand on the remaining part of her amputated leg, which was missing from the knee down, "God is not punishing you, and you haven't disappointed anyone. Life isn't easy, and it rarely goes the way we expect. But there's always hope, always change, and always something greater to remember and stay connected to. It's a choice, isn't it?

"I know that your children want you home, and your community misses you as much as you miss them. If we're going to get you back soon, you can help by lifting your own spirit. 'Standing tall' is something we feel inside; it's not about your legs or how fast you move. Try to pray more, and think of the good times that might be waiting ahead. What else can you do with the time you have? Remember springtime at home, and the fresh smell of rain on those muddy country roads."

She smiled and held my hand tightly as I got up to go. "You'll come back?" she asked.

"Of course. Every time I'm here." And I did. I visited her every time I was on the unit. She and I became friends, and her mood and energy steadily lifted. Even though she had to have part of her other leg amputated, I watched the changes in her attitude and her resilience grow from one visit to another.

One day when I arrived on the unit, one of the nurses stopped me in the hallway and asked me to be sure to visit Vera. I asked if she was okay. The nurse explained that she'd been doing well emotionally but was experiencing pain in her newly amputated leg.

"Every time you visit," the nurse explained, "her discomfort goes away. We don't have to give her any pain meds for at least 12 hours or more after you leave. When you aren't here, though, she needs them every four hours. Whatever you're doing, keep doing it!"

I was surprised to hear this and felt honored, but I knew in my heart that I wasn't doing anything for Vera. She was doing it, and a Higher Power was at work. Her faith, prayers, and commitment to see the positive whenever possible was her medicine. I was just the lucky person who got to be a part of it.

Love All, Serve All

Vera helped me see that every person—no matter how sick, broken, sad, or angry—has a story and a precious heart within. We all have a tender soul and a life of memories. Each of us lives with the longing to be in the presence of love. As that love in me grew for Vera, I found it easier to "turn it on" for others in need. I found that when I left the hospital, all the love and attention I thought I'd "given away" was somehow still within me. Even after some of the hardest days, I felt tremendous love and gratitude. As I gave, I received.

After I met Vera, I never left depleted or depressed about the suffering I encountered. I walked to my car and made the drive home with a sense of awe and gratitude. I felt filled with love and privileged to be part of the healing journey of so many. Instead of despair, I found myself awakening to the spirit of God and the goodness in all things. The Sacred isn't just in nature, beauty, and good fortune. It also resides in hard times, sad occasions, and tragedies—maybe more so. I found light in the darkest moments, hope in the broken, and lessons from the lost. The miracle of love and service is that it's like a lit candle. It can light the flame of other candles. The flame burns without going out or being diminished, no matter how many new candles it lights. This is the path of service.

My practice of service allowed me to realize that the presence of The Sacred can be in all things, in all people, and at all times. Good or bad, happy or sad, healthy or sick, we can feel the presence and power of a Higher Love and Wisdom that is there for everyone who reaches for it, regardless of culture or religious beliefs. Giving of myself to others gave me more than I could have ever imagined.

The essence of the path of service is the desire to honor The Sacred in the created world through a commitment to help and heal. Rather than turning our attention and energy to an intangible force or experience, we seek to know The Sacred in the everyday moments of our lives. We choose an act, career, or volunteer work through which we can show our devotion and express our gratitude. The writings and recorded lectures of the celebrated American spiritual teacher and healer Ram Dass were profoundly helpful and instructive in my exploration of the path of service. To this day, I recommend his book *How Can I Help?* to anyone interested in this practice.

Get Involved

The path of service isn't about writing checks to charities or recycling waste at home (although both are important actions). The path of service involves openhearted action—that is, rolling up your sleeves and getting your hands dirty. It's about caring for and working with others without a desire for reward or compensation. It's about being a part of the healing of this world with the awareness that in true healing there's no hierarchy—there's no line to be drawn between the helper and the helped. All people can be healers, and everyone is in need at times.

Your path of service could involve working with children or animals or even healing the environment. You may also wish to help those who are battling poverty, illness, or loneliness. There's no limit to the myriad situations and causes that require support. The key is to give yourself freely, without any self-serving intentions. Honor The Sacred in yourself and what you serve. You might volunteer your time, talent, labor, or experience. The path of service simply asks that you make your service an intentional and regular commitment.

Don't let the simplicity of the practice deceive you. To serve without judgment or attachment will test you in many ways. The harshness and injustice of life can defy logic; true service may make you uncomfortable at times. It's always easier to do nothing or claim that the practice isn't right for you. Despite the reasons for resistance, the path of service promises a personal experience of the transformative power of the human spirit. When you seek to love and serve all, you'll find miracles in every step you take.

Much the way Vera taught me years ago, the path of service is about learning to live from the heart. I didn't have to *do* much to help her. I just had to be honest with myself and fully present with her. I had to trust that I'd never have all the answers, and that would be good enough. To be able to walk with others in the face of life's tragedy and mystery with our hearts vulnerable and eyes open is the cultivation of spiritual awakening.

You Are the Gift

The greatest gift we have to offer is our presence: unconditional, loving, and affirming what is. In service, we come face-to-face with the Spirit of life and know its astounding capacity to triumph, as well as its delicateness in the midst of uncertainty. If we look at what *we* resist when we serve, in time it will set us free.

The way we help heal ourselves is a precious dance. Reflecting on his life and the relationship between service and spirituality, Ram Dass commented, "I am arriving at that circle where one works on oneself as a gift to other people so that one doesn't create more suffering. I help people as I work on myself and I work on myself to help people."

Chapter Twelve

THE GURU-GUIDED PATH

The Master Teacher

The One Who Walks You to the Edge

Summer in South Dakota surges like a wave of green across the rolling hills and wooded riverbanks. Even though farmlands dominate the landscape, the ancient seas of grasses and western sandstone canyons refuse to surrender to the plow . . . and their voices are never far from those who still listen.

If you allow your mind to be as open as the vast blue sky, traveling the back roads and Native American lands will transport you to simpler times. You'll witness the age when the great buffalo herds were masters of the prairies, and wolves and eagles guided people to a life in rhythm with the earth.

The Native American Sioux territories are a place of extreme seasons, from the frigid winter winds to the gentle wildflowers of springtime. At the heart of the year beats the heat of summer and an intensity often underestimated by modern tourists and travelers. Temperatures regularly soar well over 90 degrees Fahrenheit and often reach over 100 degrees. I came face-to-face with this natural power one summer while in the midst of an incredible Hanblecha ceremony.

Hanblecha (literally meaning "to cry for a dream") is the Lakota word for what's commonly referred to as a "Vision Quest," one of the oldest rites of passage on Earth. For thousands of years, people all over the world have sought spiritual guidance and insight through fasting (abstaining from food and water) and meditating in isolated places.

In the pure energy of nature, removed from the distractions and preoccupations of life, "questers" spend their time in prayer, meditation, and supplication with the intent to make direct contact with the Spiritual Forces that guide and watch over us. Some go with the purpose to communicate with Spiritual Guardians; and others remain intent on communing with God, the Great Spirit, Mystery, and Creator.

Hanblecha is an ascetic practice (which we'll discuss in more detail in the following chapter). It seeks to draw forth the very spirit of a person by overcoming the attachments to the body, mind, and even the emotional self. All is set aside to focus on nothing but the openness to receive help from the Spiritual World. In some cases, this practice is done to express gratitude to the Spirit World; and for healers and spiritual leaders, it's sometimes a process used for releasing the psychic and energetic burdens of their work. It's a time to purify, receive, and recharge.

In the Lakota way that I was taught by my spiritual teacher Wanagi Wachi and adopted community in eastern South Dakota, the Hanblecha begins long before the seeker retreats into the wilderness. It begins with a commitment, starting the moment a spiritual leader is asked to conduct the ceremony and supervise the process. From that time on, seekers turn their attention to their intention, preparations, and the guidance of their teacher.

Seekers must provide specific ritual objects for themselves and supplies for the spiritual leader. Four days before the time of seclusion, seekers begin a process of purification, including a series of *Inipi* (Sweat Lodge) ceremonies. This involves very special rituals of purification and healing in a dome-shaped, tentlike steam bath.

After the last of the four Inipi, there's a ritual procession and process to lead the seeker out to the site of seclusion.

The site is marked by sacred prayer flags and other items that protect and delineate the small space that the seeker will remain in until the spiritual leader determines that the Hanblecha is complete and retrieves the seeker. The space is usually a circle about eight feet in diameter. A "quest" may last on average anywhere from 24 hours to four days. No food or water is allowed. In addition, in our community, a shelter was *not* typically permitted. When I first started learning about this, I ventured out with only the minimum clothing necessary to survive. Some years I had only a pair of shorts and a blanket, regardless of the extreme heat, rain, or cold that might have occurred.

The year after I was adopted by Wanagi Wachi as his son and student, I experienced my first Hanblecha. It was only two days and a night, yet it was a beautiful and powerful experience. Because of my spiritual work throughout the year and my unspoken desire to learn, Wanagi Wachi expected me to endure another Hanblecha the next year. As my spiritual teacher, I didn't question his reasoning or even ask why, because I trusted his guidance and judgment. *Guru* isn't a word that the Lakota would ever use, but Wanagi Wachi was my guru for years. He was my mentor, and I was devoted to his teachings and guidance. He will always be my spiritual father.

My Teacher Taught Me How to Learn

Wanagi Wachi rarely taught me much using words. He didn't give long instructions or philosophical teachings. He did speak at length with large groups, but when it was just the two of us, we spent a lot of time in silence. When we were together, we'd be busy running ceremonies, traveling, and helping people. We also laughed a lot. And when we did speak, it always began and ended in a joke. Sometimes Wanagi Wachi's jokes were meant to teach a lesson; and other times they were just his way of playing with words, images, and ideas. His endless humor always reminded me that life is never what it seems, and nothing is as serious as we make it.

When it came time for my instruction, Wanagi Wachi left much of it to the Spiritual World and direct experience. He trusted in the ancient rites and ceremonies, and I had faith that he knew both my potential and my limits. That's the mark of a true spiritual teacher.

Wanagi Wachi's way of teaching through experience wasn't only a reflection of traditional methods of instruction, but it was also designed to break my old learning styles, challenge my assumptions and attachments, and encourage me to be more connected with my heart and body. As my mentor, he knew that I wanted things explained and that in my daily life, I spent too much time "in my head." He may have even known that I aspired to lead ceremonies one day. He also understood that *directly giving* me what I wanted would have left me empty-handed in maturity and spirit. He knew that information is easy, but knowledge and wisdom must be earned.

One day when I couldn't resist my eagerness any longer, I asked a question about a ceremony that was maybe more advanced than my current stage of development and learning.

He replied, "There's a power and responsibility that comes with knowledge. In your culture, everyone expects equal access to all knowledge, and then they don't know what to do with it. They hurt themselves and others. Take your time. Soon you'll see that true learning requires *earning*."

The only way our relationship could work was if I completely trusted his guidance, and I knew that I had to treat him as my guru until he let me know in some subtle way that it was no longer necessary. None of this was discussed—it was all unspoken but mutually understood, unfolding with an uncanny perfection.

After that second year of Hanblecha came a third and fourth. Soon we had a joke between us: every year he'd say, "Once you've completed your fourth year, you can choose if you'll fast (Hanblecha) again." The implication was that until then I'd do as he said and take part in the fasting ceremonies. The joke began after my fourth year when he continued to say the same thing! Then he said it again *after* my fifth and sixth times fasting (he still says it to this day). It seemed like it would never end. Each year he'd lead me in the ceremony, and I always looked forward to it until I encountered the severity of a Lakota summer.

Over the years, my Hanblecha experiences were extraordinary. Truly amazing dreams, visions, and realizations blessed me on each occasion. In different ways at different times, I journeyed into the dimensions of The Sacred. Although I'd encountered some extremes of cold, rain, and even a couple of severe storms that set off the tornado warning sirens in the nearby town, every year was inspiring and deeply rewarding.

As Far As You Can Go

The summer of my next fast had been unusually hot, and the days of preparation were difficult. The temperature reached over 100 degrees Fahrenheit by noon each day. I recall one night we held an Inipi ceremony. Although the sun had set and we waited to begin our ceremony, when we lifted the door of the dome-shaped steam bath, we felt a rush of hot air come *into* the Lodge from outside. I began to get nervous and feared it would be so hot during my Hanblecha that I wouldn't be able to withstand it.

On the day I finished preparations and would be led to my place of isolation, the temperature settled in the mid-90s, and I felt almost comforted. Knowing that I had no shade structure, the drop in temperature was encouraging, and I assumed it would continue to decline.

The first day was hot, but I remained focused on my prayers, contemplations, and gratitude. I stayed intent on my meditation, and the day passed quickly. The slightly cooler night was a blessing, and I experienced the presence of Spirits watching over me. I felt at ease and rested well. The next day began with a blessing.

I sat in a low valley between two hills. About 50 feet to the west and north of me were bushes and trees, and to the east and south, there were only hillsides and tall grass. The first light of day revealed an incredible sight over the eastern horizon. Clouds gathered and formed to look exactly like a massive heard of buffalo. I rubbed my eyes, stood up straight, and looked again. As clear and distinct as the earth beneath my feet, I saw the buffalo forms—horns, heads, and large heaving backs! There were rows and rows of buffalo in the sky.

My heart leapt. These majestic animals were sacred guardians of the Lakota Sioux, and I felt like it was a sign letting me know that I'd be protected or maybe visited by spirits and blessed in some way. I believed that they were coming to teach me something. With fresh zeal, I began my morning prayers and watched for the clouds to cover the sun, freeing me from the worries of comfort so that I could focus on my contemplation . . . but my wish didn't come true.

As the buffalo moved toward the sun, they began to scatter, fragment, and fade. Before long, the sun was climbing from the horizon, and there wasn't a cloud in the sky. By the time it reached its midmorning position, the heat came crashing in like a tidal wave. It was steady, growing, and inescapable.

The world turned into an oven, and I was a prisoner of my body and even worse: my mind. Inside my head, a battle raged. I wanted to run, to go home. I couldn't remember why I was doing this. My discomfort grew worse, and the sun was relentless. I watched it move so painfully slowly across the sky. It felt easily well over 100 degrees, and even the breaths of wind were hot. There was no shade or water—no break whatsoever.

Finally sunset approached, and I left my circle briefly to relieve myself in a nearby set of bushes (it was the only instance when I was permitted to leave my sacred space). I rushed to the edge of the tall grass, and as I relieved myself, I grieved the loss of fluid. I also noticed that my quick steps had sent a rush of blood to my head. Once finished I turned around to return to my circle and suddenly felt faint. I took a step, the world turned dark, and I fell to the ground.

The next thing I knew, I heard Wanagi Wachi's footsteps. I don't know how long I'd been laying there, but it seemed as if he'd appeared the moment I collapsed. However, there was no way for anyone to see me in my secluded location. He must have sensed my dire situation and came to check on me.

Only the medicine man or woman who leads the Hanblecha can travel to the site and observe from time to time. Sometimes Wanagi Wachi would only come once in three days to visit me. Because spiritual leaders are in the ceremonial space and are used to dealing with spirits, they can safely join the quester. No one else should ever do so, however, because it's believed that harm could come to those who break the spiritual codes of the Hanblecha. The Divine Energy has the power to heal *and* hurt, if disregarded.

"Can you get up?" he asked without stooping to help. He stared off into the distance.

I rose to a sitting position. "Yes, I think I can."

"Wachekiya," he insisted, which means "to pray." He wanted me to return to my prayers, but I wanted him to take me home.

I got up slowly, returned to the circle, and sat on my blanket facing the setting sun. My skin burned—my body was hot from the inside out. He just stood there, looking far off in the distance.

"You're going to be okay," he said. I nodded my head in agreement. Inside I wanted to cry and beg him to let me stop early. But I remained quiet, and he left.

That night I tried to recover my sense of calm and focus and remember my prayers. Suddenly in the middle of the night—it must have been past midnight—I heard something over the hill. It sounded like a heartbeat, and then came a voice. Wanagi Wachi was singing and drumming in the near distance. It was a healing song, and he sang for a long time. It was comforting. I realized that I had one day left. I was discouraged but now felt some hope. My teacher had never sung for me before.

The next day came and it was hot again, but I tried to remain positive. I distracted myself with thoughts of returning to the world: a cold shower, swimming, unlimited water. I remembered seeing bottles of grape-flavored Gatorade in a gas-station refrigerator the day before I fasted. It didn't look too good to me then, as I avoid drinks with sucrose syrup, glucose-fructose syrup, and coloring. But now it was all I could think about. It didn't matter what was in it; I wanted it! Eventually, I heard the drum and procession calling for me. The ceremony was coming to an end.

The closing ceremonies were beautiful. Most of my local friends and family members were there. They talked about the heat and how it was in the triple-digit range—everyone had suffered. They talked about all the helpers, fire keepers, and the people who'd come out to the country during the days and evenings to pray for me. I thought of Wanagi Wachi and how he'd set his life aside for me during this process. When did he have time to rest?

I realized that I wasn't the only one who'd been suffering and sacrificing. I began to wonder if I'd let my mind get the best of me, but I knew that it had, and I felt sadness inside. My mind had been out of control and I gave in, in so many ways.

Wanagi Wachi and I got into his truck to leave the ceremonial grounds. He sat for a moment without saying a word, but then said, "I know you had a hard time. You don't realize it, but I'm out there with you—physically sometimes and always in spirit. Wherever I am, I can see you."

He pointed to his forehead and said, "It's not easy for me either. It's hard to feel my son suffer, but it is your commitment. I'm only helping you keep it."

Then he reached into a brown paper bag beside him and pulled out a grape-flavored Gatorade.

"Next time, son, try not to think about this so much. I was trying to watch the basketball game back home, but all I could hear in my mind was 'Grape Gatorade! Grape Gatorade!'"

We laughed, and then he became serious again. "Don't forget how powerful your mind is. Don't forget the amazing and terrible things it can do. You think it's nature that you experience out there, but in the ceremonial ways, it is *yourself* whom you experience."

I was amazed that he'd read my thoughts, but I understood more than he said. It was a gentle teaching at a challenging time.

He started up the truck and began to pull away, saying, "Once you've completed your fourth year, you can choose if you'll fast again." I laughed, and then fell silent. My heart sank at the realization that I'd have to face the sacred circle another time. The thought of enduring the heat again was more than I could stand.

The next year came like a flashback of the one before, and the days prior to my Hanblecha just kept getting hotter. Once again, it was 100 degrees as we made the preparations, and weather reports called for 110-degree days for the coming week. I kept getting more and more nervous until it was the day before, and I felt sick to my stomach. Fear gripped me like nothing I'd ever known. Finally, I had to say something.

I found Wanagi Wachi in the laundry room of his home in the early afternoon. It took all my courage to speak up, and it would be the first time I resisted his instruction.

"A'te (Dad)?" I asked for his attention. "I've been thinking a lot about this. Last year was so hard . . . I guess it was a bit like a trauma to my body. I'm reacting so strongly to this. Maybe it would be good for me to skip a year—just to regain my confidence and heal. I feel sick and tense; my mind is full of fear. It's making me crazy."

Wanagi Wachi put his hand on my shoulder tenderly, and said, "Good. Now get yourself ready. You have to get out there soon."

What happened over those next days was hard to describe. The heat was intense, even worse than the year before. I knew I had to concentrate on my prayers and meditations, but I also had a new focus. I remembered to pray for all those helping me and for Wanagi Wachi. They were all working in the oppressive heat to help me keep this commitment. I prayed for the mercy of God on us all. I knew that people and spirits were watching over me. If it got too hard, someone would come with a song or medicine to help. I was so sure.

It did get hard and soon became overwhelming. Three days I spent in that heat, and each day grew worse. The middays were silent—not a creature or even an insect moved in the searing heat. From dawn to dusk the air was on fire, and the earth was a bed of coals. I emptied my mind again and again. And I collapsed on the ground again and again.

No one came to help. Wanagi Wachi didn't come to check on me. There was no song, no medicine, no water, and no magic spirit to take away the pain. My only visitors came in the cooler moments of the day at sunrise and sundown: the birds, grasshoppers, and mosquitoes. There was no sign of help; there was only the dry hum of the relentless summer days. All I could do was let go of everything possible, releasing my expectations and distractions. Only prayers, only emptiness of thought, could help. By the end of the second day, it felt like my life was slipping away from my body. I'd never been so empty, so tired.

Somewhere Beyond Yourself

The last night before the third day I wept. Sobbing, I was stunned, and wondered, *How can anything be so hard? Can I last for one more day? Will I go insane or perhaps die? It wasn't supposed to be like this!* However, during the evenings, I saw and felt many things. There were profound moments of clarity and insight, as I felt the presence of The Sacred whispering in my ear . . . until the next day came upon me like a hammer striking me on the head.

I woke to oppressive heat even before the sun was up. *This is it,* I thought. *I have nothing left to give. Wanagi Wachi thinks I can do this. If this is what I'm here to do, then I'll give everything. If God wants me to die this way, then I will die on this hill.*

The sun hit the horizon, and the day roared in like wildfire. I couldn't stand up, so I was slumped over while praying. "Why? Why is it so hard?" I pleaded to God. "Look at the great mystics and masters who survived much worse! Gandhi went 30 days without food, Jesus spent 40 days in the desert, and Mohammed and the Buddha both withstood hardship and tests. Why can I not do this?!"

I fell over and my face hit the dirt. My mouth was so dry that my saliva turned to a cottonlike paste that clung to my lips. I was totally broken and unable to move. I could barely think. The world was silent, within and all around me.

I can't do this, was my final thought. *I just can't do this.*

Then like lightning, something struck me inside. *I* can't do this—"I" am the barrier! As long as I think that I'm alone in this world, that I'm the one who makes things possible, I'll always suffer. The very thought that there's a "me" who's separate from God and Nature is a lie, and that is what's torturing me. I wasn't alone!

I was waking up to the reality that we're never alone; we are, in fact, *all one.* "I" is the ego, the persona that tries to control and judge everything. It's only the persona, the ego, that suffers. Of course "I" couldn't do it. The ego doesn't do anything alone—that's just a way of thinking to make me feel like I was actually in control. I *don't* do this alone; I never have. There were always people helping in all kinds of ways. Friends, family, and spirits assisted and supported me. Only through the grace of God—The Sacred—does anything happen. Nothing is left of me but spirit, and the spirit is never alone. The soul never dies, as it's connected to all things. It's in the hands of God; it's a part of God. The very idea that *I* have to make things happen and *do* something is what gets in my way—not just now, but always!

Somehow the complete collapse of all self-worth, self-concept, and self-control thrust my awareness into a new and soaring state. Heat was just a feeling. Dryness, thirst, and even the aches in my body were just sensations. They would pass. I didn't need to do anything with those feelings; I simply acknowledged them, allowed them, and felt them. Suddenly, I felt a strange comfort emerging, a calm and peace within my broken body. *I am not my body,* I thought. *This is only the vehicle of my spirit. It will be fine again one day.*

A rush of life flowed into me. It was as if I were filled with the Spirit of Creation. I became alert, strong, and awakened. I felt energy everywhere around me and from within. There was no difference between the force of the sun, the growth of the trees, and my own vital force. When I had no more to give, I connected with the only thing I truly am: Spirit.

I stood and began to sing my prayers out loud with joy and gratitude for the invisible web of love and support that carried me throughout my life that I had never truly realized. I cried with joy and gratitude, and prayed with strength until the ceremony came to an end. When I heard the drumbeat in the distance signaling the end, I was filled with a new sadness. I was sad to leave this precious world of Spirit and the awareness of the infinite power in everything. My time had come, and my lesson was clear and complete. The final rituals were carried out, and I climbed into the truck with Wanagi Wachi to head back into town. He never physically visited me during this Hanblecha and never asked how it went. He knew that it was a harder, hotter year than the one before, but he just looked at me with a soft smile in his eyes.

"Now you understand," he said. "You don't need anything because you have it all already. This year was just as hot or more so than the last. *Wakantanka* (God, the Great Mystery) is the only reality. You can fight it and try to control it, but that will only make you suffer. The fight to be separate from God—that is why we suffer. Instead, you can experience it and simply know that you're in a moment of truth. Whether or not it's comfortable, if you release your mind, you'll find that every instant can be such a moment of truth."

That Hanblecha changed my life forever. It was the farthest edge of myself that I'd ever touched, and I couldn't have done it without Wanagi Wachi—without trusting in him, and in his guidance and experience. More than the community, more than the ceremony, and even more than the practice was the bigger context and path that led me safely to my own limits: my total trust in my Lakota father. He wouldn't have liked to be called my guru at the time, but that's what he was, and he guided me from my self to the experience of God within.

One Step Ahead

"Can a blind person guide a blind person? Will not both fall into a pit?"
— Luke 6:39–40

In my use of the term *guru,* I'm referring to master spiritual teachers as the original Sanskrit term implies. I'm not referring solely to Hindu teachers or to those who have devotees and centers. These are Western stereotypes. I'm referring to spiritual leaders whose gifts lie in their depth of knowledge, wisdom, mystical connection, *and* capacity to impart those same things through teachings or systems that they've created. When we look to universal and ancient spiritual practices, we see that the devoted following of a master spiritual teacher appears as a path in itself. This is more than working with a coach or guide; this is a devoted relationship committed to working with a highly advanced teacher who can take us to the edge of our reality and awaken us to the depth of The Sacred.

Years ago I was talking with a Native American man who had known Wanagi Wachi most of his adult life. "You're lucky to have a teacher like that," he said. "It's not that I think he's perfect. Oh, I know he's human like the rest of us, but what makes him such a great teacher is that he can take you beyond yourself and still be one step ahead. My grandpa was a medicine man, and that's what he always told me. You want a teacher who's been down the road that you want to travel—at least as far as he or she is going to take you. I wouldn't trust anyone else." That thought stuck with me and it says something important about the role of a guru.

The word *guru,* common in Eastern traditions, simply refers to a teacher or spiritual guide. In the West, it has come to signify one who is an "expert"; however, today the term is too often said with a sarcastic tone or used to refer to a scandalous sort of cult leader. Understanding a guru (Master Teacher) relationship is difficult for people who are raised seeing the world through the lenses of fear and authority. The very idea of turning over one's spiritual direction wholeheartedly to another seems like madness from that vantage point.

In my personal experience with mentors and through my guru relationship with my Lakota father, I've discovered an extraordinary bond and mutual trust that can exist in the exploration of the self and Spirit. When I first met Wanagi Wachi, I wasn't looking for a teacher or mentor. The relationship came naturally and spontaneously, and it evolved over time. Having a guide allowed me to place my energy in the practices and experiences he introduced me to rather than spending effort on searching, starting over and over again, or trying out different paths.

In this book, I share many practices and experiences that I've tasted and tried, but it was the lasting, profound experience of Wanagi Wachi's traditions and teaching style that made it possible for me to enter the depths of the practices that made the biggest impact on me. He helped me maintain my focus, knew what was next for me, and always kept me working toward my growing edge. That deep discipline gave me the centeredness and groundedness from which to travel and explore without getting lost or distracted along the way.

Stereotypes of dangerous cults and spiritual teachers who take advantage of willing students cloud the ability to see the gift in an authentic guru relationship. Nevertheless, it's absolutely true that some gurus—like many people in positions of authority—have abused their power. Some have been crippled by their popularity, and others have struggled as their shortcomings became exaggerated under increasing opportunity and scrutiny. In a healthy guru-student relationship, none of this is common. The guru will frequently invest and sacrifice as much as the student. It isn't an easy job or relationship for either committed party.

The spiritual journey is complex, including the range of possible experiences, the number of paths available, and all the choices along the way. The role of a guru is to help you simplify the process and focus on the experiences and practices that will be most valuable to you at your current state and stage. Gurus also teach and are like a living spiritual text, bringing inspired wisdom to each question and session of instruction.

Often gurus will focus on the lessons that you experientially learn through spiritual disciplines. Just as in the previous story about my Hanblecha ceremonies, little of the lesson had to do with anything my teacher *said*. Most of my learning came from the experiences he guided me into and the limits he knew he could push. Accordingly, some gurus and students may only see each other once a year, while others may spend extended periods of time together. The guru's presence can be healing and instructive. A great deal can be passed between two people at the level of energy and consciousness.

In some traditions, a guru is to be avoided out of fear of losing focus on the process toward enlightenment. There's an old Buddhist expression that says, "If you meet the Buddha on the road, kill him!" This means that the only source of enlightenment is yourself, and you must remove any distraction or temptation to externalize your wisdom. It's said that the Buddha's own dying words were, "Be a lamp unto yourselves. Be your own Buddha." As with all the Master Paths, the primary concern is fit and function, not choosing the best or "right" path. That is a question of ego and the controlling mind.

Despite these cautions, the role of a spiritual guide, mentor, or master is timeless and essential for many. In fact, numerous Eastern traditions assert that spiritual awakening isn't possible without a guru. In a similar way, many Christian communities believe that people can't go to God directly but need a priest or minister as an intercessor. The term *rabbi* in Judaism means "teacher" or more literally, "my great one," or "my master." The title is much like the term *guru*. Sometimes when we're resistant to the teachings of a spiritual guide, we're reacting to our own fears or to something we've seen that we don't agree with or understand.

Two Guru Types: The Master Teacher and the Divine Incarnation

Looking around the world, we see two main types of guru. First, we have what I call the "teacher-guru," a highly experienced and evolved spiritual teacher to whom you entrust your training and awakening. I refer to the second type of guru as the "Divine-guru," a person you truly believe to be a spiritually extraordinary being or prophet—a direct representative of The Sacred, an incarnation of God. The Pope, Dalai Lama, the Buddha, Mohammed, Jesus, Sai Baba, and Bahaullah of the Baha'i religion are all good examples. The Divine-guru is predominantly found in Hindu and related traditions where practitioners believe that God can actually exist in multiple forms as well as human incarnations. In other cultures, these figures tend to become heads of sects and societies, such as St. Francis and Joseph Smith of the Mormon tradition.

Teacher-guru

Teacher-gurus are accessible and aren't thought to be a Divine incarnation by the community that's dedicated to them. Rather, they're assumed to be spiritually experienced and profoundly spiritually awakened. They may be seen as Divine messengers, but they aren't treated as direct representatives of God.

Some might think of popular modern teachers such as Joel Osteen, Thich Nhat Hanh, Oprah Winfrey, Ram Dass, Andrew Cohen, Thomas Merton, Brother Wayne Teasdale, Wayne Dyer, Marianne Williamson, John Rogers, or Tony Robbins when they hear the word *guru* or think of teacher-gurus. The leaders of many religious groups and personal-growth movements are people who not only offer insight, but also the capacity to harness, share, and amplify their wisdom to the masses. Their gift is usually in close mentoring relationships or the ability to have a lasting impact guiding and instructing large groups.

Divine-guru

It's not uncommon in India to find living saints—that is, individuals who are believed to have been born holy. These people are usually recognized at a young age as having a special connection to The Sacred. They often demonstrate wisdom and supernatural abilities, and naturally become the center of spiritual communities, teachings, and the originators of spiritual practices. Sometimes the division between these two types can be unclear.

My wife went to India and spent a month at the ashram of the renowned gurus Sri Amma and Bhagavan, Master Teachers who are supported and adored by millions of people. They're seen as a single consciousness inhibiting two bodies, transmitting Divine messages and healing power. Like many Divine-gurus, they have huge humanitarian projects, properties, and human movements dedicated to peace on Earth and the unity of all races and cultures. Founders of the global "Deeksha," or oneness blessing phenomena, many have witnessed firsthand their remarkable gifts as teachers, healers, and conduits of tremendous energy. Although my wife went as an invited guest and not a converted follower, she left feeling that there was a true Sacred Presence and Power at work in these people.

My dear friends Jay, a physician, and Natasha, an artist, are well-educated and well-traveled spiritual seekers who've achieved an "advanced" level of spiritual study and maturity. Frequently they go to India to see their guru, Sri Sakthi Amma Narayani, an Indian man in his 30s who was born with special markings and aptitudes that led people to recognize him early in life as a direct incarnation of The Divine. Sri Sakthi Amma Narayani is well known for his clairvoyance, clairsentience, mystical brilliance, and ability to perform miracles—the likes of which my friends have seen in person. He's also the driving force behind a host of hospitals, schools, and community programs that are offsprings of his spiritual organization. The positive impact of this man on millions of people is truly amazing.

Jay and Natasha's involvement with Sri Sakthi Amma Narayani varies from time to time; nevertheless, their love of him has become a channel through which his blessings constantly flow. He's shaped their lives and understanding of The Sacred through direct teachings, and the works of his community, as well as powerful spiritual experiences in his presence. Transformed by this relationship, they remain devoted yet fully conscious of their own autonomy to direct their own lives. Their devotional relationship is intentional and inspired; and there's no coercion, tithing, or force of any kind placed on my friends. They enjoy and benefit from the relationship with little need and complete willingness.

What sets Divine-gurus apart is their unique consciousness, energy, and talents. They typically are people who not only embody a Divine presence, but have been conscious of it throughout their lives and know how to direct their abilities. Divine-gurus usually have a very clear sense of mission and purpose, and accept themselves as Divine prophets or messengers. The cultural response to such people determines how they are received. In the Jewish and Christian traditions, such people are the saints and prophets of the past. The Messiah might fit this category as well. In other traditions where such beings are expected and sought, they would simply be given a revered place among the many Divine-gurus over time.

More Than a Teacher

Despite the examples I provide, it's important to remember that fame and popularity don't define a guru, and in some cases, it may even indicate a lack of credibility. Spiritual teachers such as Wanagi Wachi don't seek public attention or try to build wealth from those who study with them. Fame may or may not follow a guru.

What marks the guru *path* is the nature of the *relationship* between student and teacher. This is a relationship that goes beyond instruction. There's a sharing of energy and intention and a deep love that pervades the connection. I've had many teachers who've inspired me and taught me a great deal, but I wouldn't call them gurus of mine simply because my encounter was brief and the relationship never became intimate in an emotional or spiritual way.

Finding a "true guru" of either type is not always easy. Sometimes you can find a guru in a familiar setting such as in a church or synagogue, or you may receive a recommendation from a friend. Other times, you must expose yourself to a number of teachers by attending lectures, workshops, and classes before you can choose. In most cases, the best gurus arrive unexpectedly.

For me, meeting Wanagi Wachi was a fortunate accident of timing. While in my undergraduate program, it had been recommended that I study his successful work as a counselor who integrates spirituality in his addiction and trauma work. When I set out to meet him, I had no idea that he was a spiritual leader or that he'd eventually become my spiritual father and mentor.

Gurus can be spiritual counselors of one form or another. The distinction lies in their degree of knowledge, experience, and ability to guide a person into direct contact with the Divine and their Divine nature. You might consider them a "master." While I've heard the word *guru* used around the world, I've heard similar and interchangeable words in many cultures, including *master, maestro, sensei, holy man/woman, prophet, lama,* or *avatar.* Even the terms *venerable, reverend,* and *rabbi* have been used to refer to and honor gurus in various cultures.

If you're interested in working with a guru, you'll most likely need to be patient. In the meantime, you may find an excellent soul coach, chaplain, counselor, or spiritual director who can help keep you on track with your other spiritual practices and experiences. Don't let my use of the "foreign term" *guru* throw you off track; your guru could be living next door to you. It's easy to be overcautious in this search, and many discard gurus' teachings in favor of self-instruction. Don't get caught in the trap of resisting teachers because of their egos: you may end up becoming caught up in your own. Even the greatest masters themselves gleaned insight and wisdom from mentors.

PART V

Soul-Centered Practices

It began so innocently
Was it a taste?
A glimpse?
A fragrance on the wind?

Somewhere, somehow we were touched
by something Truly Sacred
It was beauty and bliss
The most intoxicating Essence

It was a knowing so complete
A peace unbelievable
And it drove us into an extraordinary madness
Forsaking everything

Not Death
Nor the breaking of this fragile body
Nor the loss of family or friend mattered
There was nothing left for us in this world

Without It
The haunting call was constant
In sleep, dream, and waking
It drove us from our lives

We took refuge in the Temple
Found Solace in the high caves and cliffs
We lay at the feet of Your Doorways
Burned days and nights like old paper

We gave it all
Until there was nothing left but
The Only Thing There Is

— J. H. Ellerby

Chapter Thirteen

ASCETIC PRACTICES

Only Spirit

My eyes were closed in prayer as my body swayed to the deep drumbeat. Thoughts and emotions were dissolving into a blackness within me. For a moment, I thought I was going to pass out; instead, I opened my eyes. What I saw and felt I will never forget.

The world had become translucent. All things maintained their form and color but somehow gave way to a pure light shining from within. It was almost as if the physical world were the shadow of a more substantial existence—a place of Energy and Light. There are no words to describe the presence of that Light and its blissful, beautiful, sacred quality. It was peace and wisdom, yet nothing was said or thought; there was just the radiance of the world.

I couldn't have imagined a more magnificent experience in such an unlikely time and place. Just when I thought there was nothing left within me, I felt more vital than ever before in my life. Not only did I see and feel the energy of the world around me, but I also knew with certainty that I, too, was only energy. I was a shining soul, a brilliant spirit, radiating through a carriage of skin, bone, and blood.

I could feel my body breathing in sunlight through my skin. The air was rich and sustaining like water, and the earth beneath my feet radiated a life force that was delicious and nourishing. With each step I absorbed more and more energy until I was full. I could feel my body and soul feeding off the life force of the natural world around me: the vibrations of the great drum and the prayers that circled us like butterflies and eagles.

I felt like I was shining—in fact, *everything* was shining. I closed my eyes and sensed the purity of surrender and trust in something greater. Suddenly my mind traveled back in time. I was in northern India when I first saw a Tibetan Buddhist monk in prostration. He stood, raised his arms in prayer, bowed, bent, kneeled, and lay in devotion on the hard earth. His forehead was bloody from the repetition. His hands were padded but still torn. I felt disdain and disgust at the time, but now I saw something different.

Again the scene changed in my inner vision, and I was in Israel silently watching rows of Christian monks in robes passing into a cathedral. Their lives were spent in study and silence, and their rooms were tiny cells. When I first saw this, I was stunned and couldn't understand their strict lifestyle.

My mind continued to fly around the earth. I saw Mexican Christians self-flagellating at Easter and visited ancient times where rabbis were fasting in the desert. I watched Hindu devotees pierce the skin on their cheeks, chests, and backs. And that scene turned to Zen Buddhist monks sitting nonstop for hours at a time that turned into days—doing nothing but endlessly sitting, sitting, sitting.

I saw the deep compassion in the eyes of a Venda African healer I once met and felt the *years* she spent living alone in a cave. (I've known many such healers who lived for weeks or months isolated from others. In Peru, a great spiritual healer I spent a few weeks with told me of the month he wandered the jungle with no food or shelter; he only had water, prayer, and the simplest clothing.)

Everywhere my awareness traveled, I saw myriad examples of the deep practice of ascetics. Originally, I'd feared and judged practitioners of this Master Path. Although I knew not all could have walked with purest intent or heart and some must have chosen extreme rituals to satisfy their egos, I somehow could go beyond that and witness their unfathomable longing for The Sacred.

I understood the depth of longing, the promise of one precious moment that would change everything. It required a choice that would seem irrational to most people. Yet there in the moment, I knew that I was, am, and will ever be nothing more or less than spirit moving toward Spirit.

🜨 🜨 🜨

It had been three full days since I'd had anything to eat or drink, but I felt more full of health and life force than ever before. I'd been active in the ceremony from sunup to sundown each day, and there was one more day left to go. It was nothing like the painful hours of meditation in northern India or the sleepless ritual dances of Africa, nor was it like the Hanblecha (Vision Quest) or wilderness fasts I'd experienced in the past.

The *Wiwangwacipi,* the Sundance ceremony of the Lakota Sioux, was very different from anything else I'd experienced in the world. Over the years, I'd attended more than a few traditional Sundance ceremonies and was also a helper at a large one in western South Dakota. Every experience was a part of my preparation, yet in the very depth of that ritual, I'd encountered a moment unlike any other.

Wiwangwacipi is an ancient Lakota Sioux ceremony that marries all of the most profound and central elements of Lakota spiritual life into one amazing, radiant community event. The Sundance ceremony incorporates nearly all of the 12 Master Paths but focuses on the ascetic practices of the Sundancers. At the heart of the Sundance is a four-day ceremony of dance, prayer, purification, and self-sacrifice. The greater community ceremony lasts at least 12 days (or more, depending on the community), and practitioners may be involved in a variety of important ways.

In the central four days of the Sundance, men and women make a commitment to fast from food, water, and social contact for a period of one to four days. This is typically expected to repeat over four years. My commitment, for example, was to dance for four days each year for four years. Many of the Sundance leaders in my community had made four-day commitments for more than 12 years in a row.

During the period of fasting, the time is spent in a prayerful ritual dance that follows a sacred pattern. Sundancers follow the movement of the sun through the sky—from the time it rises until after it sets. In many ceremonies, there are also special rituals in which some of the dancers will make sacrifices that involve piercing and tearing their skin. (The details regarding this practice are considered deeply sacred and private. I won't recount this dimension in any more detail, but it may be further researched in the writings of Thomas Mails.) Each Sundance is different, and significant variations in practices are found. I can only describe the essence of the Sundances that I participated in.

The event always takes place outside in a wilderness area. A large clearing is found or made, and an enormous circular shade structure is set up. The center is open to the sun. From above, it looks like a great hoop: a ring that's open in the middle. The ring of shade is usually only about six to ten feet wide. The structure, called an arbor, can be anywhere from 40 to 100 feet across or more, depending on the size of the ceremony and number of dancers. Most of the arbor is open to the sky.

Sections of the arbor are marked with sacred colors and ritual objects in order to honor and evoke spiritual power, creating an energy of potential and protection. Every aspect of the ceremony has meaning, intent, and spiritual purpose. In fact, the inner arbor is a giant altar—a gateway to the Spiritual World—and only dancers and purified healers and helpers may enter. There are special times when community members are brought in for healing and blessings; otherwise, they sit and stand under the shade structure, offering supportive prayers and meditations.

The great hoop of the arbor delineates the sacred grounds, and large camps are established. On one side, the dancers have a space that's secluded from all human contact aside from helpers, ceremonial leaders, and other dancers. Men and women sleep in separate quarters in tents and tepees, and the only amenities are the bedrolls that people bring and portable toilets. A sacred fire that burns throughout the entire ceremony guards the dancers' site and heats the stones for the frequent Inipis (Sweat Lodges). On the other side of the arbor, far away from the dancers, supporters erect tents and tepees and set up camps. At a distance, a cook shack is built to feed the many workers and individuals who come to pray and ask for healing through the power of the event.

At the center of the great hoop stands a single tall cottonwood tree that has been placed in the ground by people in the community, Sundancers, and supporters. Around it the earth is clear and typically just grass covered. The Sacred Tree becomes the axis of the ceremony. A sort of spiritual anchor and antenna, it holds the prayers, guides the energy of the ceremony, and watches over the dancers. A tree might be picked for this role months or even a year before the ceremony begins. Prayer flags of blue, green, black, red, yellow, and white are tied up the length of the tree before it's erected in the center of the circle. There's amazing beauty and vibrancy at the sight of a Sundance ceremony.

Our days began long before sunup with an Inipi ceremony, and then we entered the sacred altar—the inner arbor—in a ritual procession at sunrise. The dancers wore simple outfits in the colors that marked the sacred directions: men were dressed in only a kind of ankle-length skirt, and women donned a simple one-piece cotton dress. Everyone was barefoot. Humility and simplicity are essential in a Sundance ceremony.

We moved to the rhythm of the large buffalo drum, pounded in unison by male singers of mixed Native heritage. The "dance" is a manner of moving on the spot, which looks much like walking in place. This was done to the beat of the deep drum and kept alive by local and visiting male drum groups all day long. Often female singers, who were mostly Lakota and Dakota, gathered around to support the effort. People had traveled from other communities and nations to join in and offer their assistance, including Nakota, Anishinabe, and Menominee.

After sundown and throughout the night, we participated in Sweat Lodge ceremonies; received teachings from our spiritual leaders; and reflected, prayed, and slept. Sundancers accept an intense and difficult time of sacrifice, deprivation, and focused prayer. At times, it seems that an inhuman strength and faith is required. Although the dancers give deeply of themselves in a humble and profound way, it must be acknowledged that everyone involved in the ceremony makes sacrifices.

All those who help give deeply, including the fire keepers, singers, cooks, security, ceremonial leaders, and the numerous other roles that are necessary to conduct such a ceremony. These jobs require time, energy, and long hours. None of this work is paid, and the days are strenuous and spent outside in the elements. Before it even takes place, many people work throughout the year organizing and planning, while others work long hours preparing the grounds. A great dedication, devotion, and love is required to run a ceremony like this. Every single aspect relies on all others; every single person relies on each other.

Over the years of helping out at Sundances, I've seen many people face the very limits of their bodies, minds, and hearts. I've witnessed grown men crying uncontrollably, people passing out, and some becoming violently ill. I've observed the most profound acts of kindness and love, as well as the rage of the ego and controlling mind. The fullness of the human experience is at work in the Sundance: all that we think of as human and as Divine.

One year I was helping Wanagi Wachi at a Sundance in another community that took place during a heat wave where the temperature reached 119 degrees Fahrenheit. Supporters and helpers suffered greatly, and the Sundancers seemed to be tortured. Having grown up in a home where I never knew hunger and in a society where people always sought comfort, I struggled to understand what the possible value of enduring such pain could be. I couldn't fully grasp the power of an ascetic practice at that time in my life.

My spiritual father and teacher saw the sadness and confusion on my face. In the shade of a stand of trees during a break, we sat in silence. The heat was thick in the air and nothing moved. As always, he read my thoughts and started speaking.

"Everyone is here by choice. No one is ever forced or obliged to make such a sacrifice. The commitment is between each dancer and the Creator. Only they know why they dance, and only they know in their heart what they're truly praying for—what they're letting go of or asking for. Some dance for loved ones who are sick; others are sick in one way or another and pray for healing. This can seem strange or cruel if you look with the eyes of the ego. But if you see with the Spirit, you see only energy changing form. You see death and rebirth.

"Everything that people strive to be—strong, happy, clean, comfortable, perfect in the eyes of others—is willingly given up in this ceremony. Anything that clings to the ego will be torn away, and it will hurt if you don't voluntarily let it go. What you hold on to will hold on to you. It will become the burden you carry. In a ceremony such as this, you'll feel the full weight of who you think you are and experience the implications of your actions and choices.

"But if you release the ego, let go of your attachments, and surrender to what is in the moment, you'll find a place within you that you never knew. If you live your prayers and don't hold anything back from *Wakantanka* (God) then *Wakantanka* won't hold anything back from you. In this community, surrounded by your relatives, you'll tap into true *Wowasake* (inner strength). When you have nothing left to give, you'll experience yourself as a part of *Woniyelawoablezyeya*: the collective awareness of breath, life, and interrelationships. You'll understand why we say *Mitakuye oyasin* (We are all related).

"In that moment, you will be nothing and everything. The Sacred World is real, and you'll know it. You'll be more than who you ever thought you were and more humble, more grateful, than ever before."

Wanagi Wachi often spoke in riddles and paradoxes, but I felt that I clearly understood what he meant. They were profound thoughts to me, but they were just thoughts—a good philosophy.

He smiled as if he knew what I was thinking and said, "One day you'll know what I mean."

RETURN TO THE SACRED

It wasn't until years later, while standing in the light of the full sun, that I recalled his words as tears of joy ran down my face. In that moment, I knew he was right. When you have nothing left—not even the desire to be someone—that is when you'll realize that you already have everything you need. The truth of who you are is deeper than anything that has ever been said or done to you. You are not your body; you are a soul.

When There's Nothing Left to Give

"He fasted for forty days and forty nights,
and afterward he was famished. Then the devil left him,
and suddenly angels came and waited on him."
— Matthew 4:2, 11

To *feel* that you're a soul and *see* the world from that place within allows you to perceive the soul of all things. It's healing and transforming. When you release your ordinary way of being, you encounter a spiritual way of seeing. Ascetic practices, such as the examples described in this chapter and the previous one, are radical in what they ask for as well as in what they give.

Ascetic practices are soul-centered; their intention and foundation is The Sacred. People who participate in asceticism desire profound experiences of The Sacred—real, direct, unmistakable encounters. Many of the modern motivations for spirituality fall away when faced with an ascetic path. The deepest intent in this practice isn't stress management, happiness, or manifesting goals. All of these things may result through ascetic practice, and the benefits of such experiences can be incredible; however, that isn't the essence of this Master Path. Healthy asceticism is about touching the Spirit.

The word *ascetic* originates from a Greek term that simply refers to any disciplined practice. Ascetic practices and asceticism have come to refer to spiritual pursuits that involve extreme deprivation, renunciation, or abstinence from common daily comforts and necessities. An ascetic practice is one that typically rejects ordinary behaviors in order to contemplate the spiritual and metaphysical. Like the Sundance, ascetic practices can have community dimensions, healing functions, and many other layers. It's not just about suffering or harsh purification.

One of the great benefits of this practice lies in its potency. Radical actions often spark radical shifts in awareness and identity, which can have a dramatic and lasting impact on the practitioner. When guided safely, integrated well, and embraced with complete release of persona and ego attachment, an ascetic practice will change your life forever.

The challenge throughout history, naturally, is meeting all these important criteria. Often ascetic practices aren't conducted safely; many aren't integrated well; and people of all cultures have abused them with agendas of glory, escape, or masochism. This is *not* the beauty of the ascetic path. Be curious and open, but remain cautious when exploring ascetic practices.

Strange but True

If we search the world over, we find that most religious and spiritual traditions reject or discourage ascetic practices. In most cases the rationale is to protect seekers and affirm the sacredness of the human body—meaning that it's not to be abused. I suspect that another reason that these practices are restricted has something to do with the fear of radical behavior and activities that aren't easily managed among the masses.

Spiritual leaders have a far easier job when their community members simply trust in their guidance and don't seek direct knowledge themselves. Ascetic practices frequently provide an experience so powerful that individuals may feel an independence from their spiritual teachers and communities. This can threaten the ego of the community or indulge the ego of the seeker. It's a precarious path to travel. The motives vary, but the religious rejection of ascetic practices is common.

Ironically, we find that the saints, sages, and masters who gave birth to many of our revered traditions were actually influenced by ascetic practices, and the experiences that came from them essentially shaped modern-day practices. Virtually all the great masters—including Jesus, Mohammed, Moses, the Buddha, Guru Nānak, Bahaullah, and Black Elk—either chose to engage in ascetic-like events or were thrust into them, resulting in a pivotal shift in consciousness.

The ascetic path may involve short periods of extreme deprivation, but it may also involve longer periods of less intense renunciation. I recently met a woman who studied in Tibet with a small community of ascetic Buddhist monks. This bright young business owner recalled her time with strong affection.

"I spent a few months living alone in a cave," she said grinning. "The cave was an ancient place of fasting and meditation. There was a bed inside, a light, a fireplace, and a door. There were many other little caves like this in the area. It was a community of teachers and students; there were about 20 other people there."

I asked if it was scary or dangerous.

"No, not physically dangerous. We shared a local well with clean water, and we were fed. We had just enough to eat each day. We weren't overfed, but we weren't hungry. The senior monks didn't really teach in the normal sense; rather, they supervised. We had all taken a vow of silence, but there were certain times and places where we could talk if we needed help. Otherwise, I spent the vast majority of those months in silence, meditating in a cave."

It sounded absurd to me at the time, but she smiled so warmly as she recollected her experience, saying, "Actually, it was the best time of my life."

While I would never say that this is necessary or the "best" path for everyone, ascetic practice should be considered by the serious seeker. The most critical element is to find a teacher or community where the practice is supported in a healthy and healing way. *Be very careful* if you seek this path and wish it to complement or become a central part of your journey.

There are monasteries and religious schools in all traditions that would host you for a time, as well as contemporary organizations that will guide you on a wilderness quest. Healing centers, Zen retreats, and New Age detoxification programs would likely create an arrangement where you could live in seclusion for a period of time. If you choose to do so, find a guide or coach to help you on this path.

Chapter Fourteen

THE DEATH PRACTICE

The Great Passage

It was a strange dream. I was a baby buffalo, and my dad was a large adult buffalo. We were in the den of the home that I grew up in—a sitting room with a wall of books. As I child, I rarely played in this room because there were too many "nice" things that could be knocked over. As a buffalo, it seemed extraordinarily odd to be in this room of fragile keepsakes. I was a bull in a china shop!

When I saw my father, I was struck by how much larger and older he was than I. He was clearly a bull buffalo. Immediately, I could see that he was aging. His faced seemed weathered, his mane was gray in places, and his mouth was foaming white at the edges. This seemed unusual to me since my dad, who was 64 years old at the time, was as healthy as ever.

Suddenly, the big buffalo (my dad) began storming around the room. He was on top of the coffee table acting as if he'd gone insane. He raged and fought what seemed to be an inner battle, as if his insides were on fire. Then I woke up.

The dream still lingered in my mind as I headed off to school that morning, but I didn't tell anyone about it. At the time, I was completing an honors undergraduate degree with the University of Regina and the Saskatchewan Indian Federated College. I hadn't seen my parents in a month or so. They lived in Manitoba, the next province over. Although the feelings of the vision haunted me, I couldn't figure out what the dream meant.

Later the next day, I was on my way home from classes and stopped at the university bookstore. I'd ordered a set of anatomical charts of the brain that physicians use in training, and I'd received a message that they were ready to be picked up. (I was taking a class in consciousness studies and wanted to better understand the dimensions of the brain. I was fascinated by neuroscience and its relationship to spiritual growth.) After collecting the charts, I stopped by the hospital on the way home.

I'd recently begun a palliative (hospice) care, spiritual counseling internship with Dan, the head chaplain, and needed to check in with him about my program. He'd agreed to be my mentor in order to help me complete my requirements for the Interfaith seminary program that I was enrolled in. The focus of my training and work was counseling individuals and families on the units where people's illnesses or diseases were "terminal." After a brief visit, I headed home.

Setting my books on the kitchen table, I checked my messages and heard an urgent call from my mom, who wanted me to call her right away. The intensity of her voice on the answering machine was in the room with me. Something in my stomach dropped, and a sense of knowing what was next grew as I dialed the familiar number. The dream of the buffalo flashed through my mind, and I heard a voice in my head like a thought: *Prepare yourself. Dad is sick; it's serious.* As the phone rang I sat down and pulled out the brain charts I'd just bought that day. My mom answered the phone.

Through tears she explained that my dad had had a seizure that morning and had been taken to the hospital. By the afternoon, they'd already completed a CAT scan and found him to be in the advanced stages of lung and brain cancer. As she described where the lesions were located in the brain, according to the doctor, I followed with ease as I looked at the charts before me.

The diagnosis wasn't good. He was told that he might have anywhere from six months to a year to live. Even though my dad seemed to be in good health, he was riddled with cancer, and his doctor wanted to start chemotherapy and radiation very soon. I was 22 at the time. It was the saddest news I'd ever received, yet somehow I felt prepared for it. The dream suddenly made sense; it was the heavy feeling I'd carried around all day, thinking of my father as the sick buffalo as I watched helplessly. I felt prepared for what was to come. Later that week I saw Dan, my spiritual-care mentor, and told him the news of my dad's illness and impending death.

Dan was silent for a moment. He consoled me and then paused as if listening to something far off.

"Well," he began slowly, "when students are learning to counsel people who are facing death, and they find out that someone in their family is dying, we tend to encourage them to step out of the program or shift to another area of work. There can be too much pain and confusion, and it's often just easier to keep it all separated."

I was saddened by this statement. I wanted to continue in my learning, now more than ever.

"But," he continued, "sometimes, people can do this. In fact, for some, doing this work is just what they need. If you choose to stay, I'll support you. This could be a very powerful time in your life. There's no greater teacher than death. If you can face its sorrow and finality with an open heart, it will be your greatest teacher. It's the one thing we all have to face. Every one of us."

Intuitively, I knew right away that this was a path I needed to take. It seemed strange, but I wanted to be around death and dying. I wanted to know what everyone was afraid of; I wanted to know if it was painful. I wanted to find out if my beliefs and spiritual life would thrive or wither when confronted with life's greatest passage.

My program ended seven months later, and it was an amazing journey. I'd sat with many people during their last days, and on a few occasions, I had been there with them and their families at the very end when they left this world. Death was rarely scary, painful, or violent. It wasn't always ideal or in the ways people had expected, but ultimately, it was simple and natural. There was something easy about death. Dying and grieving weren't so easy for those who were left behind, but death itself was effortless, like an autumn leaf letting go in the fall wind.

The people I met who had terminal conditions taught me everything that I needed to know about death *and* life. Some were angry and confused, full of doubt or fear. From them I learned the poison of regret and self-doubt. They taught me to live as if every day were my last. Emotions that were never expressed haunted people. Religious fear of sin and judgment tormented people. The hard desire for control, wealth, and longevity was crushed by the finality and inevitability of death.

Death was extreme and simple in its teaching. It made it very clear to me that the real fear in people had little to do with death itself. The issue was always how they lived. Many died as they lived: happy people remained optimistic, and angry people stayed bitter. Most came to realize the lessons of death before it was too late: stay focused on the present, love all you can, make a positive difference every chance you get, look for the lessons life is bringing to you, and let go of control. Any attitude or approach other than this just makes dying harder and more painful.

More often than the miserable and confused, I met people who were calm, good-humored, and at peace. Some had always been like that, I suppose. Many were grateful to their illness for helping them realize what matters most in life. These were the individuals who found healing, even in the face of death, and these people were healers to everyone they met. Facing death challenged and vanquished the ego. The false aspects of their persona had been released; and they quickly learned to let go of anger, judgment, and control. They firmly held on to openness, humor, and kindness; and they made the most of the time they had with the important people around them.

Wherever people were open to the wisdom of death, I saw them fully enjoying life. The nurses, doctors, and support staff in hospice and palliative care were among the most amazing individuals I'd ever known. They were somehow more "real"—more humanistic and openhearted. They were people who lived with a conscious connection to the heart. It was as if the presence of death had cultivated kindness and a genuine quality of love and sincerity in each. I recall feeling the changes in myself as I began to feel gratitude for my time on Earth and each and every relationship that was important to me. It was hard to take life for granted. Any amount of life is a gift.

At the end of those seven months, I finished up my program and school for the year. Since all of my work was at the university as a tutor and Native language instructor, everything came to a natural conclusion in the spring, and I was free to head back to Winnipeg and my parents. At that time, my dad's health began to quickly decline, so I packed my belongings and moved back home to live with my mom and dad.

When I arrived at the house where I grew up, I found that the den had been converted into a hospital room for my father. A special bed had been put in since he no longer had the motor skills or strength to climb the stairs to his bedroom of the previous 27 years. I found him filled with illness and confined to the den—just as in the dream. It was sad yet somehow perfect.

Every day in those last months, I sat with my dad. We talked as much as he had strength for, and then when he was tired, I just spent time with him. Soon he lost his ability to speak but remained conscious and clear in his mind. I read him books that he liked or the news. I sat and watched television with him, and sometimes just sat in the room while he fell asleep at night. It was peaceful and quiet.

During his life, my dad, as I knew him, wasn't very emotionally expressive or at all interested in spirituality. He was interested in the business world and politics and had dedicated his time to his own business and our family. His main concerns were simple: if our family was well looked after and he could walk our dogs or spend time in nature, it was enough for him. He didn't express or articulate emotion well, but I knew he loved us all very deeply. In the days before he lost his speech, we didn't share great philosophy or wise conversations about life. We just spent time together. That was enough: he wanted me there, and I wanted to be there with him.

My mom, brother, sister, and I remained mutually supportive and closely connected throughout his journey. Certain relatives and special friends also stayed close and loving. Other friends and family grew no closer, and some even grew more distant. My mom carried the bulk of his caregiving and medical responsibilities, and to be forgotten or left out by some old friends and relatives was wounding for her. Having heard many similar stories in the hospital, it was not surprising to me. In my training, I'd come to understand that the way people deal with dying loved ones frequently has little to do with the sick person or family, and mostly to do with themselves. Death holds up a mirror to the heart and soul, and many are afraid to look.

As my dad drew closer to the end of his days, I spent more time in prayer and meditation and also studied spiritual texts. I was reading the Bhagavad Gita, an ancient and central Hindu text, and was trying to keep my focus on the mystical teachings of transcendence. "Fear not what is not real, never was and never will be. What is real, always was and cannot be destroyed," says the Gita. As I reviewed the mystical texts of other traditions, the reminder was everywhere: the most important things don't die. Every day I held the thought: *we are not our bodies.*

In the last weeks, it was frequently as if "he" was no longer there. The body was taking its time winding down, withering away. But his soul seemed free. It came and went from his body, often hovering just above like a ghost. Naturally, such a claim can be contested by anyone who has never seen or felt such a thing, and it's never been my intent to convince anyone of this movement of the soul. I've met many others—spiritual teachers, healers, nurses, and even a few doctors—who agreed that the essential self, or soul, has the ability to begin to depart even before the body has shut down. It was amazing to be so close to this dance.

One afternoon a strange thing happened. My mom and I were sitting in the backyard, and the family dog began barking and looking up at the roof. There on the roof right above the room where my dad was resting was a peacock! Not only had we *never* seen a wild or loose peacock in our residential neighborhood in Winnipeg, but this one was on our roof—specifically above my dad. It was plain as day for everyone to see.

My mom turned to me and said, "What do you think that means?"

I felt my reply first, and then replied, "I think this is the end. In some traditions, many believe that a messenger may come from the Spirit World to prepare the family and watch over the soul of the passing. It could be today, but in Native American cultures, many things happen in fours. So maybe we'll see four signs, or maybe he'll pass over in four days."

The peacock stayed on the roof for the next 24 hours. Four days later, my father passed over.

The One Sure Thing

Death is beautiful. In the modern world, this perspective is hard to accept. We live our lives driven by the desire for beauty, longevity, material gain, and control. Real death is hidden from view. We can turn on any television and see birth, sex, violence, illness, fame, wealth, and age. The death we see is false and is played out in a strange drama. Too often the "bad guys" in a film are discarded like trash, as the hero kills without remorse or grief. Computer games splatter blood and add points with each death! The occasional television series grabs at ratings with a dramatic death scene as the season ends. There's nothing normal about death anymore. The poignant portrayals exist, but they're few and far between.

When my father died at home, we followed the standard protocol: called the doctor for the pronouncement and the funeral home to come get the body. I made sure that we waited before calling the funeral home though. I wanted to be with my dad; I wanted to be with his body that had journeyed 67 years on Earth. It carried his soul, day in, day out. His hands, his brain, his heart—they worked to give life to me and my family. How could we just turn away so that the bed could be emptied and our discomfort lifted? For many, the time of death is "too hard" to see, "too hard" to bear so they avoid it and turn away.

After the body is removed, the room is cleaned, and the funeral ends, life will eventually snap back into place. No one at the grocery store will know what's in your heart, and no one at work will see your sadness. No one will ask you to give voice to the words you haven't found yet. Death opens a precious door to honor life, to honor yourself, and to call upon the presence of The Sacred. Don't let that door close if it has opened for you. In such times we find healing through feeling.

After tears and prayers, we prepared my dad to be taken away. I helped dress him in clothes that would give him the dignity he always tried to live with. It didn't matter that he was to be cremated. The trip to the funeral home would be his last, and we'd make sure it would be a good one.

🪲 🪲 🪲

Wherever in the world families care for their aging and ill family members at home, there's no hiding death. And where families are expected to be a part of the preparation of the body or the funeral ceremony, there's no way to avoid it. After you're born, there's only one experience that everyone is assured to have without exception: death. Don't fear what makes you human. Don't be afraid of the passage that will reunite you with the Great Mystery that gave you life.

The path of death, or the "death practice," is about intentionally being with death and dying. In some traditions, the role is highly ritualized. There are people trained and prepared spiritually to assist with death and dying, yet there are other ways to walk this mighty Master Path. Volunteer at a hospice, train as a chaplain, or go fearlessly to the bedside of friends and family members when they're ill and aging. Let your heart open even when you feel like running or resisting. All you have to do is learn how to stay vulnerable and compassionate. Be present without judgment, and meditate on death.

The death practice asks you to love the mystery, face the reality, honor The Sacred, and look for the lessons. It doesn't want you to enjoy illness or accidents, and it's not about encouraging diseases or violence. Rather, the death practice is about holding a space that's clear and holy for another person to do the work necessary in order to make the Great Transition.

When we sit close to a person passing, we feel the supremacy of death, and wish it upon no one. It reminds us to celebrate life—not just the lives of those we know or favor. Death teaches us to honor all life.

Training helps with this, as well as reading authors such as Stephen Levine or receiving guidance from a mentor. Most of all, being human, being natural, and being honest is all you need to do. The greatest healers and helpers I've known who work with the dying aren't all brilliant teachers. They don't all have wisdom to share or techniques to make the struggle easier. They come simply with unconditional love for the soul in transition and a deep respect for the sacred forces that are at work.

Being close to death is being close to The Sacred. Some souls already see the other side as death grows near. As some people approach death, they move into spiritual experiences of all kinds—from simple contentment to the extremes of bliss and enlightenment. Sometimes ancestors visit; at times God speaks. A purity of consciousness grows. Inexplicable events and experiences become ordinary. All this is available to the dying and to those committed to learning from death.

The death practice isn't complex, but requires intent, courage, and compassion. In the presence of death, we realize the precious gift of creation. We live with gratitude and begin to honor all of life. This practice reveals the places within us that thrive on attachment and control. Death shocks us quickly so that we see what doesn't matter and what is most precious. Anything that isn't of the soul is released, for death offers us clarity. The beautiful journey of death unveils all that is eternal. In it we find The Sacred, the majesty of life, the power of the Spirit, and endless love within each of us. In death, we find life.

Death of Awareness, Birth of Spirit

The city of Varanasi, India—also known as Kashi or Benares—has been a renowned holy place of pilgrimage for thousands of years, and that's what drew me there years ago. The chance to fulfill an ancient contract to pray by the waters of the great Ganges River had haunted me since I'd first read the Upanishads as a young teenager.

Much of the religious and spiritual activities in Varanasi focus on the Ganges. The sacred *Ganga* is a Divine feminine force, a Goddess to many. The water has the power to cleanse the spiritual body, removing sin, healing illness, and bestowing blessing. Many of the ancient scriptures describe how the Ganges carried the blessings from the feet of Lord Vishnu. This is why some call this sacred river *Vishnupadi,* which means "emanating from the lotus feet of the Supreme Lord Vishnu." Throughout my travels in northern India, it was difficult to lose awareness of Mother Ganga, for it seemed that so many sacred sites and pilgrim paths were known in relationship to the river. She is the guiding light and sustainer of many paths and practices.

While staying in Varanasi, I used to spend the better part of my days wandering the banks of the Great Mother. At the edge of Ganga were temples, guest houses, and *ghats*—wide carved stone steps leading down to the water. Her banks were teeming with life and rituals. Wandering holy men, *sadhus,* chanted and taught; individuals and families came to pray; and in certain designated areas were the "burning ghats," the areas where the bodies of the deceased were carefully placed and ceremonially cremated in an open fire. The remaining ashes were poured into the river, releasing them into the embrace of the Holy Mother. To be burned at the holy ghats by the Ganges is to advance the soul toward its release from the cycles of birth and death. It liberates the soul.

This trip came after my father's death and my work with dying people and their families. I couldn't help but feel an attraction to the fierce beauty of death. It had taught me so much, and I went humbly toward it again. Through death, I've learned a great deal about life, so I was naturally attracted to the burning ghats and spent a lot of time at Manikarnika, one of the most revered and popular cremation sites.

One day I arrived at the end of a cremation ceremony. The family, dressed in beautiful colors and cuts of clothing, were preparing to leave the area. As they left, I settled into a place to meditate and pray on top of a low wall that bordered the area. I made myself comfortable as I'd planned to rest there for a while. I closed my eyes and took a deep breath. I inhaled the strangely soothing and almost sweet smoldering scent of burned wood and floral offerings mixing with the unusual odor of human remains. Quickly, the scent of jasmine, rose, and other incense overcame the aroma. Intoxicating fragrances were sailing in from various homes, temples, and nearby markets. My eyes were still closed as images of flowers blossoming, scenes from ancient ceremonies, and sacred rites poured out in a kaleidoscope of color in my inner vision.

In the distance I heard the faint buzz and hum of rickshaws, mopeds, bells, and old diesel trucks. The vibration of life heightened my senses. A wave of sound poured over: human chatter, sacred chanting on a loud speaker somewhere, and dance music on a radio in a shop. Master of it all, the gentle song of the river whispered nearby as she washed the shore and played with the boats that crossed her expanse. Here there was no need for prayer or meditation; I only needed to open my senses. Life was prayer; becoming absorbed in the drama was a meditation.

I realized that a new family was arriving with a body to cremate. Ritual attendants and young assistants had been preparing a pyre right before me, and I hadn't noticed with my eyes closed and senses so absorbed. The priest led the way as helpers and family members followed. The body was carried on a narrow wooden platform, well wrapped in beautiful white fabric and modestly draped with flowers. The women followed in a rainbow of color and cloth. I watched the entire ceremony that day, which may be the only time I'd seen one from beginning to end.

It seemed like a long process, and much of the afternoon had passed. Toward the end, in my recollection, most of the family had left, and the funeral pyre was burning down in size and intensity.

I could still discern certain body parts; in particular, a portion of the skull was visible to me. Strangely, I felt a mix of emotions—an unfamiliar sight yet also a warm growing sense of peace. The simplicity of life was relieving. In the end, we are all fragile. The body returns to the earth, and our time is complete—no matter how long or short. I focused my attention on that vision and held the fragility of life in my heart and mind.

This, too, is me, I thought. *We'll all pass in time. The body is a vehicle for all of that which we truly are: spirit and soul. The only fear we feel in facing death arises when we cling to the illusion that this life has any permanence. We become attached and addicted to the stories and meaning we've created in our lives and refuse to see the immense story that we're all a part of. It's a story that never dies. The persona and ego we've identified with all of our lives begin to diminish, and rather than embracing the brilliant eternity within, many grasp and cling to the past.*

Cut off from a connection to a greater power, cut off from God, The Sacred, and the Divine Energy of the world, fear and resistance to death naturally emerge. For death steals away all that we think we possess. In truth, our lives are tremendously meaningful but not because of anything we do or any role we play. Life is meaningful because we're all a part of an infinite mystery, a sacred expression that unites us. We are co-creators of this universe, a part of The Sacred. We're unique reflections of God and the shining facets of the only thing that exists—all waves, upon one ocean. There isn't a single moment when the wave is separate from its origin—only that it thinks it is so. The crest and fall of a wave isn't a loss, but a return to its source and nature. So, too, are we expressions of the Sacred Origin. That fact alone is miraculous, amazing, and empowering.

There's nothing that we need to do to be sacred or important; it's our natural condition. Death reveals the false things we become attached to and shows us what matters most. Death only brings us closer to the Source of All; it lifts the veil between us and the force that is our life and importance.

🜨 🜨 🜨

I opened my eyes, and the thoughts subsided. Exhaling deeply, I closed them once again. I don't remember my next breath.

In an instant I lost myself, unexpectedly and completely. It was as if I were swimming in a still pool, released my breath, and slipped below the surface. What remained was only a vast awareness: no self, body, time, space, or object of attention . . . no thoughts, but a deep, open awareness. It contained no subjects or edges and no patterns or messages. There was only a presence and a feeling, and no separation between the presence and myself. There was no self or self-awareness, only a subtle feeling.

Looking back, I can say that this experience was without form of any kind: no objects, images, or concrete subjects. Much like some of my other mystical moments, all senses and solidity to who "I" am vanished. Yet there was something distinct about this experience: an overwhelming feeling that I'd dissolved into a pure energy of Love. This was more than limitless or unconditional, and it wasn't a love "for" anything, since in that moment there was no "thing" to love. Radiant and eternal, it was an experience of love's implicit essence and existence.

There at the edge of the burning ghats, the world dissolved into one dark expanse, and there was an endless and boundless feeling of what I can only call "creative force." It felt like love and joy infused with the power to create and destroy. It was like being blind in the depths of the ocean but also aware of the tide and currents. In this world, there's a vital impulse, a flowing force of change that emerges from the complete nonphysical, unformed depths of The Sacred; and this, too, is God. This is the dimension of God that breathes at the edge of creation—call it what you like. This is a truth that lies beyond words; a place where the mind can't enter. Even explaining it can't impart its truth.

Impossible as it may sound, this moment that was so empty of thought or self carried wisdom, a deeper glimpse into the depth and nature of The Sacred. Without ideas, I understood implicitly that all life, rhythms, and matrixes of power and matter emerge from this realm of pure creative potential and imperceptible movement. Even the Divine Energy, united and subtle in its features, is

RETURN TO THE SACRED

a circus of complexity and diversity in contrast to this moment of undifferentiated unity.

In such moments, we see behind all levels of the created world and feel the vibration of the Creator Force. We enter a domain where only The Sacred, only God, remains. This isn't the place of "God," the discerning, wise being; this is God beyond form or energy. This isn't the realm of spirits or angels; it's not a place of "things" of any kind. There's no "this" or "that" in such a moment, yet it's immense and full of a profound Love that permeates all. Some might say that experiencing the Divine Energy is like knowing the mind of God. If so, then to know this moment of Formless Spirit is to know the heart of God.

The Formless Spirit shows us a depth of The Sacred that has no features that can be grasped with the eye or mind. The heart remains the only manner of perception. Our identification with this dimension of God is so total and complete that the sense of self is immediately obliterated. There's a complete loss of ego and concept of self. There's no body, mind, or awareness. Even the idea of "God" seems absurd; and the convention, limits, and concepts all fall short of what this experience reveals.

The Formless Spirit is beyond death, before life, and within life; it's the creative impulse of the universe. In that moment, I *was* the creative impulse and felt the cycle in which death and life dissolve into one. I was one with the Force of Life and knew it to be my origin, my innermost soul, and my destination. It is the Formless Spirit behind all things, giving endless birth and uniting all things in it. When our awareness rests in The Sacred, we understand what it means to be eternal and see that death is an illusion—it's just a shift in energy and perception.

🏵 🏵 🏵

The sound of children laughing and playing nearby suddenly pulled my awareness back to my physical body. I was light-headed for a moment and felt like a stone—slow, ancient, timeless. My mind remained still. Not the least bit sleepy, I felt calm, as if I could sit for a thousand years.

But the ordinary world reached for me, and I suddenly felt a sharp pain in my leg from sitting for so long in one position. The pain came as a surprise. Having a body seemed so odd. Was this really "my" body? Had I really worried so much about protecting it and wishing it to look well? Was I really confined to bones and blood, time and space? As I laughed at the foolishness of it all, my next breath came like a rush of wind. My next movement felt like my first ever. Truly, I was confined to a body!

I felt sorrow, as well as immense honor. Still dripping with the sweet vibration of Love and endless compassion, life called me back to its unfolding: the rise and fall of forms, the cycles we call birth and death. Slowly, my senses returned and I stood up, taking in the vibrant beauty of India. I watched the world in all its chaos and creativity float by in peace, like flower petals upon the surface of the Great Mother Ganges.

Chapter Fifteen

THE LIFE PATH

The Convergence of All Paths and Practices

It was an unlikely meeting among the tall pines of Big Bear, California, and seemed more like an old religious joke than anything else, but there they were: a rabbinical student, an African healer, a Native American elder, and a yoga teacher sitting in a circle. I sat close by, taking a break from my busy day. Everyone was relaxing and enjoying the scenery. Gray jays watched closely, and crows cawed in the distance. The air was fresh and the sky was an infinite blue above.

At the time, my wife, Monica, and I were involved with Journey to the Heart, a nonprofit organization dedicated to preserving and sharing traditional spiritual teachings for the betterment of human communities and the planet. The centerpiece was an annual gathering of Indigenous elders, healers, and spiritual leaders from all over the world. For four days, they'd meet at a mountain camp and share ceremonies and teachings. The general public was also invited to participate in this incredible event. It was truly a global village and an honor to be a part of.

That year, Monica and I had volunteered to organize and run events. We'd also extended some of our contacts to Journey to the Heart and were there to see a number of our healer friends and mentors from Mexico, Peru, South Africa, and New Zealand. The event was well attended by spiritual seekers and individuals who believed in its vision and mission. Being a relatively short drive from Los Angeles, the gathering also attracted many people who were new to the spiritual search.

Few understood the protocols expected by the traditional healers, and in their earnestness, many novice participants gave them little time to rest. The small circle of spiritual teachers whom I sat near were taking a break from the afternoon heat, sharing stories about their own teachers and traditions.

The rabbinical student spoke of his studies at a yeshiva (a school for Torah and rabbinical study) and a recent trip to Israel, and the African healer talked about how much she'd learned about spiritual traditions from her family. The Native American elder shared his regret that his family had been negatively impacted by forced residential schooling, and as a result, he didn't know his parents very well. The yoga teacher was an American woman who had just returned from a year studying in India. She discussed the struggle of finding spirituality later in life and how spending a year at an ashram (a spiritual community) had transformed her completely.

This fascinating group soon caught the attention of some of the attendees. A couple approached who were dressed like a Beverly Hills vision of New Age fashion, complete with expensive-looking crystal jewelry. Unaware of their intrusion, they invited themselves to sit in the circle of teachers. The gentleman took off his oversized sunglasses, revealing the age that he'd hidden well with his stylish clothes, dyed hair, and tan. Despite his appearance, there was sincerity in his eyes and a longing in his manner.

"So," he began, "there's a lot going on here. This is all pretty cool, but how does someone like me sort it out? Is there one practice you all use? Is there one way to reach the path to enlightenment? You guys must all agree on something, right?"

Over the years, people have asked me similar questions, desperately wanting to know what the greatest practice of all is. In a world without a shortage of quick fixes and self-competition, I'm often asked: "What's the best way to get enlightened?" "Which path *really* works?" "Do you have a favorite religion?" Typically, my response is that the best path is the one that works for *you*.

Since I knew some of the people in the circle and they knew I was sitting nearby, I decided to stay quiet and listen. Their reply to the gentleman has since changed the way that I answer these questions.

The African healer spoke first. "In my culture, we have many ways of the Spirit, many ancient practices. I'm not sure how they'd work for you. It makes me think of one word that travels across our country. All South Africans know the word *ubuntu*. It's hard to explain in English, as it's more of a philosophy than a term. Ubuntu means that we're all connected. It signifies that we have many races of people but one humanity, and that we must live in openness with each other. If I treat you as sacred, then it's as if I am sacred. I am because of you, and you are because of me. There's no separation. So for me, the heart of ubuntu is to live each moment of my life as a ceremony in fellowship with all others. Each moment is sacred. That is the greatest path; and you're always on it!"

The Native American elder smiled and said, "Yes, in our culture, we also have such an idea. The Lakota term for this is *Mitakuye Oyasin*. We say it in many tribes because its meaning is universal and it unites us. We say it after a prayer or ceremony; we also say it as a prayer. I could talk for days about these words, and you'd still just be beginning to understand. It means 'we are all related' or 'all my relations.' Like this African word, it connects us to all that is. We aren't just related to the natural world and other people but to the Spirit World and our Creator. We are *all* family—one family.

"It means you have to learn to be a good relative if you want to live a life that feels balanced. Every day you're building your place in the world or tearing it down. Are *you* building up the world or tearing it down? We can't wait for ceremonies to be kind and connected. We must live it in each moment of our lives. That's why we have the expression 'walk in balance.' It means *every* step."

The rabbinical student spoke up and added, "We share this vision of life as a spiritual path in Judaism. I've dedicated much of my studies to *Tikkun Olam,* which we interpret to mean 'repairing the world.' To me, it's about how we live with harmony and integrity as we face each choice. In fact, there are movements in Judaism dedicated to this teaching and philosophy. For me, Tikkun Olam is about perfecting the world through good deeds so that the Messiah will soon return. Tikkun Olam means that everyone can be a healer in some way. The part that's most important to me, however, is the idea of 'conscious living.'

"Every day we must ask ourselves, *How can I refine the expression of my soul? How can I live for the highest good?* Good deeds and compassion are at the heart of Judaism, and a well-known story from my religion about Hillel—one of our most revered rabbis from ancient times—illustrates this. A potential convert to Judaism challenged the rabbi to teach him the entire Torah while standing on one foot. Hillel saw this as a simple task. Standing on one foot, he said, 'That which is hateful to you, do not do to others. All the rest is commentary. Now go and learn.' It's the essence of life as a spiritual path. We must see everyone as deserving of respect, including ourselves."

"Everyone is sacred," the yoga teacher remarked. "This is what my guru in India teaches us constantly. When we greet each other, we say *namaste,* a Sanskrit word meaning 'I bow to you' or 'I honor the divinity within you.' We were taught about *seva,* which means service, and *karma yoga,* which is about selflessly dedicating your work and actions to God. We never distinguished charity from work or work from life. The message is to make life your spiritual path. Each moment is an opportunity to honor The Sacred in you, in others, and in the world. Gandhi said to 'be the change you want to see in the world.' That says it all."

"So you see, my brother," the African healer said to the couple, who were listening intently, "there are many paths to God or enlightenment or whatever you call the height of spiritual growth. In the end, the highest expression is when our lives become our spiritual practice. Just work to live with compassion in each moment and you'll begin a life-changing journey."

The energy of the two seekers was now softened, receptive.

"I guess if we were living that way, we would have stopped to consider your needs before we interrupted all of you sitting here relaxing. I'm sorry," said the woman as she took off her sunglasses.

"We're just waking up to these things, and it's exciting yet overwhelming. We want to make the most of each opportunity, without coming from the old places within us—the clinging, buying, grabbing energy."

"I see it now," the man added.

"You'll be fine," offered the Native elder. "Follow your heart, and remember to always act with respect. Compassion means respect for yourself and others; it means to slow down and think and *feel* before you act. Life is the real spiritual practice."

Living from the Soul

Opportunities to make life a spiritual practice come unexpectedly and often produce surprising results. When my father died, my mom was in her late 50s and faced the greatest crossroads of her life. She chose to embrace life and reached out for help in her grieving and healing process. Many things came up for her at that difficult time, including confusing thoughts and feelings relating to the past and her relationship with my dad. However, these are normal reactions that many individuals encounter after losing their life partner.

Rather than avoiding or fixating on her pain as an impasse, she decided to explore modes and models of healing that supported her. One thing that quickly became clear to her was that she had allowed her spiritual life to be contained and muted by my dad's total lack of interest or understanding of anything related to the topic. So part of her healing work was the commitment to live her spiritual life fully—in whatever way that would come to mean.

In time, as my mom experienced Reiki, healing touch, and other energy-based healing treatments, she found herself desiring to learn more, but at the same time, she felt conflicted. How could she start a new vocation this late in life as an energy healer? Few of her friends even knew what energy healing was!

However, because she was learning to see her life as her spiritual path, she decided to take the risk and follow her heart. She dove into training methods, reading, and certifications—one course led to another and then another. With each step, she felt more vital and engaged, as if she were becoming someone new. In truth, she was just finally opening up to whom she'd always been.

Facing her loss, the past, and her longing to be and do something new wasn't easy. I recall many times when she asked me if I thought she was crazy or if I could see her being a success. I reminded her that on the spiritual path, doubt is a sign of forward movement—an indicator of something old that wants to be released. Trust and support is all we need to move through it.

"If this is truly what you were meant to do, you won't be able to *not* do it. If you weren't meant to do it, you'll know the minute you start applying yourself. Let life teach you what will work for you. You don't have to figure it out. Just listen to what you long for and take a step. Let go of your expectations and see what comes to you."

And so it was—she took one step at a time. At first she was full of self-doubt, but began practicing as a healer anyway, volunteering her time here and there. The results she received were positive and so was the feedback! Still at times she continued to doubt herself, but as her confidence grew and time passed, her critical self had less power, and she knew that she excelled at and loved what she was doing.

Years later, my mom is a vibrant and joyful woman with a potent gift for healing work. She has helped hundreds of people and continues to see patients in hospitals and at her home. My mom would have never wished to have lost my dad at such a young age, but she's been able to learn from the experience. Her story reminds us that if we let all the challenges and opportunities of our lives teach us, spiritual growth is guaranteed.

This type of opportunity doesn't only occur at major crossroads or setbacks, but also in the small moments of a day, including waiting in lines, being caught in traffic, and relating to friends. When we embrace this way of living and being, it changes us and the world. Sometimes the embrace of this vitality can even trigger a healing in the body that defies the mind and science.

The Embrace of Life Heals Life

Joe was one of my mom's clients. When she met him, he was in a palliative-care facility where he was receiving "comfort care" to ease his journey toward death. He had advanced Huntington's disease as well as bleeding lesions on his brain. The doctors had no way to control this and encouraged him to prepare for his passing.

Huntington's is a genetic disease that results in neuronal cell death in select areas of the brain; complications from it can reduce a person's life expectancy. Symptoms include erratic body movements and lack of motor skills. It also impacts mental abilities and behavior. There's no proven cure, and symptoms are managed with a range of medications and approaches. Huntington's typically only becomes terminal when complications become unmanageable.

At his worst, Joe was being fed intravenously and couldn't move his body sufficiently, bathe, or even use the toilet without help. He had lost much of his weight, and his physicians were medicating him for comfort and preparing to let him die, which everyone thought would be soon.

"They said he'd die, but he told me something else," my mom told me. "He said, 'They only know my body—they don't know *me*. They can't decide if and when I'll die. I won't let them! Something else will decide, something greater. That's one thing I know and feel in my heart.' Joe said this often. He never said it in anger, just with focus and certainty. He never acted bitter and was always a gentleman."

Shortly after, my mom started visiting Joe and doing energy work with him. She started to see some improvement and often updated me on his progress.

"He's healing; every day I can see it. It isn't me. It's *him*—his attitude and how he lives. He's so loving and patient. I think it's the force of his character that's healing his body. Gratitude, acceptance, and allowing—that's his medicine. He knows all the staff by name and always greets people, introducing individuals when he can. It's hard for him to speak, but he honors everyone he encounters. He's grateful for everyone who helps and never judges those who don't.

"One day he waited two hours for someone to bring him his pain medication. They'd forgotten about him. When the nurse finally came in, he thanked her sincerely. He's also waited hours before someone had come to help him use the bathroom, yet he never raises his voice in anger. He says that he's grateful for whatever he has and tries not to be attached to his expectations. He moves through life one moment at a time, letting go of disappointments as they come.

"One time I was acknowledging how difficult it was for him. He looked deeply into my eyes and said, 'I've worked hard all these years to learn how to let go. I used to own a hip, successful restaurant in Toronto. I played music and enjoyed all my customers, who were like friends. I worked 16- to 18-hour days and savored every minute of it. I loved the food, the people, and the music. I did it all and felt unstoppable! But now, I do nothing. I'm just lucky to be alive. I almost died, but I'm slowly coming back. I have to be happy with that. I've worked and worked at letting go, and I finally have. I've released everything in my life. And as soon as I did, everything instantly changed and became easier. I'm happy—all day, every day. I'm happy in stillness, in silence, and surrounded by noise. I like everyone here; I like all my roommates who come and go. I enjoy listening to people and the world, which has its own music. I listen carefully to everything that goes on.'"

"Joe is always happy," my mom added, "and he's always happy for others. I never feel resentment, self-pity, or envy from him. He sees that there are different ways to enjoy life and be human. They all matter; they can all be good in time. He doesn't dwell on what was—rather, he lives for what is. Acceptance, allowing, and gratitude are what keep him at peace. Don't think he's a pushover, either. This is one determined man!"

To the astonishment of his physician, Joe hasn't died yet. In fact, he's gained back much of his weight and is walking once again, which was never expected. He eats solid foods and can even go out for occasional dinners. His violent tremors have subsided, and his shaking is minimal. He lifts 60 pounds during his regular exercise routine. Still, he lives in gratitude. Every moment of every day, he sets his intention clearly, and then takes action with acceptance and allowing. When his life became his spiritual path, Joe became his own medicine.

The Pathless Path

The world is filled with extraordinary stories of faith, impossible metaphysical talents, and impressive spiritual disciplines and practices. These stories attract our attention and are important to help us awaken and learn about the world we live in. At the same time, it's critical not to let such stories become distractions. Miracles, altered states, and exotic techniques can be misleading.

If the goal of the spiritual path is the ever-deepening relationship to The Sacred—in yourself and the world around you—then the things that matter most are those that move you along that path. You must be cautious of the distractions that lead you away from your true nature and the fullest expression of The Sacred. Be mindful of stagnation or times when you feel stuck. Your soul is trying to tell you something: take a step in a new direction. Start with the way you manage your thoughts and feelings, and choose a Master Path to help.

The Master Paths must be understood first and foremost as vehicles. They are modes of travel into the heart of the self and the Spiritual World. Their purpose is to help us move beyond our egos and wake up the soul to the direct experience of the Divine. Through the Master Paths, we express and exploit our unique tendencies and spiritual personality to help us remove all that has come between us and our sacred essence. The paths show us how to reclaim our direct knowledge and expression of the Sacred Consciousness. As we do so, the deeper healing qualities of compassion, connection, service, and open-mindedness begin to blossom in our lives.

As our practices lead us to experience a new awareness of ourselves and the world, a new opportunity begins to emerge: the chance to apply our realizations in everyday life. Life itself can be a spiritual practice. Stories of the "life path" involve choices and conduct in which we make the ordinary supernatural. Releasing anger, ego, attachment, and judgment . . . and embracing love, connection, and empowerment are some of the simple yet profound ways we can make life our spiritual practice.

When someone is cruel, respond with compassion and support. When someone exhibits impatience and criticism, return it with curiosity and generosity. When you feel anger, experience the emotion but also look to its roots—you'll find fear or hurt hidden within. Always feel your emotions fully; however, don't act from them.

The life path is at work in the small moments of life. Everyday events can be viewed as opportunities to discover our barriers of fear and resistance and cultivate love for ourselves and others. The happenings in the world are viewed within a higher order and Holy Intelligence.

Our task is not to judge, but to cultivate the power of being present to the fullness of each moment. It includes learning to develop our intuition and sense of connection. We must feel the responsibility to co-create consciously.

Easier Said Than Done

The life path sounds easy and appealing to many people. They think, *I don't need a specific practice, religion, guide, or tool. I just need to be nicer to others and myself.* However, it isn't as easy as it may seem. In order to truly embrace this practice, it helps to have accumulated awareness, discipline, and spiritual understanding. *All* of the Master Paths help feed and inspire the life path.

The life path requires the same attention, discipline, and attitudes that the other Master Paths require—except the opportunity to practice it is constant. It's in our work, relationships, bodies, and breath. It's a commitment to cultivating a new perspective of the world, while refining a way of being in it. The mind-set we have in making the most of the other paths becomes the same intent we apply to every event and encounter of our daily lives. Life becomes our meditation, as well as our ceremony, our devotion, and our prayer.

Many people are very good at the life path when things are going well for them. When their expectations are being met, life becomes a blissful gift from the Divine, and every day is a joy. The true practice shows up when things aren't going so well. This happens when we fail, or when life throws us a painful surprise such as the loss of a loved one, job, or illness. Then we are confronted with the greatest challenge of this path: it is either all or nothing.

On the life path, we can't claim that everything is Divine when we get our way and then complain and moan when things don't go as we wish. Either it is all in Divine Order or not. Now this does *not* mean that we must act as if we approve of hurtful, violent, or unjust things, but it does mean that we look for the lesson in every moment.

When we face a painful situation or disappointment, we ask ourselves, *What characteristic is this calling forward in me? What can this teach me?* We use all moments and relationships to cultivate an open heart, an attitude of connection and service. We practice being fully present and releasing judgment. For those who deeply embrace the depth of the life path, the sheer mystery of life and its infinite nature blows apart any certainty of justice, righteousness, or duality.

In time, the mystical mind emerges. We see truth and beauty everywhere and encounter ordinary magic all of the time. We live the wisdom of Divine Energy and the Formless Spirit. We see that it's the only mind-set that can truly be aware and content at the same time. Only the mystical mind can hold all of the extremes and polarities of life together and say yes to them all.

When tragedy and terror in the world are overwhelming, the life path calls us to remain with an open heart and mind. It shows us that life itself is the great crucible that burns away all attachments—all expectations, limiting beliefs, anger, and judgments. When we stand in the face of life's inexplicable extremes of joy and pain—and trust that it's all in Divine Order—our old models for happiness and safety are destroyed.

As we learn from each obstacle we face, each success and failure, we must remember that the evolution of the soul is the essence of life and the life path. Since every experience helps with the evolution of the soul and the discovery of The Sacred, then *all* experiences are meaningful and significant.

PART VI

Living Balance, Lasting Peace

A precious path has led you this far
To the beauty of the chalice and the fire,
Garden and temple, drum and jewel

We sat with angels, flew with eagles
Here we healed the broken
And we too, were restored

Beyond the Sacred Doorway
After the dance and all you know
There is another world

Beyond walls and wishes
After the hope and fear
A new world waits for you

Go on, go through the ancient doorway
Let all you have tried to be
Vanish in the light of this final day

There is a star in the blue sky
That has watched over you all your life
Follow it to this forever Holy Place

Let yourself be loved and nothing more
The great sun and endless sea
Will sing to you day and night

This is what you were born of
and where you will return
This is the place where
Everything is Sacred

— J. H. Ellerby

Chapter Sixteen

Everything Is Sacred

A Simple Truth

Life is precious. All life is precious. It's astonishing when we acknowledge the miracle of its diversity, tenacity, complexity, and beauty. Life is blissful *and* horrifying. There are those who waste it, those who destroy it, and those who fight for their portion of it. And there are those who honor it, celebrate it, and share it. In this moment, existence itself is the one undeniable thing that all people and creatures—all forces of nature—have in common.

Everything that exists right now coexists with you. It is all a part of you, an extension of yourself. This existence can be analyzed and explained in a million ways. Science and art will dance and debate forever. There can be no final answer or universal agreement because existence is as personal as your own breath and as confounding as the outer edges of the universe. Regardless of the story you accept about this great existence, you have a choice: what will you do with this extraordinary gift of life and consciousness that you have?

Will you spend it attacking, judging, or trying to control the lives of others? Will you stay angry at yourself, hanging on to guilt and shame? Or will you seek to explore it, love it, and know it in its infinite depths? Will you be an intimate lover of this existence? Or will you be estranged—living in fear, disconnection, and self-doubt?

Everyone is faced with these choices in each moment of every day. It's a power more awesome than most can imagine. Once you choose to embrace this creation and its mystery, something changes within you, and you're set free to explore the possibilities—each more amazing than the next.

To embrace a spiritual practice is to make the journey into mystery *and* knowing. It is a path—if well practiced and deeply experienced—that can lead us and the world to new and incredible levels of peace, balance, and wisdom. We each need to choose our path and do our part.

Like millions of others, I've been blessed to realize an ever-deepening presence of peace and clarity in my life as a result of spiritual experiences that have helped me see myself and the world differently. While the experiences are what most often changed and informed me, it was the spiritual practices and teachers who guided me and increased my ability to open up to those experiences.

Spiritual practice is at first a vehicle to travel into the world of the Soul and Spirit. Once you've begun to enter the realm of spiritual experience, spiritual practice takes on a new role. It will help you integrate and sustain the wisdom and healing you've found. It *is* possible—peace can last a lifetime.

When you personally experience or trust those who've perceived the unitary nature of the world, respect, reverence, and relationships will become essential to your way of being. You'll see beyond the borders of fear and cultures of separation. Your practice can hold this intention for you and can be your embodied affirmation.

Every day I'm filled with gratitude and hope because I'm able to experience The Sacred in my life. When I don't wake up to that feeling of connection, I sit at my altar, invoke The Sacred, say a prayer, and quiet my mind in meditation. Life isn't always easy, but my practice keeps me connected to what matters most. You, like me, will still experience ups and downs, disappointment, joy, and pain. What we do with those moments is where the gift of a deep spiritual life lies. Enlightenment is a way of being; it's a moment to moment choice.

When things fail or falter, whether I succeed or suffer, it all becomes small in the scope of the Silent World of God that comprises all and rests within everything. Everything is made small in the vastness of consciousness, God's Eternity. All things are made holy in their union with The Sacred, and all things are made endurable in the Light of Timeless Awareness. In my most difficult moments, I draw from the memory of Sacred Experience and remember that all things shall pass, except the things that matter. The immeasurable essence of our Sacred Source lives within everyone and connects us to our eternal origin and the fabric of being. This is a knowing that lives within each of us. It isn't so much a discovery as it is a remembering.

What if our religion was each other
If our practice was our life
If prayer, our words
What if the temple was the Earth
If forests were our church
If holy water—the rivers, lakes, and ocean
What if meditation was our relationships
If the teacher was life
If wisdom was self-knowledge
If love was the center of our being.
— Ganga White

Love and Healing: The Soul of Truth

After years of study, practice, personal healing, and helping others heal, I live with the absolute conviction that the qualities of life we all innately seek—such as love, peace, security, and connection—*are* the essential traits that are revealed through spiritual practice. We come from a Great Mystery, a Divine Order, and its wisdom lives within each of us.

When we look to the distinctly "spiritual" moments that are described by the great spiritual masters who have lived around the world and throughout the ages, we find that they're more similar than different. In fact, when we look at the various descriptions of people's direct spiritual experiences (and not just at interpretations of beliefs, myths, and scriptures), it's clear that we're all encountering the same thing! Again and again throughout time, individuals' encounters of The Sacred have shown common qualities and lessons, regardless of religion, education, or social class. Spiritual experiences reveal to us our greatest potential for healing ourselves and the world. Those who learn from such experiences live from the Light they encounter.

Some would say this is idealistic. But you've experienced the evidence for yourself already. Spiritual experience isn't just for saints, yogis, shamans, sages, and monks; it's not reserved just for those who believe in Divine Forces or the supernatural. Everyone has spiritual experiences, more often than is acknowledged. People seek an encounter with The Sacred every day as they reach for connection, compassion, and the feeling of being "enough." Although you may not use the words *sacred* or *divine* to describe what you live for, your natural drive is toward the spiritual and the very qualities found in the direct experience of God and the Spiritual World.

The reason why we seek these things in our lives and why we can't remain content in a life of violence, self-doubt, disconnection, anger, or the denial of our true passions is because we all possess the memory of The Sacred imprinted on our very souls. *The nature of the Spiritual World is our nature: the complexity of our minds, the depths of our hearts, and the changing world we encounter every day.* Fundamental to the deepest transformations of self, society, and environment that we are capable of as human beings is a realization of the Universal Life Source that is beyond the limits of culture and language. *To care for the world is to care for ourselves; to care for ourselves is to care for the world.*

Dealing with Darkness: Dangerously Disconnected

When we live without a spiritual practice, it's easy to become disconnected from our true selves. We become unaware of our own Divine nature and The Sacred presence in the world. Eventually, we begin to feel a dull sense of detachment. We find ourselves successful but not satisfied or endlessly searching and never fully content. When trouble hits, we're overwhelmed and become victims to our own history and past emotions.

Swept out to the sea of demands and hasty reactions, we can feel lost, as if there's no ground to stand on or shore to reach. Yet even in our darkest days, many of us have moments when we sense that there's a power within us that we haven't yet expressed or experienced. We feel that there's something more and know that we deserve and are capable of something different. The feeling may have grown faint, but it remains. We live with a longing for a connection to a greater force—within ourselves and beyond.

Sometimes we give up the fight because the challenges we confront can feel like too much. We ignore the call of the soul and allow ourselves to grow numb in the routine of life and the roles and expectations we've accepted unconsciously. If we live without a connection to The Source long enough, we'll forget our true nature and find ourselves locked into a life of reaction and routine. We grow attracted to the illusions of control and remain vulnerable to the winds of change. In the absence of Spirit, we feel stagnant.

For some, it's as if they've fallen asleep. The richness of life slips away, and each day takes more effort to feel a sense of meaning and peace. Many people who are accomplished in a material or social sense still feel lonely or lost. Others are busy moving about in this world yet don't feel truly alive and content. Without a connection to The Sacred, there's no freedom or balance. This is because all of our energy and meaning comes with conditions and dependence on the world around us. Without an awareness of The Sacred, we become addicted to cycles and situations that are no longer healthy or healing.

It's natural to be caught by the hooks of worldly drama. The hooks that pull us out of Sacred Awareness can be subtle, such as being pressured by family members and society, or drastic, like enduring trauma or abuse. Once we've become disconnected, we rarely remember or notice how it happened, but we know that something isn't right. In the struggle to find the way home to a Spiritual Connection, people do outrageous and even horrible things.

War, addiction, violence, consumption, pleasing, fixing, working ceaselessly, and chasing wealth and perfect health are all examples of the twisting, writhing efforts of a fish out of water, longing for its true home. We grasp for answers, but all of the clinging and attachment to things that make us feel better temporarily only make us feel more hollow in the end. These acts are attempts to find The Sacred again through the twisted logic of a wounded heart.

One of the most difficult realities that spiritual growth reveals to us is how intimately involved we are in the creation of our own experiences of disappointment and suffering. This isn't to suggest that emotional pain or physical discomfort aren't real, nor does it imply that people are at fault for being a victim of crimes, illnesses, or attacks. The reality is that the degree to which we experience these things as suffering is directly related to our spiritual well-being.

The stories we tell ourselves about the world—what we fear, what we resist, what we are attached to—directly feed the suffering we experience. When we can learn to be present, open-minded, and patient and practice a mystical mind-set, even the hardest times become bearable and even fruitful. When we've experienced a direct connection to The Sacred, within or beyond ourselves, an eternal flame of hope is lit. We're reminded of the words of Rumi: "Your task is not to seek for love, but merely to seek and find all the barriers within yourself that you have built against it."

Let your spiritual practice help you to know yourself and release the barriers from your life.

Evil

Many people throughout time have taken comfort in externalizing the sources of hurt and harm in the world. Indeed, most traditions have a concept of "evil" and an admonition to war against it.

But this presents a major problem for the human community. I don't deny the possibility that there are forces, human and otherwise, that have harmful, destructive, and oppressive intentions. The world is filled with examples of terror and trauma. It's interesting to note that recognizing that evil exists, or having a belief in it, hasn't helped us to end it.

In many cases, the interpretation of "what" and "who" is or isn't evil is at the very heart of the tragedies in this world. Genocide, fundamentalism, torture, and terror are all rooted in conscious divisions of good and evil. Once we create and feed a concept of evil, there's a natural and immediate justification for fear and judgment. These two characteristics are the exact and recurring sources of trouble in our lives and the greater communities we live in. Placing attention on evil has never been a successful spiritual practice.

In the majority of cultures I've traveled among, the notion of evil is very real. Moreover, many of the Indigenous healers I've worked with specialize in protecting people from "evil energy" and healing them from its damages. I've witnessed and have even been a part of ceremonies to exorcise "demons," and I've heard countless stories of the chaos caused by dark forces. I've even worked with clients who've had—for lack of better language—"bad luck," "curses," and "dark spirits" haunting them. The important question isn't "is there evil?" but "does it really have any power in this world?" and "what can we do about it?"

I've explored the concept of evil with Christian priests, rabbis, Hindu yogis, Native American elders, spiritual healers, energy healers, and spiritual teachers everywhere I've gone; and I've asked them all the same thing: "Do you believe evil exists? If so, what can we do about it?" Their answers might surprise you.

The most common response is that evil is a dangerous concept because the boundaries of good and bad can become so easily blurred. We'll never be able to exactly prove or disprove it, and the identification of it is tricky. How do we know the difference, for example, between an evil act and an evil person? Who decides? If the criteria are written in a sacred text, who interprets it? How do we separate crimes of need from crimes of passion, or crimes of defense from crimes of political greed? The most spiritually experienced and mature teachers agree that the very idea of evil can be used to perpetuate and justify evil (violence, persecution, and power over others).

The preoccupation with evil is itself a problem and detrimental to the spiritual path. The fear of evil evokes feelings of defense and judgment and causes people to focus on what they're afraid of and what they believe they must avoid, instead of focusing on love and what they hope to become. Placing attention on evil causes us to discriminate and feed the ego's desire to be "right," rather than feeding the soul's desire to be free. We look for sources of problems and blame others when we should be investing in solutions and being a part of change.

The most common advice I've heard from spiritual leaders is that while evil may be a real energy or entity in the world, it doesn't deserve our time, effort, or attention in the ways we've been taught. What we put our attention on will grow. If we feed evil with our energy, then we become a part of it; we affirm its reality.

The spiritual teachers I've met have always suggested to focus on positive people and forces, as well as compassionate outcomes. Stay intent on love, health, and connection in your life and evil won't be an issue to address. There can be no shadow where there's a bright light. If you have a strong spiritual practice that connects you with a sense of peace and a spirit of love, the topic of evil rarely ever arises. A healthy spiritual practice will help you see how you judge people and things, and how you can live more deeply from the wisdom of your heart.

A great African healer I met in Swaziland once said to me, "It's true that I deal with evil and the dark forces, but they are only an issue for people who are unclear in the mind, closed in the heart, or weak in the spirit. If your path is about carrying a spiritual light, you don't have to worry about evil. No shadow can cross your path when you shine a light before you."

An Anglican priest I knew once told me, "Sometimes I think the concept of evil is itself evil. I see the way people blame with it, judge with it, and think they are better because of it. They use it in so many selfish ways; and in the end, they do as much harm as those they accuse. I've stopped preaching about evil because of that.

Even Jesus said, 'Let anyone among you who is without sin be the first to throw a stone.' I think his message was clear! He also said, 'Why do you look at the speck of sawdust in your brother's eye and pay no attention to the plank in your own eye? How can you say to your brother, 'Let me take the speck out of your eye,' when all the time there is a plank in your own eye? You hypocrite; first take the plank out of your own eye, and then you will see clearly to remove the speck from your brother's eye.'"

I suggest a sort of "spiritual optimism" as protection from negativity in life. This is a concept that Joan Borysenko, Ph.D., and Larry Dossey, M.D., have both written about. It's not an excuse to avoid the challenging topic of "bad things" in the world; rather, it turns your attention to what you can do about it.

As you explore the different spiritual practices, don't fear the possibility that you may expose yourself to something "bad" or "evil." Place the energy of your heart and mind on the goodness, love, and light that you wish to bring into your life and the world.

Let your practice keep you connected to all the goodness and love you know. With open-mindedness, guidance, and support, you'll navigate the surprises and challenges that come up along the way. If you have a clear intention of connecting to the highest Source and Light, darkness will find no place to take hold.

Furthermore, as you look for the good in life and practice the laws of attraction and intention, remember that it's all or nothing. It's common for people to focus on all the good things in their life and to think of them as magic, blessings, and evidence of their spiritual progress. But when things go poorly, they end up labeling and judging those things as "bad" and look for an external source to blame. They may also turn the blame inward, which is just as destructive. The self-judgment and fear feeds upon the self. Many become trapped in a cycle of personal disharmony that's projected into the world.

Spiritual practice helps us break such cycles and teaches us that life *is* the test. The challenge isn't to expect easy tests but to respond well to the ones we're given.

The Call of the Spirit

People can live their entire lives without recognizing the call of the spiritual self. It's a call for deeper wholeness, to awaken to something greater within and around us. I believe that we all hear it, although not everyone recognizes it. The call to truly know the inner dimensions of the self and the outer reaches of The Sacred comes to each of us every day. It's in each wounded moment, in the experience of stress, and in the feeling of disconnection or the sense that something is missing in our lives.

Without the awareness of the Spiritual World and the spiritual aspects of the self, many of us fail to understand the opportunity before us and the longing within. We become confused in the turmoil of emotion, the passions of greed and power, and the hunger for perfection and protection. All of it is just a grasping for something to soothe the dark fire of longing that burns for union with the Infinite. Infinite Love, Wisdom, and Connection are our origin and home.

Until we heed the call, choose a path, and begin the journey, we may wander in the shadow of fear. Until we remember our Divine Nature, we see division and pain and experience stress and depletion. Until we begin to remember that *everything* is Sacred, we struggle between perfection and comparison, forgetting that we're already perfect and worthy of complete love and abundance.

Those who heed the call will cross an invisible line on life's road and realize that there's no going back to a life of unconscious choice and reaction. We're awake and hungry for the light of day and can't wait to travel beyond what we already know. One day the fear of staying stuck overcomes the fear of change. Whatever names we give it—peace, balance, clarity, joy, love, contentment, connection—we know that it's real *and* possible.

Celebrate and pursue the health of the body, the emotional self, and the intellect. It's wise to care for the totality of this gift that we've been given, regardless of its limitations or eccentricities. We must, however, not forget that the soul needs tending to as well and requires a diet, an exercise program, and a healer. The soul, the True Self, is our genuine source of connection to The Sacred. We realize that spirituality isn't a belief system or religion. It's an experience, a practice, and a way of life. Spirituality is the awakened expression of all aspects of the self, of life, and the Great Spirit. Our spirituality is our consciousness and mind-set. Our life journey is the process of waking up to the fullness of this existence, one day at a time.

The Meaning of Life: From Longing to Belonging

When I began to teach and work as a healer, people would ask me in jest what the meaning of life is. I'd laugh and always say that it's a personal journey, a personal answer. It's different for everyone and can only be known by ourselves and for ourselves. That is an answer that works in many settings and is politically correct and safe. I do believe it.

There is another answer. It's the one I live by. It is what the majority of our great saints, sages, and masters have adhered to. The purpose of life is the evolution of the soul—to fully realize its sacred nature and express it. Each one of us has one simple task: to remember who we really are and live from that awareness. The task of discovering the True Self and the Sacred Nature of our world is what heals us.

In the blinding light of our own beauty, power, and connection, our self-doubt, pain, and uncertainty vanish. Fear is replaced by love. All problems, challenges, and needs are served by this great awakening. It is the end of *longing* and the beginning of *belonging*.

As you've learned, the path toward the True Self isn't always easy or clearly laid out before you. It isn't always comfortable, and its blessings may not come quickly. But when you persevere and follow it, it's as natural as breathing. It will feel more clear and certain than anything you've ever known. It is self-evident and a truly endless mystery that you can spend your entire life exploring, practicing, and integrating.

The Whole World Is Waiting

This is a unique time in human history when human beings have an unprecedented power over all life on Earth. As a species, we possess the capacity to destroy the planet thousands of times over with weapons built for "security." More than ever, wealth and control is pooled in the hands of the few. The distance between those with much and those with little grows exponentially every day. Factions and extremes grow among the very people who could be leading the call toward peace. Religions and political parties grasp for power and control as the simple needs of the masses go unmet.

Resources that could build schools, hospitals, and feed the poor are wasted on indulgences of fleeting gain. Our political communities spend trillions of dollars annually on projects of war. Collectively, we spend billions of dollars on distractions, appearances, and personal medications such as coffee, Prozac, and alcohol to regulate our moods—rather than seeking healing.

If we look to our precious planet, we'll find an equally disturbing reality. More than a billion people lack safe drinking water, and the availability continues to diminish annually. While the world debates global warming and the greenhouse effect, more obvious pollution from households and big businesses continue to choke the life from the land, air, and sea. Empty homes stand for sale or demolition while precious resources are poured into new developments. Through our focus on consumption and comfort, we're drowning ourselves and the natural world in our own filth.

Leading wildlife organizations such as the World Wildlife Fund have estimated that in the time it takes to read *this page,* an entire *species* will become extinct from this planet—never to be seen again. By this time tomorrow, more than 150 more will be lost forever. Looking at natural trends in nature and throughout time, experts estimate that the current rate of species extinction ranges from 100 to 1,000 times what's natural or historical.

Fish populations are declining, and the rainforests we all rely on for the stabilization of climate and air quality are still being decimated daily. Indigenous cultures and languages are vanishing just as quickly. Everywhere we look there are mounting challenges. We find the scar of human carelessness everywhere. The relentless pursuit of technology spreads like a virus seeking control over the natural world and life itself.

What does spirituality have to do with any of this? Why choose ancient practices when the world struggles for air to breathe? Why look inward, when the world around us needs help? How can we be asked to pray, meditate, dance, and fast when there are mouths to feed and wounds to heal? Is there any hope at all?

The answer is *yes*. Yes, there is hope; there are chances, changes, and choices that will turn this world around. Our ability to create change in our own lives and the world is just as great as our ability to create more problems. Religious traditions have been at the heart of much bloodshed and misery throughout the ages, but let's not forget that religious and spiritual people have always been among the great agents of social change, justice, and freedom.

The abolishment of slavery, care for the poor, and equal rights for women and other groups were pioneered by people whose spirituality was clear, active, and engaged. If we look at our human species throughout time, there has been a steady increase in quality of life, life expectancy, art, science, connection, and choice. We're currently struggling to find a mind-set that will restore balance in our hearts, security and opportunity for all, and vitality to the natural world. We must not forget that change is what we now excel at. Change is possible if we learn from our ancestors and live for our great-great-grandchildren.

Vanishing Trails

As we look to the future, we can see a crucial value and practicality to honoring our souls and exploring the Spiritual World. Not only does a rootedness in The Sacred evoke our greatest sense of connection and compassion, but we also find the tools we need to create the scale of change this world needs. Creative thinking, cooperation, intuition, and quantum leaps in science all rest on our ability to embrace the spiritual dimension of ourselves and this world. The Spiritual World evokes new senses and ways of being. As we look to discover and revitalize these aspects of who we are, we must also pay attention to those in the world who still maintain a relationship to The Sacred and the lost worlds of Spirit.

Indigenous people everywhere are under threat of extinction, from the Bushmen of the Kalahari to the traditional people of Tibet, as well as the Native American communities that have been pushed to the broken edge of American society. We must not forget that many of these cultures and communities still live with the wisdom that others have lost. Each year as industrialization and globalization lunges forward, languages, traditions, and pathways to The Sacred are lost.

Every day we make choices that impact these people and the ancient ways of peace. The clothes we buy, the governments we support, the charities we give to, and the way we conduct ourselves among friends and family are all simple acts that have a ripple effect around the world.

This isn't a matter of glorifying the past and condemning the present, nor is it about spirituality versus science or development versus the environment. This is *not* about a new war or struggle. What the direct experiences of The Sacred teach us is that all things coexist and are interrelated, and what we do with that knowledge is a choice. As individuals and societies, we determine our own priorities and the balance we live by. If we don't like what we see, then the choice for change is ours.

Learning about Indigenous cultures and supporting Indigenous causes is an example of how a person can begin to explore another way of being in the world that offers healing in addition to extending support through action, attitude, and charity. Getting to know a neighbor of a different culture or going to visit the house of worship of another tradition are also terrific ways to be touched by the beauty of the world. Let yourself be inspired to be a part of change. Look for good news stories, and ask more questions. Help someone who doesn't know how to ask. Be kind.

Even extending your relationship to the natural world can help you unlock the secrets of The Sacred while also connecting you with the very real needs and challenges that wildlife species and diverse ecosystems are facing. Spend more time outside; respect your body and Earth. Learn more about the animals in your area, and if there aren't any, find out more about the importance of biodiversity in this world. Find ways to get educated and involved, allowing you to practice many of the Master Paths in deep relationship to Creation. Find an organization that shares your values, and ask how you can help.

All One

A healthy spiritual practice is absolutely concerned with the evolution of the soul and the self. Yet, if it's vital and maturing, the process of awakening also becomes a revelation of interconnection, compassion, and integrity. Eventually, it leads beyond the self. The spiritual path is about your relationship to the world. It's about how you live in relationship with The Sacred.

There are many paradoxes within the spiritual journey. Sometimes we travel halfway around the world in order to appreciate where we are from. Sometimes we seek to know our innermost self only to find something that transcends who we are. In other cases, we seek something larger than life and find the truest experience of our unique personality and potential.

In a similar irony, we don't often adopt a spiritual practice *so* we can heal the planet. However, when we truly commit to the healing and transformation of self, we realize that at some profound level we *are* the planet and all of creation. Our healing spirals out into the world, and we come to understand that we are all related. We can no longer feel "alone," because we realize we are "all one." A strong spiritual practice has the power to shift our identity so radically that we not only rise above stress and questions of meaning, but we're able to become living expressions of our beautiful soul and the one Universal Spirit.

AFTERWORD

Lasting Change

Lasting change in the world begins in the heart and the soul of each person. It starts in your home. It's easy to find people who can tell us what to believe, what's wrong, and what to do. The big challenge lies in finding the willingness to *be the change*. Willingness can't be taught; it comes from within. It grows in love and rises up when we live with integrity and congruence—inside and out. Deep spiritual awakening helps us love ourselves, our community, and this amazing creation. Loving our world leads to spiritual awakening. We must be courageous enough to love more. We respect and heal what we love. Masters from all parts of the world have long said, "When there is peace in the self, there is peace in the home. When there is peace in the homes, there is peace in the community. When there is peace in the communities, there is peace in the nations. When there is peace in the nations, there is peace in the world."

Spiritual practice has been seen as a luxury by many, but spiritual awakening is now a necessity. Many criticize those who are overly committed to a spiritual path as being unrealistic or disengaged from the world, but true awakening couldn't be further from that claim. For instance, where we find people and communities who have committed to the path of awareness, we discover great healers, helpers, and problem-solvers. Where we find people who feel connection and compassion, we see innovation, change, and inspiration. In the embrace of spiritual experience and the access to Divine Energy and creativity, we'll find new solutions to old problems and lasting ways to honor this magnificent existence of which we are all a part.

If you strive to live your life as a spiritual journey, feed that intention with the lessons and maturity you cultivate through a regular spiritual practice. Once you make a lasting commitment to one or more of the Master Paths, you'll quickly find powerful changes within and around you. Connections, synchronicity, and intuition will come to your aid.

As you cultivate spiritual experiences through practice and intention, your inner vision will develop, your heart will open, and your mind will release the illusions that breed fear and attachment. You will become the medicine that you seek; you will be a healer to all you know. For some, it will happen in simple ways, such as showing kindness in the grocery line, volunteering, or learning not to pollute your body and the earth. Others will commit to projects and pathways of healing that will reach around the world. Every little bit helps.

Consider which of the Master Paths appeal to you most. Make a commitment to yourself to invest in one or two and give it your full attention. Be sure to allow yourself some time, at least a month or two. If it works for you, commit to a year's practice.

We know that just as exercise is good for the body, learning is good for the mind, and relationships are good for the heart, so too a spiritual practice is good for the soul. The extraordinary gift of a spiritual practice is the ripple effect it sends throughout all levels of our lives. A dedicated practice may have an impact on our physical health, sense of peace, and even on the world. It's a miracle that such a force lives within each of us, and all we have to do is choose to tap into it.

If you already have a spiritual practice and it doesn't seem to challenge or enrich you anymore, try something new. Look for the places where you've grown complacent or lazy. A vibrant spiritual life isn't about always being comfortable and happy. There are growing pains, wounds to heal, and fears to face. Accept the adventure and what you'll receive in return is *transcendence:* true freedom. The further down the spiritual path you go, the more you realize the simplicity of life and the possibility of lasting peace—no matter who or where you are.

҈ ҈ ҈

I often give thanks for the gifts of the spiritual practices that I've committed to over the years. I'm thankful for patience, compassion, and the ability to step back from a situation and release my desire to control or judge. Having a clear, soul-centered sense of vision drives my choices. Being able to release expectations and attachments keeps me in the present moment. These aren't grand metaphysical philosophies, but simple earthly truths that make the wheel of life turn a little smoother.

I think of these things at 3:15 in the morning when I wake up to change my son's diaper on a work night or when my wife and I are in a disagreement that concerns our household. I remember what I've learned in the wilderness fasting, in the temples meditating, and in the ceremonies praying. I carry those gifts into each moment of my life, consciously and intentionally.

It all helps—even while attending meetings, being stuck in traffic, facing the loss of loved ones, and maintaining the balance of life. When my current spiritual practice is steady and essential, my perspective is clear and everything falls into place. I do my best to remember that I am, at the most, a co-creator in this world: I do nothing alone. I try to stay aware that I'm an expression of the Most Sacred and that I'm a simple human being, no better than a snail or a stone. I am as extraordinary and powerful as I am insignificant and forgettable.

Spiritual practice has taught me to wake up each day with gratitude and a desire to love, heal, and grow. It has taught me that

I'm a soul evolving and all things in my path can support me in that process, especially the things I resist. I trust that everything is perfect and that there is always more work to be done. I'm honored by the gift of life and accept the mysteries of it. Each day I seek a deeper truth and release the need to know. Most incredibly, spiritual practices, such as the ones in this book, have given me the experience of my oneness with God and awakened my intimate relationship with creation. We are one in the guise of many.

In time, a spiritual practice will reveal to you that your consciousness is a precious facet of the one consciousness of all things. As you shine, we all shine. A meaningful spiritual practice nourishes the world, like water in a desert land. If you seek balance and joy in life, if you long for a world at peace, then now is the time to embrace your Soul and the Spirit of Life. Awaken to your deepest sense of The Sacred. Bring forward your gifts. Allow each moment to teach and inspire you with an open heart and mind. Release your fear. When you live with love, you'll know that everything is Sacred. Everything you seek is already a part of you right now. The world is waiting for your choice. Return to The Sacred.

There are moments when
Light turns to spirit.
The very air you breathe
Becomes an ocean of life.

Your bones will dissolve into the sea,
Your blood becomes the saltwater,
And only one thing remains.

When the mind grows still
And the work of becoming is released
The great tide and
The waves of creation and death will cease

In that moment
You will be lost completely,
Your heart
Will become the world.
And there will be nothing left to ask.

One day
You will be the answer.

— J. H. Ellerby

ACKNOWLEDGMENTS

Looking back at the journey that brought me to the writing of this book, I'm overwhelmed by the multitudes of people, communities, and organizations I feel deep gratitude for. There are so many stories in this book that are based on relationships and experiences that others have graciously brought into my life or have been a part of.

I couldn't possibly name each and every person whom I carry in my heart and feel a profound thankfulness for. To even attempt to list all who've helped me and indirectly contributed to the writing of this book is an impossible task. With respect, I'll confine my regards for those whose impact on this book has been most direct. To all and any that go unnamed, know that I thank you in my heart and I send you love and blessings.

With all my love and devotion, I thank my wife, Monica, who has encouraged me and endured the process necessary for me to write this book in the spare moments of an already full and busy life. She is one of my greatest heroes and a living model of so many things taught in this book. To my sweet and magnificent son, Narayan, I'm deeply grateful for the time you granted me to complete this project and for plunging me ever deeper into the absolute sacredness of life and love.

To my family, I also offer thanks. To my mom, for her readings of the book and for her endless encouragement and unconditional support of my spiritual unfolding. Thank you to my brother, sister, Brenda, Jess, and my father, William Ellerby (in spirit), who have all shown me nothing but love and support on my journey. Also to the many families I've been absorbed into around the world, especially the Apodaca/Montoya gang—thank you!

In South Dakota, my love and gratitude to Wanagi Wachi; to every member of his extended family; and all those in Wase Wakpa. You are all wonderful, *wopila!* To the Wase Wakpa Sundance Society, you know what I mean when I say, "Smug me I'm snuffering."

In Africa, my love and gratitude to Ramaliba, for being such a great and enduring friend and teacher; Mandaza, for your brotherhood and wisdom; and for Sammy who opened the door. To all those at Tshungani and the many healers I've learned from in southern Africa: *Ndivhuho. Ri tshimbila na midzimu!*

At Canyon Ranch, I send my love and gratitude to one and all for allowing me to be a part of such an extraordinary place of work and service. In particular, to Jerry, Mel, and Carrie, for believing in me, bringing me into your family, and supporting all of my efforts, including this book. Also gratitude to my extended CR family. To the great doctors Jim (and Amma) and Gary for your wise and loving counsel. You've both offered much worthy encouragement and support.

To the "Council of Twelve" and the Circle of Cooperation, each one of you have traveled this road of writing with me indirectly and tolerated my endless updates and musings. Thank you for your loving support—you know who you are. Special thanks to Catherine for your reading, guidance, and feedback.

To Dr. Morgan and the amazing people at the Graduate Theological Foundation. You helped make a dream come true. I offer deep respect and gratitude to the great Dr. Ewert Cousins for agreeing to be my adviser and for making possible my defense at Oxford.

To my new Hay House friends and family: you've all been so kind and generous with your attention and help. Special gratitude to Reid Tracy for believing in me and offering me this opportunity. To Jill Kramer, Lisa Mitchell, Charles McStravick, and Nancy Levin for working with me on edits, covers, and appearances. Thanks to all the Hay House authors I've met who've been so encouraging and caring. You are all wonderful and live the wisdom you promote.

To my new, wonderful friend and fellow on the path, Michael Green, for your cover artwork and heartening energy, thank you. Thanks to Ganga White for your good words.

Love and gratitude to the great *Jambavan,* my dear friend and agent, Ned Leavitt. Thank you for your wisdom, wit, tenacious spirit, and fearless feedback. More so, for your stories and songs, thank you.

And to those friends and mentors who have inspired and walked alongside me (whether or not you know it): Mark Samuel, Sophie, and family; Mark Thompson; James Pappas; Mark Naseck; Peter Beach; Jane Rigby (yes, you too); Larry and Barbie Dossey; Ramakrishna; Black Elk; Yogi Bhajan; Ram Dass for your inspiration; and the amazing Joan Borysenko, who helped me turn a spark into a flame. Thank you all, thank you.

Finally, to the Sacred Source, the One True Spirit, expressed through all these Divine manifestations, the many guiding Spirits, and your infinite Grace and Love—with all that I am, I thank you, I thank you, I thank you.

RESOURCES

If you're looking for organizations that can support your exploration of the practices and philosophies featured within this book, consider the following programs and people. Many of the centers listed offer workshops addressing practices from various cultures and religious traditions, including Western (Christian, Jewish, Muslim), Eastern, and Indigenous. Consult their calendars for more details. Web addresses are provided.

Jonathan H. Ellerby, Ph.D.
To learn more about my work, retreats, events, and international spiritual travel opportunities, and for more information and resources that will support your experience of this book, please visit my Website.
www.jonathanellerby.com

Spiritual Mentorship, Counseling, and Ongoing Training

Claritas Institute

The Claritas Institute offers excellent spiritual growth and mentorship programs, as well as interfaith dialogue and education.
www.claritasinstitute.com

CMED Institute (Caroline Myss Education)

The CMED Institute offers programs in medical intuition and spiritual growth.
www.myss.com/CMED/home

Spiritual Directors International

Spiritual Directors International is a great resource to locate local spiritual counselors and mentors from a range of backgrounds and traditions.
www.sdiworld.org

Integral Institute

The Integral Institute offers education, training, and events that foster intentional, behavioral, cultural, and social self-awareness. The Institute unites esteemed spiritual teachers and professionals of diverse backgrounds to help global leaders from all arenas improve the human condition.
www.integralinstitute.org

Soul Coaching

Soul Coaching by Denise Linn offers training to enhance your skills and development as a healer and helper. The organization provides educational and certification opportunities.
www.deniselinn.com/Soul-Coaching.htm

Wilderness- and Indigenous-based Training

The Four Winds Society
The Society offers workshops, travel, and training based on Indigenous models of energy medicine and healing.
www.thefourwinds.com

Wind Spirit Teachings
Wind Spirit Teachings offer Indigenous-run desert intensives, enhancing personal growth and reconnection with nature and the Spiritual World.
www.windspiritteaching.com

Sacred Passages
Sacred Passages provides intensive retreats and programs in wilderness settings, focusing on energy work and solitary contemplation in nature.
www.sacredpassage.com

The Animus Valley Institute
The Institute conducts intensive and diverse workshops, retreats, and programs in wilderness settings.
www.animas.org

Society for Shamanic Practitioners
The Society for Shamanic Practitioners provide a helpful Web resource for locating credible and professional non-Indigenous, modern shamanic journeywork practitioners.
www.shamansociety.org

Meditation and Yoga

There are many excellent programs around the world. Here are a few examples to get you started.

Spirit Rock Meditation Center
Spirit Rock Meditation Center offers excellent spiritual growth workshops and retreats, including special programs in meditation.
www.spiritrock.org

Tassajara Zen Center (The San Francisco Zen Center)
The Tassajara Zen Center conducts excellent Buddhist-oriented spiritual retreats and meditation training.
www.sfzc.org/tassajara

Kirpalu
Kirpalu is a renowned center for yoga instruction, featuring diverse forms of yoga, chanting workshops, and other spiritually related programs.
www.kirpalu.org

Yoga Journal
The magazine *Yoga Journal* and the events page on its Website are very helpful in directing people to yoga related events and training.
www.yogajournal.com/conferences

Where to Attend Weekend Workshops and Retreats

In addition to the previous listings, the following organizations offer or coordinate a wide range of spiritually related programs of various lengths, styles, and orientations.

Hay House (events across the United States and Canada)
www.hayhouse.com

Omega Institute (East Coast USA)
www.eomega.org

The Crossings (southern USA)
www.thecrossingsaustin.com

Hollyhock (West Coast Canada)
www.hollyhock.ca

Integrative, Holistic Health Programs with Spiritual Offerings

Canyon Ranch Health Resorts

A longtime leader in the world of wellness vacations, prevention education, integrative medicine, and vital living, Canyon Ranch features world-class professionals, state-of-the-art facilities, and luxury accommodations for the ultimate in life enhancement. Comprehensive spiritual workshops, lectures, and services are ongoing (including, but not limited to, yoga, meditation, energy medicine, Spirit Lodge, soul coaching, rites of passage, shamanic journey, retreats, sound healing, astrology, Tai Chi, Spirit Hikes, and intuitive services).

www.canyonranch.com

Path of Service Suggestions: Organizations to Help You Get Connected, Educated, and Involved

Bioneers

Bioneers remains one of the most innovative, cooperative, and holistically oriented organizations addressing issues relating to the environment.

www.bioneers.org

Save the Children

Save the Children is dedicated to addressing the challenges of children in need, including poverty, disaster relief, and feeding programs. This organization is known for its high rate of revenue to service ratio. In 2007, 90 percent of donations went to programs and services.

www.savethechildren.org

ONE

This American-based organization is uniting organizations and huge numbers of people in the global effort to end poverty and the HIV/AIDS epidemic.

www.one.org

Amnesty International

A longtime champion of human-rights issues, Amnesty International works toward global peace and justice.

www.amnesty.org

World Wildlife Fund

The World Wildlife Fund is a global leader in addressing issues of ecology, pollution, and sustainability.

www.wwf.org

The Nature Conservancy

Based on science, partnership, and an intent to protect biodiversity and ecosystems on land and at sea, The Nature Conservancy is known for its high standards and effective work.

www.nature.org

Journey to the Heart

Journey to the Heart is dedicated to the protection of Indigenous traditions and healing systems through cross-cultural awareness and the formation of collaborative partnerships to support grassroots projects.

www.journeytotheheart.org

ABOUT THE AUTHOR

Jonathan Ellerby, Ph.D., has spent more than 20 years dedicated to the personal, professional, and academic exploration of spirituality, healing, and consciousness. Throughout his journey, he has traveled the world meeting and studying with spiritual teachers from more than 40 cultural traditions. With a doctoral degree in comparative religion and an ordination as an interfaith minister, Jonathan has worked as a healer, teacher, and consultant with individuals and groups in settings as diverse as hospitals, major corporations, prisons, community groups, conferences, and some of the world's leading holistic health resorts. His work and training has taken him deeply into the worlds of Indigenous healing, corporate culture, and integrative medicine. Currently, Jonathan is the Spiritual Program Director for the acclaimed Canyon Ranch Health Resort.

Born in Winnipeg, Canada, Jonathan now lives in Tucson, Arizona, with his wife, Monica, and son, Narayan. Traveling and spending time in nature remain their great joys while they continue to explore and share in the spiritual traditions of the world.

Website: **www.jonathanellerby.com**

NOTES

NOTES

NOTES

NOTES

NOTES

NOTES

NOTES

NOTES

NOTES

NOTES

NOTES

Notes

NOTES

NOTES

Notes

NOTES

HEAL YOUR LIFE ♥

Take Your Soul on a Vacation

Get your daily dose of inspiration today at **www.HealYourLife.com®**. Brimming with all of the necessary elements to ease your mind and educate your soul, this Website will become the foundation from which you'll start each day. This essential site delivers the latest in mind, body, and spirit news and real-time content from your favorite Hay House authors.

Make It Your Home Page Today!

www.HealYourLife.com®

HAY HOUSE

www.hayhouse.com®